Original photograph of the aftermath of the Adair, Iowa train robbery committed by the Jesse James Gang July 21, 1873. Known as the first robbery of a train west of the Mississippi, the robbery is also called the world's first robbery of a moving train.

the SUM TOTAL

A Search for Levi Clay (1843-1917)
and Jesse James (1847-1882)

the SUM TOTAL

A Search for Levi Clay (1843-1917)
and Jesse James (1847-1882)

Barbara Inman Beall, Ph.D.

Aventine Press

Published by Aventine Press
750 State St. #319
San Diego CA, 92101
www.aventinepress.com

ISBN: 1-59330-694-6

Library of Congress Control Number: 2010917471

Printed in the United States of America

"Every man is a sort of modified sum total of his ancestors."[1]

--Robertus Love (1925)
The Rise and Fall of Jesse James

---

1   Robertus Love, *The Rise and Fall of Jesse James* [Lincoln: University of Nebraska Press] 21.

Table of Contents

List of Photographs and Photo Credits

- **Cover Photo and Frontispiece:** Original Photograph of The Adair Train Robbery, July 21, 1873. Viola Clay Inman Photo Collection now owned by Barbara Inman Beall

- **Section 1 Cover Photo**: The John Clay Family, ca. 1843, Summit Co., Ohio. Viola Clay Inman Photo Collection now owned by Barbara Inman Beall

- **Section 1 Photos:**

- John Clay Grave, Grill Cemetery, Summit Co., Ohio. Photo taken by Barbara Inman Beall, May 1996.

- Mary Hoy Clay Barn, Willow, Berreman Tp., Jo Daviess Co., Illinois. Photo from the Collection of Jeremy Clay. Used with permission from Jeremy Clay July 27, 2010. Ancestry.com website. Available at http://www.ancestry.com.

- James Kirkpatrick Tombstone, Glade Run Presbyterian Church Cemetery, Dayton, Pennsylvania. Photo taken by Barbara Inman Beall, Summer 1993.

- Levi Clay, 1869, Rockford, Illinois. Viola Clay Inman Photo Collection now owned by Barbara Inman Beall

- Mary Elizabeth Stillians Clay and her sister, Sarah Jane Stillians, 1869, Rockford, Illinois. Viola Clay Inman Photo Collection, now owned by Barbara Inman Beall.

- **Section 2 Cover Photo:** The Samuel-James Family, Clay Co., Missouri. Jesse James Gedcom Page, Rootweb.com. Accessed September 27, 2010. Available at http://www.rootsweb.ancestry.com/~daisy/jamesged.htm

- **Section 2 Photos**

- Robert Sallee James. Awesome Stories Website. Accessed September 27, 2010. Available at: http://www.awesomestories.com/assets/robert-s-james-father-of-jesse-james

- The James Farm, Kearney, Missouri. Excelsior Springs Chamber of Commerce Website. Accessed September 27, 2010. Available at http://www.exspgschamber.com/jessejames/farm.html

- Why Jesse James Never Smiled for Pictures. Photo taken at the Jesse James House Museum, St. Joseph, Missouri, March 2006 by Barbara Inman Beall.

- Painting of Jesse James titled "Dingus" by George Warfel. Photo taken at the Jesse James House Museum, St. Joseph, Missouri, March 2006 by Barbara Inman Beall

- Jesse James, 1875, Nebraska City, Nebraska. Encyclopedia Britannica Online Website. Accessed June 5, 2010. Available at http://www.britannica.com/EBchecked/topic-art/299846/120621/Jesse-James

- **Section 3 Cover Photo:** The Jesse James Historical Site, Adair, Iowa. Photo taken by Barbara Inman Beall May 2002.

- **Photos for Section 3**

- Construction of Adair, Iowa. Summer 1873. Viola Clay Inman Photo Collection now owned by Barbara Inman Beall

- Early Construction Photo, Adair, Iowa, Summer 1873. Viola Clay Inman Photo Collection now owned by Barbara Inman Beall

- Site of the Adair Train Robbery, July 21, 1873, showing the Embankment. Photo taken by Barbara Inman Beall, May 2002.

- Part of the Original Track, Adair, Iowa. Photo taken by Barbara Inman Beall, May 2002.

- The Oldest House in Adair—The Section House Built in 1868 where the James Gang ate before the robbery. Photo taken by Barbara Inman Beall, May 2002.

- Monument in Adair Park, Adair, Iowa. Photo taken by Barbara Inman Beall Summer 1999.

- **Cover Photo for Section 4:** The Jesse James House Museum, St. Joseph, Missouri. Photo taken by Barbara Inman Beall March 2006.

- **Photos for Section 4**
- Marker at 1318 Lafayette Street, St. Joseph, Missouri, where the Jesse James house was originally located. Photo taken by Barbara Inman Beall March 2006.
- Painting of Jesse James by George Warfel depicting Jesse James shortly before his death. Photo taken at the Jesse James House Museum, St. Joseph, Missouri by Barbara Inman Beall March 2006.
- Parlor of the Jesse James House Museum, St. Joseph, Missouri. Photo taken by Barbara Inman Beall March 2006. Bob Ford sat on the chair beside the organ when he shot Jesse James.
- Hole in the Wall, Parlor of the Jesse James House Museum, St. Joseph, Missouri. (Souvenir hunters have enlarged the hole over the years.) Photo taken by Barbara Inman Beall March 2006.
- Jesse James Display, Jesse James House Museum, St. Joseph, Missouri. Photo taken by Barbara Inman Beall March 2006.
- Jesse James Gravestone, Mt. Olivet Cemetery, Kearney, Missouri. Jesse James by Random Things Website. Accessed September 27, 2010. Available at http://www.flickr.com/photos/87458344@N00/2960404738/
- Frank James at the James Farm, Kearney, Missouri, photo on an old post card. The American Legends Website. Accessed September 27, 2010. Available at http://www.legendsofamerica.com/mo-hauntedjamesfarm.html
- **Cover Photo for Section 5:** The Levi Clay House, Adair, Iowa, taken 1880s/1890s. Viola Clay Inman Photo Collection now owned by Barbara Inman Beall
- **Photos for Section 5**
- The Levi Clay House, Adair, Iowa, taken November 11, 1892. Viola Clay Inman Photo Collection now owned by Barbara Inman Beall.
- Levi Clay, ca 1880s, Adair, Iowa. Viola Clay Inman Photo Collection now owned by Barbara Inman Beall

- The Adair Machine Shop (originally Levi Clay's blacksmith shop), Adair, Iowa. Taken by Barbara Inman Beall, May 2002.

- The Levi Clay Family, ca 1909. Viola Clay Inman Photo Collection now owned by Barbara Inman Beall.

- Levi and Mary Stillians Clay Grave, Sunny Hill Cemetery, Adair, Iowa. Photo taken by Barbara Inman Beall May 2002.

- **Cover Photo for Epilogue:** Adair Happy Face Tower, taken by Barbara Inman Beall, May 2002.

- **Photos for Epilogue**

- Downtown Adair, Iowa. Taken by Barbara Inman Beall, May 2002.

- Another View of Downtown Adair, Iowa. Taken by Barbara Inman Beall, May 2002.

- Monument at Jesse James Historical Site. Photo taken by Barbara Inman Beall, May 2002.

- Site of the Levi Clay House, Adair, Iowa. Photo taken by Barbara Inman Beall, May 2002.

- "New Home Where Old Home Once Stood." Photo taken 1925 by Viola Clay Inman, now owned by Barbara Inman Beall.

- May 2002 Version of the "New Home." Photo taken by Barbara Inman Beall, May 2002.

Forward

Late one Sunday afternoon in the mid-1950s, my family clustered around our television set in order to watch a program that had become a ritual. Hosted by Walter Cronkite, *You Are There* focused on a different historical event each week. This particular episode—*The Capture of Jesse James*—dramatized the killing of the outlaw by another gang member named Bob Ford on April 3, 1882 in a house in St. Joseph, Missouri.[2] The part of Jesse James was played by the actor John Kerr while a young rising star by the name of James Dean appeared as Bob Ford. I was around ten years old at the time and only remember the shooting in the program. What I distinctly remember, however, is the conversation at the dinner table after the program ended.

"Jesse James robbed a train in Adair," Dad told us. "My grandfather was there and saw the whole thing. He chased Jesse James through the night all the way to the Missouri border."

The story impressed me, of course, but I heard nothing further about it. I didn't know which grandfather he was talking about, nor did I know the location of Adair. Presently, I forgot the story.

Then in July 1958, my family decided to take a vacation trip to Colorado where some of my mother's relatives were living. We left Cedar Rapids, Iowa and traveled west across the state on Highway 6, a road that took us through the town of Adair.

"My granddad had a blacksmith shop right over there," Dad stated.

---

2   You are There: The Capture of Jesse James. Director: Sidney Lumet. Release date: 8 February 1953. Narrator: Walter Cronkite: Cast: James Dean as Bob Ford; John Kerr as Jesse James. CBS Television Network. Information available at IMDb website, Accessed September 25, 2010. Available at: http://www.imdb.com/title/tt0751918/.

Granddad? Adair?

"What was his name?" I asked.

"Levi Clay. He was Grandma Inman's father."

I don't remember asking anything else, because I was busy soaking in the information. Levi Clay would have been my great-grandfather. I recall seeing his name on an ancestral chart one of my cousins had sent my parents a few years previously. So, I filed away all of the new information in my brain and forgot the whole story again. In 1963, a newspaper article in *The Cedar Rapids Gazette* rekindled my interest, and the article specifically referred to the train robbery in Adair on July 21, 1873. I saved that article in a scrapbook for future reference, something I would not look at again until the late 1980s.

This book is the story of my 22-year search for facts and information surrounding the first train robbery west of the Mississippi—an event that has also been called the world's first robbery of a moving train. In compiling my information, I focused not just on the robbery—but on the people involved as well. Much of this book is devoted to a genealogical search for the ancestors and descendants of Levi and Mary Stillians Clay, as well as the ancestors and descendants of the James and Cole families. Operating from a thesis that we are all more or less the sum total of our ancestors, this book has been divided into five main parts, with the first two sections being devoted to genealogical research:

Part 1 focuses on the Clay, Stillians and allied families. Genealogical information was initially obtained from the author's cousin, and subsequent information was obtained by the author through her own genealogical research. Levi Clay was born into a farming family in Summit Co., Ohio in 1843. His father John Clay died when Levi was only six months old. The family subsequently moved to Jo Daviess Co., Illinois. Levi Clay remained in Illinois until he was grown, and he eventually relocated to Iowa, where some relatives had already settled. He married Mary Elizabeth Stillians in Rockford, Illinois in 1869. The family eventually settled in Adair, Iowa, where the Clays remained for the rest of their lives. Main family names include *Klee/ Clay, Heu/Hoy, Stillings/Stillins/Stillians, Lee,* and *Dilley/Dille/Dille.*

Part 2 focuses on the James, Cole and allied families. The genealogical portion of this section is based on the work of Phillip W. Steele, *Jesse and Frank James: The Family History*. Jesse James was also born into a farming family in Clay Co., Missouri in 1847. His father Robert Sallee James was a Baptist minister, who became one of the founders of William Jewell College in Liberty, Missouri. Jesse's family came from Kentucky, where his older brother Alexander Franklin James was born in 1843. Jesse's father journeyed to California during the Gold Rush. Shortly after his arrival there, he contracted a fever and died. Jesse then experienced two different fathers. Situated in an area called "Little Dixie", Clay Co., Missouri became a focal point for unrest before, during and after the Civil War. Jesse and Frank James fought with guerilla units during the war and continued the fight as outlaws after the war ended. Jesse James' outlaw image was portrayed as a modern-day Robin Hood in the press, an image that was projected by John Newman Edwards. Main family names include *James, Cole, Mimms, Woodson, Poor, Dorsey,* and *Howard.*

Part 3 deals specifically with the train robbery. It opens with a look at the early establishment of Adair, Iowa, and it also incorporates a chapter on the Reno Gang of Indiana, the first peacetime train robbers. The Adair train robbery would later be known as the first train robbery west of the Mississippi River and also as the world's first robbery of a moving train. Details of the robbery were obtained from actual newspaper accounts from papers in Iowa and Missouri.

Part 4 examines the demise of the James gang and the impact of the Pinkerton Detective Agency on the James and Younger families. It also examines the "crime of the century" when the Pinkertons bombed the James farmhouse, killing Jesse and Frank's half-brother, Archie Samuel, and maiming their mother. It focuses on additional robberies committed by the James gang, culminating with the robbery in Northfield, Minnesota, a debacle that led to the final downfall of the gang. The chapter also looks at the lives of the James brothers in Kentucky and Tennessee before Jesse's return to Missouri and his brief life in St. Joseph and his death there as Thomas Howard.

Part 5 deals with the aftermath of the train robbery in Adair and the lives of the Clay family. This section incorporates newspaper accounts that deal with two major fires in Adair in the late 1800s. It focuses on the Levi Clay family and provides information about the children and grandchildren. The section ends with the deaths of Levi and Mary Clay.

The Epilogue provides a general wrap-up. It opens with a 2002 visit the author made to the town of Adair. It compares and contrasts the two main individuals featured in the book—Levi Clay and Jesse James—and attempts to answer a question concerning society's attraction to the dark side. Reference is made to other historical places in western Iowa, as well as in other parts of the state.

* * *

This book is dedicated to my father, Gordon Loren Inman (1908-1974), whose stories instilled my interest! It is also dedicated to my grandmother, Adelia Viola Clay Inman (1869-1951) daughter of Levi Clay, who told these stories to my father, and who saved all of her original photographs.

This book is also dedicated to my cousin, Charles Gordon Inman, who provided me with the initial information--and to my husband Howard and children Brian and Debbie—who encouraged me to continue writing--all of whom made this book possible!!!

Barbara Inman Beall

September 30, 2010

Prologue

He ran!!!

Half walked!

Half jogged!

Half ran!

Night fell! Darkness engulfed the Iowa prairie. A figure sped down the path with only the moonlight guiding him in the direction of Casey.

Not too far!

Or was it?

Would he have time to seek help? Would help arrive quickly?

A thousand possibilities swirled through his mind as he raced along in the darkness. He stumbled and fell but regaining his feet, plunged forward into the night.

What had he seen?

Who were these men?

What happened before the crash?

Four miles!

He only had four miles to Casey and to the telegraph office where he could signal for help!

Help?

What about the people back there?

Were they all dead?

The only thing he could hear was the roar—the roar of the screeching train and slamming metal—the screams of the people still ringing in his ears.

And he saw the masked men!

Who are they?

What do they want?

As he stumbled along in the darkness, he remembered the warnings given to the brakemen and as well as to the other railroad workers— all of them bearing a name:

Jesse James!

Jesse James in Iowa?

Would Jesse James leave Missouri for the Iowa prairie to rob a train?

The moon beamed brightly overhead, its light falling on the path before him.

He had to get to the telegraph office in Casey!

And he had to get there quickly!

The figure lunged forward into the night with one name imprinted on his mind—

Jesse James!

Part 1: Beginnings: Origins of Adair and Guthrie County., Iowa Clay and Stillians Families

The John Clay Family, ca. 1843, Summit Co., Ohio. The back of the photo reads "John Clay Family, Centre County, Penn and Summit Co., Ohio. This photo was taken about the spring of 1843. John Clay and his wife Mary Barbara Hoy are seated. The infant is Christina Magdalena, who was born April 24, 1842. Jeremiah Clay (age 13) is the young man standing behind his father. The two females are Mary Barbara (age 15) and Catherine (age 12). Alfred Sidney (age 17) is standing next to Catherine, and William Clay (age 23) is on the end. George, Peggy, Henry and Rebecca had already died. Sarah, John, and Elizabeth were married and living elsewhere. Hiram (age 10), Daniel Reuben (age 7), and Margaret Christina (age 4) are not pictured.

Chapter 1: Early Summit County, Ohio

Mid-May 1996. Howard and I sped along the interstate in the direction of Pennsylvania, where I was scheduled to defend my dissertation proposal. Always seeking routes to avoid Chicago traffic, we took I-80 across Illinois to Highway 30—and 30 across Indiana and Ohio to I-74. Our goal was to reach Indiana, Pennsylvania by evening. My defense would take place the next morning. And then we would be on our way home to Colorado once again.

Traffic increased significantly as we drew closer to Akron. I remembered this location well since we had visited a cemetery just off this route three years previously. My great-great grandfather, John Clay, and his family resided in Summit County, Ohio in the 1840s, and I had discovered the name of the cemetery where his grave was located. We visited that cemetery in 1993, but had no plans to visit it this time.

We traveled in silence, and I spotted the sign for the Cleveland-Massillon Road which led down to the cemetery. As we passed the exit, I remember saying, "Well, it's just four miles straight down that road, but we don't have time to stop there today. Maybe—if we head back this way on our return trip—we could stop then."

A car pulling a flat-bed trailer sped around us and pulled on ahead. The vehicle moved into the right lane with cars surrounding it on all sides. I don't remember the speed we were traveling, but I know it was at the limit.

Just then, the entire right rear wheel and axel broke free of the trailer. I gasped when I saw it! The wheel and axel rolled off to the side of the road. The car and the rest of the trailer continued down the highway. We expected the wheel and axel to stop in the ditch beside the road, hoping that would be the end of it. Then as though with a mind of its own, the wheel and axel rolled up an embankment and sped across the highway in front of our car. It rolled down in the center median, where we thought it would surely rest.

It didn't!

With a new burst of speed, the wheel and axel rose out of the ditch and sped across the highway in the direction of the opposite embankment, barely missing a string of cars as it crossed.

"It has to stop there!" I exclaimed as it disappeared inside a ditch off the opposite shoulder.

It didn't!

Instead, the wheel and axel rolled up that embankment and then with a sudden burst of energy, tore across the highway again, this time in the direction of our car. I yelled. We heard a loud crunch as the flying missile connected with the side of a large semi heading in the opposite direction. By now, the car hauling the trailer pulled off to the side of the road when the driver became aware of what happened. We were shaken and could say nothing until reaching the outskirts of Akron.

"I think we're going to stop and visit that cemetery on our way back!" I said.

* * *

From a passing traveler's perspective, Summit Co., Ohio appears as a peaceful scene of rolling hillsides, tall trees, and nodding grasses bobbing in the wind. Its colorful hillsides dotted with farms, its mid-nineteenth century villages and towns, and even Akron reminds the traveler of a more peaceful time, inviting further exploration. But while Summit Co. shows a pleasant image to the world, its history reveals something less than bucolic in its nature. Not only was Summit Co. the home of a number of industrialists, it was also the home of a raging abolitionist, whose activities would change history. And it was the setting for a fiery religious fervor a few years after the county's creation!

Ohio was first explored by the French in 1669. Almost one hundred years later, Americans took control of The Northwest Territory. The Treaty of Fort McIntosh in 1785 extinguished Native American title to the lands and in 1786, Connecticut relinquished all land in this region except for an area called The Western Reserve. The Northwest Territory was created by Congress in 1787 which included Ohio, Indiana, Illinois, Michigan and Wisconsin. The first permanent settlement was at Marietta in 1788.

Ohio became a territory in 1799; however, the formation of the Indiana Territory reduced Ohio's original size the following year. Also in 1800, Connecticut released its jurisdictional claim and on March 1, 1803, Ohio officially became the 17th State admitted to the Union. Various counties were formed after Ohio became a state: Columbiana in 1803, Portage (which was organized from Trumbull) in 1808, followed by Stark (from Columbiana) that same year, and Medina from Portage in 1818.

On March 3, 1840, Summit County was carved from Portage, Medina and Stark Counties, and acquired its name from "the highest land on the line of the Ohio canal, originally called *The Portage Summit.*"[3] Its rolling hillsides were conducive to producing fruit, and a large amount of bituminous coal lay beneath its soil. The lush hillsides lured settlers from further east long before Summit County was established, many of them arriving from Pennsylvania. Part of the attraction stemmed from the presence of a number of natural lakes that were formed from glaciers centuries ago. Known as The Western Reserve, the region became the western-most boundary of the United States after the Treaty of Fort McIntosh in 1798. David Hudson established the first Summit County settlement in 1800—a little town known as Hudson that is 24 miles from Cleveland and 13 miles northeast of Akron. Abolitionist John Brown spent some of his early days in the town of Hudson, and the county history enumerates some of his activities there. In fact, the first burial in the old cemetery was of John Brown's mother in 1808. A Baptist clergyman named William Miller, the founder of "Millerism", not only preached in Akron, but traveled throughout the

---

3   Summit County-Ohio History Central: A Product of the Ohio Historical Society. Accessed June 2, 2010. Available at http://www.ohiohistorycentral.org/entry.php?rec=2016.

region. Summit County was later the home of Industrialists Benjamin Franklin Goodrich, Ferdinand Schumacher, Frank Seiberling, and Harvey Samuel Firestone, to name a few. The State of Ohio later became the birthplace for five U.S. Presidents. This narrative focuses on two individuals: John Brown and William Miller.

Born in Torrington, Connecticut May 9, 1800, John Brown came from a family that was devoted to anti-slavery principles for three generations. His father Owen took part in the forcible rescue of some slaves who were claimed by a Virginia clergyman in Connecticut in 1798. When he was five years old, his family relocated to Hudson, Ohio, where John Brown worked in his father's tannery and at farming until the age of 20. He learned surveying and later became postmaster at Randolph, Pennsylvania when Andrew Jackson was President. He was back in Ohio in 1836 but by 1844, he moved to Massachusetts. By 1849, he purchased a farm in Northern New York. Then in 1855, he followed five of his sons to Kansas. His sons had settled near Osawatomie the previous year. Kansas was the site of the "Free-State Party", and John Brown wanted to aid in those activities. Some of his activities while living in Hudson provide indications of what he would later do in Kansas and elsewhere. Brown definitely believed that he was chosen by God to end slavery. On the day of his execution for his raid on Harper's Ferry, he handed a note to one of the guards:

> *CHARLESTOWN, VA., Dec. 2, 1859. I, John BROWN, am now quite certain that the crimes of this guilty land will never be purged away but with blood. I had, as I now think, vainly flattered myself that without much blood-shed it might be done.*[4]

Brown's conviction was manifested in a religious fervor, and such fervor in Summit County could only be matched by a Baptist minister named William Miller. Miller became absolutely convinced that Christ's Second Coming would occur by April 4, 1843. As a result of his conviction, Miller began preaching fire and brimstone sermons painting a terrifying picture of hell and damnation to large audiences. People needed to repent and convert immediately or they would per-

---

4   Henry Howe, *History of Summit County*, Historical Collections of Ohio, Vol.II [G. J. Krehbiel & Co., 1888] 625-656

ish. As a result, he acquired a huge following that was mostly confined to the northeastern part of the United States.

Miller arrived at his conclusion after seven years of extensive Bible study with a special focus on the books of Daniel and Revelation. He built his theory from historical occurrences and specific biblical references and created such an elaborate hierarchy, thousands of people were convinced that the end was near and that they needed to convert immediately. As many as 100,000 people gathered on hillsides, awaiting the Second Coming of Christ. Many of those people were from Summit County. Miller taught "that a great trumpet from heaven would sound, Jesus Christ would gather up the faithful, and the wicked would be destroyed by fire."[5] When the appointed time arrived and Christ didn't return, many in the crowd grew restless and walked out. One person complained that Miller hadn't taken the differences in latitude and longitude between Palestine and the U.S. into account.

One of Miller's associates, Samuel Snow, decided that Miller was off by one year in his calculations. Snow was certain that Christ would return on October 22, 1844 at midnight. Miller eventually endorsed the new date, and both men maintained there was no possibility of making a mistake this time. Media reaction was spontaneous. Reporters covered the speaking engagements and newspapers were flooded with stories. Fifteen hundred Millerites traveled across the United States proclaiming that the Advent was near. People quit their jobs and disassociated themselves from former congregations who disavowed the preaching. On the appointed date, many people waited on hilltops, dressed in ascension attire, believing they would be caught up in the air. As was true with the first prediction, nothing happened.

Miller and his cohorts probably did more to discourage believers than they did to encourage them since many of the fifty thousand followers shucked their faith completely. Others formed the Adventist group. The majority, however, returned to more traditional churches. And even though they were tricked twice, a number of the followers believed that Christ had indeed returned to earth October 22, 1844 but they claimed he could not be seen since he was invisible! Miller felt

5   Sylvester Bliss, *Memoirs of William Miller, generally known as a lecturer on the prophecies, and the second coming of Christ.* (New York: AMS Press, 1971) 278.

compelled to write a note to his followers: "Brethren hold fast; let no man take your crown. I have fixed my mind on another time, and here I mean to stand until God gives me more light, and that is today, today, and today, until he comes."[6] Miller spent the next five years rereading the books of Daniel and Revelation and rechecking his charts, wondering how he had miscalculated such an important date!

Summit County returned to its blissful routine, but "Millerism" left a definite scar on the minds of people for many years.

---

6   Bliss, *Memoirs of William Miller*, 278.

Chapter 2: From Klee to Clay

When the John Clay family relocated to Stark Co., Ohio in the early 1820s with John's parents, they were looking for suitable farmland and a place where they could spend the rest of their lives. Born February 26, 1794 in Centre Co., Pennsylvania to Mathias Clay and Anna Maria Fromm, John married fifteen-year old Mary Barbara Hoy in 1815. A large German family, the Clays had seventeen children of their own and after his John's death, his widow adopted three more. A list of their children follows:

George Clay (Dec. 26, 1815, Centre Co., Pennsylvania-Jan. 29, 1834, Franklin Tp, Summit County, Ohio);

Sarah Clay (April 14, 1818, Centre Co., Pennsylvania-March 1, 1858, place unknown)—married William Brady;

John Clay (1819 or 1824, Centre Co., Pennsylvania [Note: if the birth date is 1824, he would have been born in Stark Co., Ohio] – married Louisa Rex (1848);

William Clay (1819-20, Center Co., Pennsylvania-July 15, 1894, Adair Co, Iowa)—married Eliza Fickler [or Fickles];

Elizabeth Clay (March 27, 1821, Brush Valley, Centre Co., Pennsylvania-July 23, 1912, Berreman Tp., Jo Daviess Co., Illinois)—married (1) Abraham Brubaker, Summit Co., Ohio; (2) Clevidence;

Peggy Clay (1824-died in infancy);

Alfred Sidney Clay (March 23, 1826, Stark Co., Ohio-February 7, 1905, Willow, Illinois)—married Lydia Church, February 28, 1856;

Mary Barbara Clay (March 19, 1828, Stark Co., Ohio)—married Abe Collins;

Jeremiah Clay (February 22, 1830, Franklin Tp., Stark Co., Ohio-May 21, 1890, Willow, Illinois)—married Martha Staley, September 20, 1855, Freeport, Illinois;

Catherine Clay (September 5, 1831, Stark Co., Ohio-July 3, 1912, Willow, Illinois)—married (1) John Bottorf; (2) George Schlafer, 1860, Willow, Illinois;

Hiram Clay (May 28, 1833, Stark Co., Ohio-Dec. 22, 1860)—married Martha Hiscox;

Daniel Reuben Clay (March 9, 1835, Stark Co., Ohio-May 2, 1858, Mt. Carroll, Illinois)—married (1) Christina Bruce, May 2, 1858, Pleasant Valley, Jo Daviess Co., Illinois; (2) Julia Bermer, November 28, 1907;

Henry Adam Clay (1837—died in 1837);

Margaret Christina Clay (Oct. 2, 1839, Stark Co., Ohio-May 27, 1911, Dickinson, North Dakota)—married Anderson Palmer, 1857, Pleasant Valley, Illinois;

Rebecca Clay (1840—died in 1840);

Christina Magdalena Clay (April 24, 1842, Dutch Hollow, Franklin Tp., Summit Co., Ohio-Aug. 14, 1920, Marble Rock, Floyd Co., Iowa)—married James Daniel Anthony;

Levi Clay (December 12, 1843, Franklin Tp., Summit Co., Ohio-June 24, 1917, Adair, Guthrie Co., Iowa)—married Mary Elizabeth Stillians, February 7, 1869, Rockford, Illinois.[7]

The family surname was originally *Klee*, a German word meaning "clover." John Clay's great-grandfather, Johan Nicholas Klee, arrived in Philadelphia with his wife and his father-in-law aboard the ship *Loyal Judith* September 13, 1739. He was naturalized as a resident of

---

7   Charles Gordon Inman, Notes on the Clay (Klee) Family, January 9, 1992

Bern Tp., Berks Co., Pennsylvania in April 1761.[8]

Born in the year 1708 in Rohrbach, Birkenfeld, Oldenburg, Germany to Heinrich and Anna Maria Klee, Johan Nicholas Klee married Lisa Margaretha Staudt, daughter of Abraham Staudt and Anna Katherina Geiss on November 2, 1738 in Wolfsweiler, Saarland, Germany. The Klees had twelve children:

Abraham Klee, married Katherina Grim;

Anna Margaretha Klee, born or baptized March 9, 1741;

Jeremiah Klee;

Christina Klee, who remained unmarried;

Christian Klee;

Jacob Klee, who was born before 1755;

John Klee;

Barbara Klee, married Adam Blatt or Platt;

Mathias Klee, b. after 1755;

Mary Elizabeth Klee, married Solomon Neidig;

Eva or Eve Klee, married Martin Bender;

Catherina Klee, married John Rhiel or Riehl.[9]

Johan established a farm in Bern Tp, Berks Co., where he died in 1763. It has been long established that he and his wife are both buried in the Bern Church Cemetery. However, no tombstone for either of them has ever been found there. Two of Johan Nicholas Klee's children are important to this narrative: Christian and Jeremiah. (Jeremiah will be discussed in a later chapter.)

The grandfather of John Clay, Christian Klee, was born in 1745 in Bern Tp., Berks Co., Pennsylvania to Johan Nicholas and Lisa Margaretha Klee. Around 1772, he married Mary Barbara (wife's

8   Don C. Shaw, *A Genealogy and History of Some of the Descendants of Johan Nicholas Klee*, 1968.
9   Shaw, *Johan Nicholas Klee*, 1968

surname is unknown), and they had seven known children. The oldest
child was Mathias Clay, father of John. Two records have been found
for Christian's Revolutionary War service. He was reportedly a private
in Baloys Company, Heister's Battalion, 6th Berks Co. Pennsylvania
Militia. (The records have been lost for Heister's Battalion. However,
Heister's tombstone is in the Bern Church Cemetery.) The second record has Christian listed as a private in Capt. Emrick's Co., 5th Class
of the 3rd Battalion, Berks Co. Pennsylvania Militia. He reportedly
served under Heister from August 10 to September 9, 1780.[10]

After his father died, Christian inherited land from the estate, and he
farmed that land until shortly after 1800. Thereafter, he and his oldest
son, Mathias, migrated with their families to Farmanagh Tp., Mifflin
Co., Pennsylvania. Centre County was formed in 1810, and parts
of Farmanagh Tp. became Potter and Miles Tps. in Centre County.
Christian Clay's farm was located in Potter Tp. This is where Christian
died in 1805. The children of Christian and Mary Barbara Klee/Clay
were:

Mathias Clay, born 1774, Bern Tp., Berks Co., Pennsylvania;

Christina Clay, who married George Neacker;

Susannah Clay, who married Jacob Nidoch;

Christian Clay, born October 10, 1786, Bern Tp, who died May
27, 1844 in Franklin Tp., Summit County, Ohio, and who married
Catherine Wolf in Centre, Pennsylvania;

Jeremiah Clay;

Frederick Clay;

Martha Clay.[11]

John Clay's father, Mathias, was born in 1774 in Bern Tp., Berks Co.,
Pennsylvania. His wife was Anna Maria (or An/Ann Mary) Fromm,
whom he married in Berks Co., Pennsylvania ca. 1793. Their children
were:

10   Betty Duvall Pollard, DAR National Number 577008-A481 for Christian
     Clay (Klee), February, 1974.
11   Inman, Notes on the Clay (Klee) Family, January 9, 1992

Rebecca Clay;

Margaret Clay;

John Clay—b. February 26, 1794; d. May 6, 1844;

Magdalena Clay, born 1801;

Catherine Clay, born 1802;

Simon Clay, born 1805;

Adam Clay, born 1810;[12]

David Clay, b. 5 Feb 1819; d. 18 Sept. 1902.[13]

The 1810 Census finds the family in Farmanagh Tp, Mifflin Co., Pennsylvania[14] but by 1820, the family relocated to Nimishillen, Stark Co., Ohio.[15] Mathias' brother, Christian, and his uncle, Jeremiah, had previously moved to Ohio—Christian settling in Stark County, and Jeremiah settling in Trumbull County, respectively. Two of Mathias Clay's sons, Simon and David, relocated to Seneca Co., Ohio by 1825, where they appear on the tax lists,[16],[17] and by 1840, Mathias and An

12 Mathias Clay Overview, McCabe Family Tree, Public Member Trees, Ancestry.com, Provo, Utah, Accessed June 15, 2010. Available at http://www.ancestry.com

13 David Clay, Armstrong Cemetery, Reed Tp., *Seneca County Ohio Cemetery Inscriptions*, Compiled by the Seneca County Genealogical Society, Seneca Chapter OGS

14 Christian and Mathias Clay. 1810 Census, Farmanagh Tp, Mifflin Co., Pennsylvania, Ancestry.com, Provo, Utah. Accessed June 4, 2010. Available at http://www.ancestry.com.

15 Mathias and John Clay. 1820 Census, Nimishillen Tp., Stark Co., Ohio, Ancestry.com, Provo, Utah. Accessed June 4, 2010. Available at http://www.ancestry.com.

16 Clay, Simon and David Clay. 1825 Tax Lists, Loudon Tp., Seneca Co., Ohio. Seneca Co., Ohio History, Records, Facts and Genealogy. My Ohio Genealogy Website. Accessed June 17, 2010. Available at http://www.myohiogenealogy.com/oh-county-seneca.html.

17 Clay, Mathias and John Clay. 1830 Census, Nimishillen Tp., Stark Co., Ohio, Ancestry.com, Provo, Utah. Accessed June 4, 2010. Available at http://www.ancestry.com.

Mary also relocated to Loudon Tp., Seneca Co., Ohio, where Mathias died in November of that year.[18]

The text of Mathias Clay's will follows:

> *The last will and Testament of Mathias Clay deceased produced at a Special Session of the Court of Common Pleas begun and held at the Court House in Tiffin in and for the County of Seneca and State of Ohio on the Twenty-sixth day of November in the year of our Lord one thousand, eight hundred and forty, proven and ordered to be recorded.*
>
> *Loudon Township, Seneca County, Ohio, June the 29 in the year of our Lord one thousand, eight hundred and forty that I Mathias Clay make known by these presents that I am weak in body but sound in mind and do declare this to be my last will and testament, that after my funeral expenses are all paid, that I will and bequeath unto my widow all the beds in my house, bedsteads and bedding and all the kitchen and household furniture and all the dresser ware and my old red and white spotted cow and all my hogs and all the grain and vegetables and potatoes now growing on my place and further I will and bequeath unto my daughter Margaret my boom and all the grass and weeds thereto her bed and bedding and my young red and Brindle cow and I also will and bequeath that my widow remain on my farm as long as she lives with the exception of Robert Youngs lease to be and remain for eight years yet from the first of April last.*
>
> *Witness my hand and seal.*
>
> *Mathias Clay*
>
> *Attest present: Henry Ebersole*
>
> *Jacob Croan*
>
> *And the proof of said will as taken by said Court is in the words and figures following to-wit:*

---

18 Mathias, Simon and David Clay. 1840 Census, Loudon Tp., Seneca Co., Ohio, Copy obtained from Tiffin-Seneca Co., Public Library, March 19, 1993.

The State of Ohio, Seneca County, ss:--Special Session of the Court of Common Pleas of the County aforesaid held on the 16 day of November A.D. 1840—Personally appeared in open Court Henry Ebersole and Jacob Croan two of the subscribing witnesses to a certain paper writing now exhibited to them in court purporting to be the last will and testament of Mathias Clay late of Seneca County and State of Ohio deceased—and being carefully examined, cautioned and sworn respectively depose and say that they were present and saw the said Mathais [sic] Clay sign said last will and testament that he then declared it to be his last will and testament and published the same as such in the presence of said witnesses thereto and requested them to subscribe it as witnesses as aforesaid which the[sic] severally did in the presence of said Mathais [sic] Clay and that the said Mathias Clay at the time of executing the same as aforesaid was of full age, sound mind and memory and not under any restraint.

Henry Ebersole, Jacob Croan

Subscribed and sworn in open Court this 26 day of November A.D. 1840.

John Elder Deputy Clerk

I recorded the above Will to-gether with the Proof thereof as taken by said Court

John Elder Deputy Clerk[19]

Mathias Clay's widow An Mary (Anna Maria) died in Summit County, Ohio in 1842.[20]

* * *

"I need to ask you a question. On your records, you indicate that John Clay's middle name was *Christian* or began with the letter *C*. Where did you get that? I will admit it is an excellent possibility since his

---

19   Clay, Mathias. *Seneca County Ohio, Will Record, 1828-1849. Vol. 1,* FHL Film 388,625.84-85.

20   Ann Mary Fromm Overview, Public Member Trees, Accessed June 15, 2010. Ancestry.com. Provo, Utah. http://www.ancestry.com

uncle and his grandfather were both named *Christian*, but where did
you get that C? I have never found that anywhere!"

This question appeared in an email received approximately fifteen
years ago from a Clay researcher. Her question made me wonder:
Where did I see that letter C? "His tombstone," I suggested, which
produced her quick response: "No, I have visited his grave, and there
is no letter *C* for his middle name. He is only listed as *John Clay*. Now,
where did you get that middle initial?"

The answer is found in a letter dated March 10, 1993 from the Stark
County Chapter of the Ohio Genealogical Society as set out below:

> *...In the 1820 census John Clay is in Stark Co., Lake Tp on page
> 181 and Mathias Clay is in Stark Co., Nimishillen Tp, on page
> 183. In the 1830 census John Clay is in Stark Co, Franklin Tp on
> page 311 and Mathias Clay is in Stark Co, Nimishillen Tp. Page
> 236. So is Simon Clay in Stark Co, Nimishillen Tp, page 233. In
> the 1840 census **John C Clay** is in Summit Co., Franklin Tp, page
> 254 and Mathias Clay is not listed.*

John C. Clay--John Christian Clay, which can be easily deduced from
the 1840 Summit Co., Ohio census!

The letter continues:

> *1820 John Clay, Stark Co, Lake Tp: Males 1 0-10; 1 26-45.
> Females: 1 16-26*

> *1820 Mathias Clay, Stark Co, Nimishillen Tp: Males: 3 1-10; 1
> 16-18; 2 16-26; 1 45 up. Females: 2 -10; 2 10-16; 2 16-26; 1
> 26-45; 1 45 up*

> *1830 John Clay, Stark Co, Franklin Tp: Males: 2 0-5; 2 5-10; 1
> 10-15; 1 30-40. Females: 1 –5; 1 5-10; 1 10-15; 1 30-40*

> *1830 Mathias Clay, Stark Co, Nimishillen Tp: Males: 1 50-60.
> Females: 1 20-30; 1 50-60.*

> *1830 John Clay, Seneca Co, Reed Tp: Males: 2 0-5; 1 5-10; 1
> 10-15; 1 40-50. Females: 1 15-20; 1 30-40. I do not believe this
> one is yours.*

*1840 **John C Clay**, Summit Co, Franklin Tp: Males: 2 5-10; 2 10-15; 1 15-20; 1 20-30; 1 40-50. Females: 1 0-5; 1 5-10; 1 10-15; 1 20-30; 1 40-50*

1840 John Clay, Seneca Co, Reed Tp: Males: 1 0-5; 2 10-15; 1 15-20; 1 50-60. Females: 1 5-10; 1 40-50. I do not believe this one is yours.

In Volume D, page 21 of the Stark County Land Records there is a purchase dated 28 Jun 1818 for 50 acres for $302 at Range 8, Township 12, Section 18 which is Lake Tp. He paid taxes on this land each year through 1825. John Clay in Franklin Tp shows up on the tax list in 1825 and continues from there for 79 acres in Range 10 Township 2 and Section 8. There is no record of a purchase of 800 acres by John Clay. That would be a full section of 640 acres plus a quarter section 160 acres. Apparently Mathias Clay owned no land of his own. There are other Clays who owned land in Stark County: Isaac, David and Christian.

All records for Franklin Tp after 1840 would be in Summit County. In Grill Cemetery in Franklin Tp. of Summit Co. are the graves of Christian Clay along with your John. Whereas John Clay died 6 May 1844, Christian died 27 May 1844, and Catharine Clay, wife of Christian, died 8 Aug 1844. a Mary Clay died Aug 1844 and a Susan Clay died 12 Sep 1844. That is five Clays dying in 1844.

I can find no information about Mathias Clay. He does not appear in any of the Stark County cemetery books of Stark County, I have come to the conclusion that Stark County records will not reveal the information you are seeking.

Sincerely,

Clifford T. Wig

Corresponding Secretary[21]

Nine days later, I received a letter from the Tiffin-Seneca Public Library in Tiffin, Ohio, enclosing a copy of the 1840 Census Record with the following Clays in Loudon Tp.:

21 Clifford T. Wig, Stark County Chapter, OGS, Letter dated March 10, 1993

David Clay—Males: 1 under 5; 1 20-30; Females: 1 5-10; 1 20-30

Simon Clay—Males: 1 under 5; 2 5-10; 1 10-15; 1 30-40; Females: 1 under 5; 1 5-10; 1 30-40

Mathias Clay—Males: 1 5-10; 1 60-70; Females: 1 20-30; 1 60-70.[22]

It is interesting to note that Henry Ebersole, one of the witnesses of Mathias Clay's will, is also on this same census record, as is Jacob Croan. Mathias' daughter, Margaret, would have been the female aged between 20 and 30, and the small boy could have been her son (name unknown).

While the John Clay family continued to reside in Summit County., Mathias Clay and his wife joined their children who were living in Seneca Co., Ohio. The exact burial site for Mathias Clay and his wife An Mary is unknown. More than likely, they are buried in Sheller Cemetery in Loudon Tp., where members of the Simon Clay family are buried:

Joseph Clay, son of Simon & Barbara, d. February 1, 1843

Margaret Clay, daughter of Simon & Barbara, 13 y 11 m 9 d; d. May 31, 1848

Oscar Clay, son of H & E, d. Nov. 5, 1852, 1 y 6m 17 d

Clay inf, son of U & R, d Feb 15, 1865, 1 m

Clay, inf, son of U & R, d. April 22, 1866, 23 d

Hiram, son of H & R, d Aug. 22, 1854, 1 m.[23]

Simon and Barbara Clay last appear in Loudon Tp., Seneca Co., Ohio on the 1850 Census.[24] By 1856, they were in Palermo, Grundy Co.,

22   Jane B. Wickham, Tiffin-Seneca Public Library, Tiffin, Ohio, Letter dated March 20, 1993.

23   *Sheller Cemetery Records, Loudon Tp., Seneca County, Ohio,* compiled by the Seneca County Genealogical Society, OGS., Date Unknown.

24   Simon Clay, 1850 Census, Loudon Tp., Seneca Co., Ohio, Ancestry.com, Provo, Utah. Accessed June 24, 2010. Available at http://www.ancestry.com.

Iowa, just two counties below Floyd, where members of the John Clay family eventually settled.[25] They finally appear on the 1860 Census for Felix, Grundy Co., Iowa.[26]

The David Clay family is buried in Reed Tp, Seneca Co., Ohio in the Armstrong Cemetery:

> *David Clay, Feb. 5, 1819 - Sept. 18, 1902*
>
> *Irvin Clay, s/o David and Elizabeth, April 15, 1867, Jan. 22, 1870*
>
> *Lucy B.Clay d/o David and Elizabeth, June 21, 1853- Sept. 20, 1885*
>
> *Elizabeth Clay, wife of David, Nov. 30, 1830 – Oct. 2, 1892.*
>
> *Elizabeth Clay, wife of Isaac, Jan. 14, 1851; 63 y. 3 m*
>
> *Irvin Clay, s/o I & E, June 22, 1850, 12 y 9m 7d*
>
> *Lucy Ann Clay, Daughter of C & C, June 30, 1849, 1 y, 3m 26d*
>
> *Caroline Clay, wife of Conrad, May 16, 1849; 25 y 3m 20d.*
>
> *John Clay, July 30, 1844, 68 y.*
>
> *Elnora Clay, Daughter of L & M.J., Nov 18, 1867 2y 20 d.*[27]

[Note: John Clay of Seneca Co. and Isaac Clay of Seneca Co. were sons of Jeremiah Clay, son of Johan Nicholas Klee, and first cousins once removed of John C. Clay of Summit Co.]

25 Simon Clay, 1856 Iowa Census, Palermo, Grundy Co., Iowa, Ancestry. com, Provo, Utah, Accessed June 24, 2010. Available at http://www. ancestry.com

26 Simon Clay, 1860 Census, Felix, Grundy Co., Iowa, ancestry.com, Provo, Utah. Accessed June 24, 2010. Available at http://www.ancestry. com.

27 *Armstrong Cemetery, Reed Tp., Seneca County Cemetery Records*, compiled by the Seneca County Genealogical Society, OGS., Date Unknown.

Chapter 3: Death and Transition

Levi Clay was born December 12, 1843—the youngest child of John and Mary Hoy Clay. Sometime during the year 1843, the Clays had a family picture taken, and that photograph appears at the beginning of this section. Some of their older children and an infant appear in the picture with them. No doubt, Levi's mother gave the picture to him in later years, as it appears framed in the background of many family photos taken in Adair, Iowa. It later passed on to my grandmother, Adelia Viola Clay Inman, who displayed it on top of her piano in her home in Marble Rock, Iowa, where it appears in the background of photos taken there. The back of the photo is labeled: "John Clay Family, Centre County, Penn. Summit County, Ohio."

The State of Ohio was afflicted with a serious cholera outbreak in the 1830s and 1840s.[28] Records of the Grill Cemetery, Franklin Tp., Summit Co., Ohio show a number of Clay deaths that happened relatively close together:

CLAY, John--May 6 1844--50y m 11d

Christian--May 27, 1844--57y 7m 17d

Catharine w/o C--Aug 8 1844--51y 11m 9d

George--Jan 29 1834--18y 1m 3d

Mary w/o C & d/o C Hively – Aug - 1844 — 22y 4m

Susan d/o C & C--Sep 12 1844--20y 5m 27d

---

28 Cholera Epidemics—Ohio History Central, A Product of the Ohio Historical Society. An Online Encyclopedia of Ohio History Central. Accessed June 5, 2010. Available at http://www.ohiohistorycentral.org/entry.php?rec=487

Levi--Sep 18 1849--21y 3m 26d

Matilda d/o J & R--Jan—1852

John--Dec 27 1852--39y 10m 21d

John (s/o Rebecca)--Sep 12, 1853--17d²⁹

This Christian Clay was the brother of Mathias Clay and John Clay's uncle. His wife was Catharine Wolfe. Mary, wife of Christian and daughter of C Hively, died August 1844 and was Mary Hively who married Christian Clay, son of Christian, April 14, 1844 in Summit Co. Jacob Clay, son of Christian, married a Bergner. George Clay was the first son of John Clay and Mary Barbara Hoy Clay. John Clay, who died Dec 27 1852, was also a son of Christian Clay.

According to the *Cemetery Records of Summit Co.* concerning the Grill Cemetery:

> *This cemetery, which should properly be called BERGNER CEMETERY, is located behind St. Peter United Church of Christ, 6385 S. Cleveland-Massillon Road. The cemetery is owned by the Franklin Township Trustees and is not owned by St. Peter's. This one acre cemetery is still active. Monument orientation is West.*

> *Although adjacent to a church, records indicate that this cemetery was never owned by a church, but was a private family cemetery, then a community cemetery, and was finally turned over to the township under Ohio law. The cemetery bears the name of John Grill, who owned the land on which the church now stands.³⁰¹*

Cholera entered the United States in 1832 from European immigrants via the Great Lakes and followed the Ohio and Mississippi Rivers and also the canals. Cleveland was the first Ohio city struck by the disease. Many canal workers died of cholera, and as many as 8,000 people died in Cincinnati. Former President James K. Polk was the most famous person to die of cholera in 1849 while a resident of Tennessee. The epidemic reached its peak in Ohio in 1849, causing people to flee for safety. Many refugees took the disease with them, however. Since

---

29 *Grill Cemetery Records, Franklin Tp., Summit Co., Ohio, Vol. 2* (Summit Co., Chapter, OGS, 1980) 28-34.

30 *Grill Cemetery Records*, 28.

these Clays all lived close together and were part of the same family group, it is highly probable that cholera claimed their lives.[31]

Levi Clay was only six months old at the time of his father's death. His mother and the children who survived may have been living in another house at the time and thus avoided contracting the illness. John Clay and members of the Christian Clay family were victims. Perhaps John Clay was working at Christian's farm when he fell ill, and he remained there.

Levi's mother Mary Hoy Clay remained in Summit Co., Ohio until 1849. John Clay died intestate, so quite possibly it took that long to settle his estate. According to the John Clay 1844 Estate File[32] and Levi Clay 1845 Guardianship file[33] for Summit County, John Grill was appointed guardian of Levi Clay. Christina Magdalena Clay also had a guardian by the name of Henry Drake. The last entry was dated October 12, 1848, where Lucius Peck appears as Clerk of Court. It seems that John Clay and Christian Clay had so many overlapping business matters, that the two estates were probated simultaneously. Most of the documents in these files are illegible, but there are approximately fifteen pages of data. Papers pertaining to the Christian Clay estate also appear in the John Clay estate file. He may have died intestate as well.

* * *

Mary Barbara Hoy was born April 22, 1800 in Centre Co., Pennsylvania to George Hoy (b. September 10, 1775, Bern Tp., Berks Co., Pennsylvania; d. April 16, 1863, Madisonburg, Centre Co., Pennsylvania) and Elizabeth Klee (b. 1774, Bern Tp., Berks Co., Pennsylvania; d. March 1813, Centre Co., Pennsylvania.) George Hoy was the son of Albrecht Hoy (Heu) and Susanna Sneavely/Schnable. Elizabeth Klee was the daughter of Jeremiah Klee and Catherine (Surname unknown). This Jeremiah Klee was the brother of John Clay's grandfather, Christian Klee, and is the same Jeremiah Klee who

---

31   Cholera Epidemics, http://www.ohiohistorycentral.org/entry.php?rec=487
32   John Clay Estate File, 1844, Court of Common Pleas, Summit Co., Ohio
33   Levi Clay Guardianship file, 1844, Court of Common Pleas, Summit Co., Ohio

relocated to Weathersfield Tp., Trumbull Co., Ohio. Mary Barbara Hoy and her husband John Clay were first cousins once removed. The children of Jeremiah Klee follow:

> Elizabeth Clay, b. ca. 1776, Bern Tp., Berks Co., Pennsylvania; d ca. 1813, Centre Co., Pennsylvania; m. George Albert Hoy, 1797, Bern Tp., Berks Co., Pennsylvania;

> John Clay, b. Oct. 27, 1786, Bern Tp., Berks Co., Pennsylvania; d July 30, 1844, Seneca Co., Ohio; m. Julia Ann Hair ca. 1816;

> Isaac Clay, Sr., b. Dec. 21, 1781, Bern Tp. Berks Co., Pennsylvania; d Aug. 18, 1874, Maumee, Wood Co., Ohio; m. Elizabeth Wise, ca 1806, Pennsylvania;

> Abraham Clay;

> Catherine Clay, m. Reuben Gall;

> Benjamin Clay, b. ca 1788, Pennsylvania; d. Aug. 9 1829, Trumbull Co., Ohio[34]

[Note: The John Clay listed here is the same John Clay who is buried in the Armstrong Cemetery, Reed Tp., Seneca Co., Ohio.]

George Albert Hoy, father of Mary Barbara Hoy Clay, was born in Berks Co., Pennsylvania September 10, 1773. His family lived in the Little Swatara area near Lebanon, Pennsylvania and in 1802, he and his brother moved to Brush Valley. They purchased 400 acres from Andrew Apple and divided it equally between them. George married Elizabeth Klee ca. 1797 and had eight children. His children by his first wife Elizabeth were:

> Albert Hoy, b. in Pennsylvania, Nov. 29, 1798; d. March 15, 1849; m. (1) Magdalena Weckerly; (2) Mary Niehart (Newhart);

> Mary Barbara Hoy, b. April 22, 1800, Centre Co., Pennsylvania; d. Nov. 12, 1867 in Berreman Tp., Joe Daviess Co., Illinois; m. 1815, John Clay, Centre Co., Pennsylvania;

> Elizabeth Hoy, b. in Pennsylvania ca. 1802; m. John Brungart (or Brumgart);

---

34 Lois P. Wilson., Jeremiah Klee Family Group Sheet, October 1, 1993.

George Hoy, b. in Brush Valley, Centre Co., Pennsylvania, 1805; d. 1864; m. Susannah Ziegler;

Jeremiah Hoy, b. in Brush Valley, March 1807; d. May 13, 1885, buried in a cemetery on Route 192 near Madisonburg, Pennsylvania; m. Elizabeth Bucher;

Susan Hoy, b. in Brush Valley ca. 1809; m. John Vanada (or Voneda);

Sarah Hoy, b. in Brush Valley, Aug. 29 or 31, 1812; d. Savanna, Illinois May 17, 1894; m. Oct. 7, 1832, James Parkinson.[35]

Elizabeth Klee Hoy died in March 1813. George Hoy married Catherine (surname unknown), and the couple had the following children:

Mary Magdalena Hoy, b. in Brush Valley; m. John Roush;

John Hoy, b. in Brush Valley; m. Mary Kline;

Margarete or Rebecca Hoy, b. in Brush Valley; m. Samuel Kline;

Henry Hoy, b. in Brush Valley.[36]

Between 1804 and 1812, George Hoy built both a large house and barn. He has been described as a good farmer and businessman and willed each of his children five thousand dollars. While his sons learned to read and write, his daughters did not. George died April 16, 1863 and is buried in the Lutheran Cemetery at Madisonburg, Pennsylvania. His second wife Catherine was born December 28, 1779 and died January 10, 1861. She is buried in the same cemetery as her husband.

The Hoy/Heu family originated in Germany and came to America as part of the large Palatine migration. Albrecht Hoy/Heu was born May 30, 1737/1738 and arrived with his parents in 1751. Albrecht and his brother Bernard took the Oath of Allegiance before Peter Spyker May 25, 1778. In both 1786 and 1794, he owned 212 acres in Tulpehocken Tp., Berks Co., Pennsylvania. About 1795, he migrated from Berks Co., to Buffalo Valley, Union Co., Pennsylvania in 1795. On April 17, 1759, he married Susanna Sneavely (Schneable). [She was the daughter of Johan Jacob Schneable, who died April-June 1772, and

35 Inman, Notes on the Clay (Klee) Family, January 9, 1992
36 Inman, Clay Family, 1992.

Barbara Eberle, both of them coming from the Alsace Lorraine, and
settling in Lancaster, Pennsylvania. Susanna was born June 22, 1738
in Berks County, Pennsylvania. On July 19, 1816, she made a deposi-
tion in the settlement of her son Charles's estate in Centre County,
Pennsylvania.] Albrecht Hoy died ca. 1810, and his wife died ca. 1820
in Centre Co., Pennsylvania. The children of Albrecht and Susanna
Hoy/Heu were:

   Elizabeth Hoy, bapt. Feb. 10, 1760, Berks Co., Pennsylvania;

   Karl Hoy, bapt. Aug. 21, 1763, Berks Co., Pennsylvania; d. Centre
   Co., Pennsylvania, no later than 1816; m. Elizabeth (surname
   unknown). (Karl—Charles—and wife are buried at Rebersberg,
   Pennsylvania;

   Phillip Hoy, bapt. Feb. 25, 1765, Berks Co., Pennsylvania; d.
   January 21, 1844; m. Anna Maria Gilbert;

   John Hoy, bapt. April 25, 1767, Berks Co., Pennsylvania;

   George Hoy, bapt. Sept. 10, 1773, Berks Co., Pennsylvania.[37]

Albrecht Hoy arrived with his father Carl Hoy/Heu and his mother
Maria Eva (surname unknown) in Philadelphia September 25, 1751
aboard the *Phoenix*. The Hoys/Heus came from the south bank
of the Rhine in Germany and were probably among the last of the
large Palatine migration. Carl settled in Tulpehocken Tp., Berks Co.,
Pennsylvania and was naturalized in Philadelphia April 1, 1764. He
took the Oath of Allegiance before Peter Spycker in Berks Co. May
30, 1779, and was a member of the Evangelical Lutheran Church.
In 1789, he was still living in Berks Co., Pennsylvania. His children
were:

   Albrecht Hoy, b. in Germany, May 30, 1737/1738;

   Maria Elizabeth Hoy, b. in Berks Co., Pennsylvania October 7,
   1753; m. _____ Helm;

   Bernard Hoy, m. Margaret _____;

   _____ Phillip Hoy[38]

37 Inman, Clay Family, 1992.
38 Inman, Clay Family, 1992.

After John Clay's estate was settled, Mary Barbara Hoy Clay took part of her family and relocated to Jo Daviess Co., Illinois where she bought 640 acres of land in Berreman Tp. from the Government. For this purchase, she used some of the money she inherited from her father's estate. While Mary Clay could not read or write and signed her name with an "X" on the release for her father's estate, her children were literate and no doubt aided her tremendously in making these transactions. Their schooling was limited, however. Levi Clay had four years of formal schooling. Alfred Clay was not educated until almost reaching his majority. Jeremiah Clay was educated in the common schools of Summit County. Daniel Reuben Clay attended the district school in Summit County., and obtained a thorough understanding of the subjects taught at that period of time. Mary Clay settled on her land in Berreman Tp., and raised her family there. Family lore suggests that after her removal to Jo Daviess Co., Illinois, Mary adopted three more children.

The first dwelling was a rude log cabin built by Daniel Reuben Clay (who was 14 by then) and another of her sons. The cabin was clapboarded (the nails were manufactured by the Clays at home). It also had a dirt floor and a door hung on leather hinges. The door opened by means of a latchstring and was always out since the family welcomed travelers. According to the *Jo Daviess County History*, it rained every day while the cabin was under construction. The Clays made themselves as comfortable as possible at night—some of them sleeping under the wagon box while the rest sheltered themselves under the shingles, which they used for blankets. This cabin was later used as a church meetinghouse. One wonders why Mary Barbara Clay and her children would move so far away from familiar surroundings to a life of uncertainty.

The first permanent settlements in Jo Daviess County were in 1820 and in 1827, the county was formed. It was named after Maj. Joseph Hamilton Daveiss, U.S. Attorney General from Kentucky, who was killed in 1811 at the Battle of Tippecanoe. Historians have noted that the major's name is consistently misspelled! Jo Daviess people pronounce the name "Davis."[39]

39 *The History of Jo Daviess County*, Illinois, H. J. Kett and Co., (Chicago, 1878).

Jo Daviess Co., Illinois was the site of numerous lead mines that were discovered in 1700 by a Frenchman named LeSueur.[40] Early maps indicate that by 1820, the Galena River was labeled "The River of Mines." It should also be noted that during the 1840s, a number of Mennonite families settled in Jo Daviess County.[41] While the Clays and the Hoys came from German Reformed/Evangelical Lutheran backgrounds, there were Mennonites in the Hoy/Sneavely (Schnaeble) line. The presence of German people would certainly appeal to the Clays. And the county was definitely a lure for other people as well, including Ulysses S. Grant, who arrived in Galena with his family in the spring of 1860. The Grants rented a home there and after the Civil War broke out, Grant's attention was turned toward battle. On August 18, 1865, a victorious Grant returned to Galena, where some grateful Republicans presented him with a house. After he was elected President, Grant spent little time in the house. His final visit was in 1880. Grant died July 23, 1885 of throat cancer at the age of 65 in Mt McGregor, New York.[42]

For the Clays, however, a combination of factors encouraged their move from Ohio to Illinois: cheap land, which was being sold at five dollars an acre, the presence of numerous lead mines, fear of the cholera epidemic in Ohio, bright prospects for the future and a willingness to start over and put the past behind them.

A brief discussion of this family is found in the *Jo Daviess County History* (1889):

> *John Clay, was born in Centre County, Pa., Feb. 26, 1794. He grew to manhood in his native State, and there married Miss Mary B. Hoy. She was a native of the same county as himself, and was born of German parentage, April 22, 1800. After their marriage they*

40 *Jo Daviess Co. History* (1878).
41 Hazel N. Hasson, *The Early Mennonites of Joe Daviess County*, Mennonite Heritage, March 1977. Genealogy Trails: Jo Daviess Co., Genealogy & History. Accessed June 3, 2010. Available at http:// genealogytrails.com/ill/jodaviess.
42 *Portrait and Biographical Album of Jo Daviess County, Illinois.* Chapman Bros., (Chicago, 1889).

removed to Ohio, and settled in Summit County, where the death of Mr. Clay occurred in May, 1844. He was a worthy man, and a consistent member of the Presbyterian Church. The mother of our subject died Nov. 12, 1867, in Jo Daviess County. To them were born seventeen children, eleven of whom are now living: William, Elizabeth, John, Alfred S., Jeremiah, Catherine, Hiram, Daniel R., Margaret, Christina Magdalene, and Levi. William, a gardener of Adair County, Iowa, married Eliza Fickles, of Summit County, Ohio, and they have eight children - Alfred, Elizabeth, Daniel R., William, Caroline, Emma, Hamilton, and Polly Ann; Elizabeth married Abraham Brubaker, a farmer of Berreman Township, and they have seven children - Mary Ann, Susan, Elizabeth, Catherine, Isabella, Lucy, and Hiram; John, a farmer of Floyd County, Iowa, married Louisa Rex, of Summit County, Ohio, and they have seven children - Harriet, Mary, Aaron, William, John, Rebecca, and Cassius; Alfred, a resident of Jo Daviess County, married Lydia Church; they have no children of their own, but have adopted two - William and Mary Brady. Catherine married for her first husband John Pottorf, who died, leaving her with one son, Alfred Pottorf. She subsequently became the wife of George Schlafer, of Germany, now a farmer in Berreman Township. Seven children have been born to them - George, John, Molly, Ward, Lena, Mary, and James, the last two being deceased; Hiram, an express and freight agent at Marble Rock, Iowa, married Martha Hiscox, of Floyd County, Iowa, and they have the following children - Albert, Pearl, and Jewett; Daniel R. (see below); Christina married Anderson Palmer, of this county, who is now engaged in mining in Grant County, Wis., and they have eight children - Jeremiah, Jasper, Grant, Francis, Jane, Nellie, Alfred, and Eddie; Magdalene married James Anthony, a carpenter and joiner of Morrison, Whiteside Co., Ill., and they have five children - John, Belle, Albert, Edith, and Clara; Levi, a drayman in Adair County, Iowa, married Mary Stillions, and they have the following children - Viola, Lizzie, and Jennie.

Mr. and Mrs. Clay [Daniel R. Clay] were married in this county May 2, 1858. Her maiden name was Christiana Bruce, and she was born in Centre County, Pa. April 2, 1833, her parents being William and Hannah (Meace) Bruce, natives of Virginia and

Pennsylvania. Of this Union seven children have been born: William H., James W., Walter E., Christiana, Milton A., George L., and Kiner F.[43]

Mary Clay died November 12, 1867 in Berreman Tp, Jo Daviess Co., Illinois. She is buried in the Clay Cemetery in Jo Daviess Co., Illinois, where a number of her family members are also buried. There is no marker on her grave.

43 *Portrait and Biographical Album of Jo Daviess County, Illinois.*

Chapter 4: The Stillians Connection

The records do not reveal how Levi Clay and Mary Stillians met, but more than likely, they met at church. Mary Elizabeth Stillians was the daughter of William Stillians (1826-1907) and Catherine Lee (1826-1852). She was born June 30, 1849, and her death certificate lists Pennsylvania as the state of her birth. However, this family moved frequently, and the boundaries shifted between Pennsylvania, Virginia, what was later West Virginia, and Maryland. According to Charles Gordon Inman, great grandson of Levi and Mary Clay:

> A later 1957 letter from Mrs. Lula (Clay) Splawn—daughter of Levi and Mary Clay—(never mailed, but found by her daughter, Loraine (Baker) Scott in 1969) gave the birthplace of Mary Stillians as Grandville, Virginia. The Postal Guide of 1851 lists no Grandville in Virginia. A West Virginia atlas of 1876 shows a Granville in Monongalia Co., however. This is the county in which Morgantown is located.[44]

By 1850, the William Stillians family had moved to Cumberland Tp., Greene Co., Pennsylvania. Mary's place of birth is listed on that census record as Pennsylvania.[45] By 1860, the William Stillians family resided in Jo Daviess Co., Illinois, and Mary's place of birth is listed as Pennsylvania.[46] The rest of the available census records identify Pennsylvania as her birthplace. Her parents were married in Granville,

---

44 Inman, Clay Family, 1992.
45 Stillians, William. 1850 Census, Cumberland Tp., Greene County, Pennsylvania, Ancestry.com, Provo, Utah. Accessed July 18, 2010. Available at http://www.ancestry.com.
46 Stillians, William. 1860 Census, Woodbine, Jo Daviess County, Illinois, Ancestry.com, Provo, Utah. Accessed July 18, 2010. Available at http://www.ancestry.com

Monongalia Co., Virginia May 9, 1848.[47] It is possible that she was born in Granville, Monongalia Co., Virginia (today, West Virginia) and the family moved to Pennsylvania shortly after her birth.

The records are just as confusing about her father William Stillians. A number of family history researchers have identified him as "John William Stillians" in recent years, but I have never found "John" associated with his name. His name was William Stillians. If he had a middle name, I have yet to find it. It's possible some people are confusing William with his father and his grandfather.

William Stillians was born December 29, 1826 in Pennsylvania[48], Virginia[49], or Maryland[50] to William and Mary Stillens. He died in Bear Grove Tp., Guthrie Co., Iowa October 13, 1907. The 1850 Census for Cumberland Tp., Greene County, Pennsylvania lists his place of birth as Maryland. It is interesting to note that the 1860 Census is the first reference to Pennsylvania as his birthplace. The Pennsylvania reference continues until 1880.[51] His birthplace appears as Virginia for the first time on that record. However, his daughter, Sarah Jane Stillians Tift identifies his birthplace as Pennsylvania.[52] William's father, William M. Stillens[53], was a Methodist Circuit Rider, a judge and a doctor. This family traveled throughout Western Pennsylvania, Virginia (what is today West Virginia) and parts of Maryland and Delaware. To add further confusion, the name is spelled differently everywhere they went! In all likelihood, the name was originally

---

47   Inman, 1992.
48   William Stillians, 1860 Census, Jo Daviess, County, Illinois
49   William Stillians Death Certificate, October 1907, State of Iowa
50   William Stillians. 1850 Census, Cumberland Tp., Greene Co., Pennsylvania
51   William Stillians. 1880 Census, Bear Grove Tp., Guthrie Co., Iowa, Ancestry.com, Provo, Utah. Accessed July 18, 2010. Available at http://www.ancestry.com.
52   William Tift. 1885 Census, Manning, Carroll Co., Iowa. Ancestry.com, Provo, Utah. Accessed July 18, 2010. Available at http://www.ancestry.com.
53   William M. Stillen. 1840 Census, Greene Tp., Greene Co., Pennsylvania. Microfilm No. M704, Reel 40, p. 351. National Archives Annex, 6th & Kipling, Denver, Colorado.

Stillings or Stillins—possibly Stallions--and the family originated in England, settling first in Maryland.

* * *

Mary Stillians Clay's great-grandfather was John Stillings who died in June 1785 in Cecil Tp., Washington Co., Pennsylvania.[54] John Stillings' name first appears on a Maryland list of runaway convict servants:

> *Stilling (or Stillin), John. Reported as a runaway 4 September 1766 to 23 October 1766 and 12 July 1770 to 9 August 1770, MG [Maryland Gazette] Near Annapolis. Thomas Rutland. The 1770 advertisement states that he probably will change his name "as he did once before when he ran away."*[55]

John Stillings was probably born in England ca. 1750. Cox describes the typical convict servant as follows:

> *The typical escaped convict servant appears to have been English, male, about 28 years old, from Anne Arundel or Baltimore counties, and possessing a wide variety of skills. The majority of the servants identified by nationality were English, mostly from the western part of the country; the remainders were predominately Irish. Of the nearly 800 convicts reported in the newspapers, only 32 were women, a percentage probably not reflective of the nature of the trade in the Chesapeake. The ages of the runaway convicts tended to be on the youthful side, with slightly over 69 percent of those with ages reported being between 20 and 30 years; however, the ages of these convicts ranged from 14 to 70 years. The geographical concentration of the servants is the result of the location of the main urban centers. Baltimore and Annapolis, where these servants were likely to be employed, in demand, and*

---

54   John Stillings Estate File, 1785-1786, Washington Co., Pennsylvania
55   Richard J. Cox. *Maryland Runaway Convict Servants 1745-1780. National Genealogical Society Quarterly,* Vol. 68, No. 2, June 1980, 105-215.

imported through, and the fact that the colony's only newspapers were based there (the Maryland Gazette in Annapolis, and the Maryland Journal in Baltimore). Although less than one half the servants were reported as having skills, these skills were varied. A total of 64 different occupations were listed, led by farmers (38), shoemakers (33), sailors (27), weavers (26), tailors (20), and blacksmiths (20). Many convicts claimed to have a certain skill, however, which proved to not be true once purchased and set to work.[56]

Mary Elizabeth Stillians Clay's great grandfather is quite possibly the John Stilling/Stillin who appears on a 1766 passenger and immigration list for Maryland[57]

John Stillings was successful in his 1770 escape attempt and appears to have made it to Harford Co., Maryland, where a Jacob Stallion appears on Harford and Frederick County records. John Stillings may have also known John Webster, a convict transported to Maryland in 1772.[58] It is possible that they knew one another in England, John Stillings having been transported in 1766 and John Webster in 1772. They may have been "partners in crime" or they may have met one another in prison.

In any event, after John Stillings arrived in Harford Co., he encountered a family of Quakers named Webster, who owned the Brush River Iron Works.[59] Partners in the Iron Works included brothers Johnny Lee Webster, Isaac Webster, James Webster, and John Bond and Jacob Giles. Johnny Lee Webster was a planter and a money lender.[60] Brumbaugh notes that Johnny Lee Webster "acted as a bank and

56 Cox, Runaway Convict Servants, 107-108
57 *Passengers and Immigration Lists*, 1357.2, p. 293 (1987 Index Supplement)
58 Peter Wilson Coldham. *More Emigrants in Bondage: 1614-1775.*, 186. [Baltimore: Genealogical Publishing Co., 2002] 217p
59 Johnny Lee Webster File, Maryland State Archives, Annapolis, Maryland. [File folder consisting of penciled notes.]
60 Webster file, Maryland Archives.

loaned money to hundreds.[61] His occupation was sometimes dangerous. Thomas Hall threatened his life on September 9, 1780.[62]

According to the John Lee Webster File at the Maryland Archives,
Johnny Lee Webster was born March 6, 1731 in Baltimore to Isaac
Webster and Margaret Lee, and he died June 9, 1795 in Harford Co.,
Maryland. His father Isaac died in 1759, and was the son of John
Webster, a Quaker, who died in 1753. Margaret Lee was the daughter
of James Lee, a planter from Baltimore. The Children of Isaac and
Margaret Webster follow:

> Isaac Webster (b. 1730; m. Elizabeth);
>
> Johnny Lee Webster (b. 1731; m. Elizabeth);
>
> Hannah Webster (b. 1724; m. Samuel Glover, a Quaker in
> 1742; m Nathan Richardson, a Quaker in 1756);
>
> Margaret Webster (b. 1725/26; m. John Talbot of John (a
> Quaker);
>
> Mary Webster (b. 1728; m. 1748 Robert Pleasants of John (a
> Quaker)—he m. 2dly Mary Hill, mother of H. M. Hill 1760,
> who m. Benj. Ogle;
>
> Susannah Webster (m. 1759 Robt. Pleasants Jr. of Thomas (a
> Quaker);
>
> James Webster;
>
> Cassandra Webster, (m. 1763 Jonathan Masser of Aquilla (a
> Quaker);
>
> Elizabeth Webster (m. a Robertson);
>
> Sarah Webster (d. by 1769; m. 1761 William Coall (a Quaker);

61 Gaius Marchas Brumbaugh, *Maryland Records Vol. II.* (Baltimore:
    Genealogical Publishing, 1928) 154.
62 C. Milton Wright, *Our Harford Heritage: A History of Harford County,
    Maryland.* (French-Bray Printing Co., 1980) 176.

Aliceanna/Alisanna Webster (d. by 1805, m. John Wilson of
Christopher and Sarah of Cumberland, England;

Ann Webster (m. a Jewett);

Samuel Webster (m. a Tanner)[63]

John Lee Webster appears on the 1776 Census for Spesutia, the Lower
Hundred, Harford Co., Maryland with his wife Elizabeth, his year old
son John, and a 14 year-old girl by the name of Elizabeth Webster,
who was living in his household. Mary Webster appears on the same
record, and Mary is listed at age 38.[64] The Harford County Websters
were from Baltimore. It is quite possible that Mary came out of one
of those families. Young Elizabeth may have been her daughter, and
she may have been living with the John Lee Webster family to help
take care of the year-old son. There is the possibility that fourteen-
year-old Elizabeth may have been a daughter of Johnny Lee Webster.
I believe that about 1778, this young Elizabeth Webster became the
wife of John Stillings. John Stillings appears to have been a rascal,
(something that is implied in his records), and his wife was probably well-connected. He needed money in order to "operate," and he
appears to have had money in order to do that.

In 1778, John Stalions took the Oath of Fidelity in Anne Arundel
Co.,[65] so perhaps John settled the situation with Thomas Rutland
through the Webster influence prior to his marriage to Elizabeth.
John and Elizabeth Stillings moved to Yohogania Co., Virginia (today
Washington and Greene Counties, Pennsylvania) shortly after their
marriage.[2] A document in the John Stillings estate file indicates they
were in Yohogania County by 1779:

---

63 Notes in Johnny Lee Webster File, Maryland State Archives.
64 John Lee Webster.. 1776 Census, Spesutia, Lower Hundred, Harford
    Co., Maryland. Maryland Census 1772 to 1890, Accessed July 18, 2010.
    Available at Ancestry.com, http://www.ancestry.com
65 Margaret Roberts Hodges, Editor. An Alphabetical List of those who
    took the Oak of Fidelity and Support of the State of Maryland in Anne
    Arundel County, 1778. Genealogical Department, National Society,
    Daughters of the American Revolution, Annapolis, Maryland. FHL Film
    0006302

*Washington County, P: Came personaly before me the subscrib-
ing Justice for the County aforesaid, William Anderson and being
duly sworn deposeth and saith that in the year 1779 he this deponent was present when John Stillion late deceased measured and
took three bushels of wheat and one bushel of rye the property of
William Laughlen who was then fled from his plantation for fear
of the Indians and this deponent sayeth that he heard said John
Stillion say at same time he would be forth coming to William
Laughlen aforesaid for said grain and further this deponent sayeth not: Sworn and subscribed before me the 31ˢᵗ day of Oct. 1785.
William Anderson[66]*

Washington Co., Pennsylvania was formed from Yohogania Co.,
Virginia. According to the *Lists of Inhabitants 1800 or Before:*

*Settlers by the thousands poured into southwestern Penna in the
1770's. Many stayed, while in later years others pushed on to
Kentucky or Ohio. In 1771 the territory was organized as a part
of Bedford Co; in 1773 it was made a part of Westmoreland Co;
in 1781 it became Washington Co...Virginia claimed this territory
until 1780 and held courts 1775-1780.[67]*

John Stillings appears as *John Stilliongs* as a Sergeant 5ᵗʰ Class in Capt.
Joseph Beelors Militia Company on December 24, 1781 in the Second
Battalion, Washington Co, Pennsylvania. George Vallandigham was
Lieutenant Colonel. The Major was William Pollock. The Captains
were Thomas Parkeson and ??? Cunningham[68] He appears as *John
Stillings* on a return for the , 2ⁿᵈ Battalion, Washington Co., Militia,
ordered to rendezvous June 14, 1782.[69]

In 1784, John Stallions appears on the list of inhabitants of Cecil Tp.,
Washington Co., Pennsylvania.[70] John Webster and William Mitchell
also appear with him on the list. John Stillings' granddaughter, Lydia,

66 John Stillings Estate File, Washington Co., Pennsylvania
67 Raymond Martin Bell, Compiler. *Lists of Inhabitants in Washington
    County, Pennsylvania 1800 or Before,* (Dated 1981)
68 Arrangement of Militia 1781-1782, *Pennsylvania Archives 6ᵗʰ Series, v.
    2*, 25-26
69 Arrangement of Militia 1781-1782, *Pennsylvania Archives, 6ᵗʰ Series, v.
    2*, 46
70 Bell, *Lists of Inhabitants,*

later married Isaac Gibson Mitchell in Washington Co., Pennsylvania.[3] And this John Webster may have been the convict transported to Maryland in 1772.

By 1784, John Stillings became involved in land speculation with Johnny Lee Webster, James Webster of Harford Co., Maryland and James Crawford of Monongalia Co., Virginia. On February 10, 1784, John Stillings of Yohogania Co., Virginia sold 400 acres on Raccoon Creek to John Lee Webster of Harford Co., Maryland. The text of the deed identifies John Stillings of Yohogania County and com- monwealth of Virginia, "farmer" for and in consideration of "three thousand five hundred pounds Continental money to me in hand paid by James Crawford of Monongahala County [sic], state aforesaid on behalf of John Lee Webster of Hartford County Commonwealth of Mariland have granted bargained and sold by these presents do grant bargain and sell and convey unto the said Lee Webster..."[71] Then On April 28, 1785, John Stillings ordered 350 acres of land surveyed in Washington Co., Pennsylvania.[72]

John Stillings died prior to June 27, 1785. On that day, Letters of Administration were issued to Elizabeth Stillings, William Williams, John Madow, and Ephraim Burwell all of Washington County, Pennsylvania. Elizabeth Stillings and William Williams were ap- pointed administrators of John Stillings' estate. Elizabeth signed her name with an "x". William Williams, John Madow and Ephraim Burwell signed their names. Other names appearing in the records: James Webster, William Laughlin, and William Anderson. Items in John Stillings' estate Include:

> *bed and bedding and "waraing" clothes, three books, lather and shews; one pare of chanes and old ax and old iron; boles and puter knifes and forks & pare of pots, hooks and ???; thread woll; sedall bridle and hambs; 6 horses, cash; three bonds.*[73]

---

71   John Stillings/John Lee Webster Deed, February 10, 1784, Washington
     Co., Pennsylvania
72   John Stillings Survey Note, April 1784, Washington Co., Pennsylvania,
     Pennsylvania Archives.
73   John Stillings Estate, 1785, Washington Co., Pennsylvania, Pennsylvania
     State Archives.

The final entry for the Orphans Court Record October 29, 1785 reads:

William Williams acting administrator of John Stillions, Deceased (Came into Court) and produced an acct. of his administration by which it appears that there is a balance of one hundred and eighty six pounds nine shillings two pence in the hands of the said administrator subject to distribution according to law, part of which consists of bonds (viz) one bond on William Still for seventeen pounds seventeen shillings and nine pence due to the Estate of the said Deceased the last day of November 1785 one other bond on William Still for twelve pounds two shillings and three pence due the last day of November AD 1785 one bond on John MaDow for twenty seven pounds ten shillings to be paid in Horses ninth May 1786 one other on the said John MaDow for twenty seven pounds ten shillings to be paid in Horses at cash price on the ninth May 1787 one other Bond on said John Madow for twenty seven pounds ten shillings to be paid on Horses at cash price on the ninth May 1788 one other Bond on the said John MaDow for five pounds five shillings to be paid on the first day of September 1787 one other Bond on Rowley Boyle for three pounds payable twenty ninth October 1785 and Bond on James Kirkpatrick[1] for three pounds twelve shillings payable first September 1787 and one Note on Thomas Boyle for four pounds ten shillings due the twenty ninth day of October 1785....By the Court.[74]

John Stillings' estate was recorded as closed February 1786.

The record grows silent after the death of John Stillings. A Joseph Stealions appears on the 1790 Census for Derry Tp., Alleghany Co., Pennsylvania, which is today Westmoreland, Co.[75] The record identifies two males over 16, one male under 16, and four females. Joseph Stealions would have been too old to have been another child of John and Elizabeth Stillings, but he may have been John's brother, a nephew, or a cousin. I believe Elizabeth Stillings may have moved into

74 John Stillings Estate. Orphan's Court Records, Washington Co., Courthouse, Washington, Pennsylvania, Vol. 1, 27
75 Joseph L. Stealions 1790 Census, Derry Tp., Alleghany Co., Pennsylvania. *Heads of Families at the First Census Taken in the Year 1790*. (Washington DC: Government Printing Office, 1908).

the Joseph Stealions household in Derry Tp., since it is near the area
where she last appears on a census record (Hanover Tp.) and her son
apparently married in Beaver County. On the 1790 Census Record
for Derry Tp., her son would have been the child under 16. She would
have been one of the females.

John Stillings' widow last appears on the 1800 Census for Hanover
Tp, Washington Co., Pennsylvania as Widow Stillian.[765] She does not
appear on the 1810 Pennsylvania Census Records. There is the possibility that she may have remarried, but to date, I have found no marriage record for her. And she may have died sometime between 1800
and 1810. It does not appear that she returned to Maryland.

While the records do not specify the number of children for John and
Elizabeth Stillings, their son William appears to be the only child.
William Stillens was born in 1781, a name and date confirmed by
1820, 1830 and 1840 Census Records and the Stillians Family Bible.[77]

There is some confusion in later records about William Stillens' name
as well as the location of his birth. Some later records refer to him as
"John" while earlier records substantiate that his name was William.
Some later records claim that he was born in England while earlier
records state that he was born in Pennsylvania. The 1840 Census
for Greene Tp., Greene Co., Pennsylvania lists him as William M.
Stillens. Perhaps his middle name was Michael, if in fact his maternal
grandfather was Michael Webster, or he may have been named for
another Michael Webster in the family! For clarity's sake, I will refer
to him here as William M. Stillens. He was the grandfather of Mary
Stillians Clay.

And the records are equally confusing about William M. Stillens'
wife Mary. Apparently, Mary was raised by the William Inghram
family of Greene Co., Pennsylvania. She was born in 1795, a year
that is substantiated by the 1850 Census for Amwell Tp., Washington

76 Widow Stillians. 1800 Census, Hanover Tp., Washington Co.,
    Pennsylvania. *Lists of Inhabitants in Washington County, Pennsylvania
    1800 or Before with Maps of the Early Townships.* Raymond Martin
    Bell, Compiler. (Washington and Jefferson College, 1961).
77 Stillians Family Bible, in the possession of Bruce Stillians, Villisca,
    Iowa

Co., Pennsylvania, where she appears in the Elisha Lacock/Laycock household[78] I originally thought that her surname was *Inghram* because she named her children after members of the William Inghram family. A trip to the Greene Co., Pennsylvania Courthouse could yield no information about her. Subsequently, I received an email from one of William Inghram's descendants informing me that Mary was not an Inghram, even though she was raised by the family. William and Mary Stillens were married in 1814 in Greene Tp., Beaver Co., Pennsylvania[79] Their children follow:

John Inghram Stillians, b. June 3, 1815, Washington Co., Pennsylvania; d. April 14, 1893, Clarinda, Page Co., Iowa; m. Ruth Gapen December 28, 1837;

Samuel Stillians, b. Dec. 12, 1817, Delaware; d. Oct. 2, 1899, Nodaway, Page Co., Iowa; m. Elizabeth Davis, Dec. 7, 1843 Monongalia Co., Virginia;

Lydia Stillians, b. Dec. 14, 1819, b. Wilmington, New Castle, Delaware; d. in Illinois; m. Isaac Gibson Mitchell, Nov. 12, 1835, in Illinois;[6]

Elizabeth Stillians, b. Aug. 1, 1821, Hampshire Co., Virginia;

Sarah Jane Stillians, b. Nov. 3, 1823, Washington Co., Pennsylvania; d. March 7, 1902, Manson, Calhoun Co., Iowa; m. Elisha Lacock/Laycock, May 22, 1846, Washington Co., Pennsylvania;

William Stillians, b. Dec. 29, 1826, Maryland, Pennsylvania or Virginia; d. Oct. 13, 1907, Bear Grove Tp., Guthrie Co., Iowa; m. Catherine Lee, May 9, 1848, Granville, Monongalia Co., Virginia; m. Rachel Dilley Aug. 22, 1852, Mercer Co., Pennsylvania;

Thomas Stillians, b. June 29, 1829;

---

78 Elisha Lacock/Laycock, 1850 Census, Amwell Tp., Washington Co., Pennsylvania, Ancestry.com, Provo, Utah, Accessed July 1, 2010. Available at http://www.ancestry.com.

79 William Stillians. OneWorld Tree, Ancestry. Com, Provo, Utah. Accessed June 18, 2010. Available at http://www.ancestry.com.

Mary Stillians, b. Oct. 27, 1832.[80]

The oldest son was born in Washington Co., Pennsylvania in 1815. The second son was born in Delaware in 1817. The family returned to Washington Co. in 1819, where the oldest daughter was born. The family appears on the 1820 Census for Hamsphire Co., Virginia. This is the only William Stillens/Stillions listed on any census record that year and again, the parents' and children's ages through 1819 match the 1830 Census for Washington Co., Pennsylvania.[81] The fourth child, a daughter, was born in Hampshire Co., Virginia in 1821. The family may have moved back to Washington Co., by 1823 because the fifth child, another daughter, was born there. Then they returned to Hampshire Co., Virginia, where they appear on the 1825 Tax Records.[82] William Stillians (1826-1907) was born in Maryland, Pennsylvania or Virginia. Earlier records support Maryland as the location of his birth, followed by Pennsylvania and then Virginia in later years. Since the family had already lived on the Eastern Shore in 1817, it is distinctly possible that William was born on Kent Island or in Dorchester, Maryland. The two younger children were born in Pennsylvania.

According to the Stillians Family Bible, William M. Stillens died May 23, 1833,[83] but I believe this is a scrivener's error and the writer intended to write 1843 instead. William appears on two census records in 1840: (1) the 1840 Census for Greene Tp., Greene Co., Pennsylvania, where he is listed as William M. Stillen;[84] and, (2) the 1840 Census for Canton Tp., Washington Co., Pennsylvania, where he is listed as

---

80   Inman, Clay Notes, 1992.
81   William Stillions 1820 Census, Hampshire Co., Virginia, Ancestry.com, Provo, Utah. Accessed July 18, 2010. Available at http://www.ancestry.com.
82   William Stillions. 1825 Tax Records, Hampshire Co., Virginia. Wilmer L. Kerns. *Historical Records of Old Frederick and Hampshire Counties, Virginia (Revised)*. Heritage Books, Inc. May 1, 2009.
83   Stillians Family Bible, in the possession of Bruce Stillians, Villisca, Iowa
84   William M. Stillen. 1840 Census, Greene Tp., Greene Co., Pennsylvania. Microfilm No. M704, Reel 40, p. 351. National Archives Annex, 6th & Kipling, Denver, Colorado.

William Stillens.[85] This family moved constantly and owned property they frequently returned to in Washington County. William was either listed twice in two locations on the 1840 Census, or someone was managing the farm for him in Washington Co. I would assume that William died in Washington Co., Pennsylvania, but so far have not found any estate records for him there. After his death, his wife Mary lived with her daughter, Sarah Jane Stillians Lacock/Laycock, who had married Elisha Lacock/Laycock, and Mary moved with the Laycocks to Jo Daviess Co., Illinois. I have not found a date of death for her.

William M. and Mary Stillens' children either moved west or died young. John Inghram Stillians settled in Western Iowa, as did Samuel Stillians. Lydia married Isaac Gibson Mitchell and eventually moved to Jo Daviess County, Illinois. Sarah Jane married Elisha Laycock, and the Laycocks eventually moved to Jo Daviess Co. and from there, to Iowa. Elizabeth died relatively young. Thomas and Mary both died young. William Stillians (1826-1907), the father of Mary Stillians Clay, was a Methodist Circuit Rider[7], a doctor, a farmer and a businessman. The *History of Adair and Guthrie Counties* suggests that he delivered many babies in that area![86]

---

85   William Stillens. 1840 Census, Canton Tp., Washington Co., Pennsylvania. Microfilm No. M704, Reel 44, p. 199. National Archives Annex, 6th & Kipling, Denver, Colorado.

86   *History of Adair and Guthrie Counties, Iowa,* 1884.

Chapter 5: The Lee and Dilley Factors

Over fifty years ago, I remember hearing an old family story concerning the presence of the Confederate General Robert E. Lee on our family tree. There is definitely a Lee line on the chart. When I first heard the story, I made a note of the connection by the Lee name and filed it away for a future investigation. Years later in the early 1990s, I began searching for my Lees and their supposed connection with the famous general and ran into a brick wall at the beginning. For one thing: my Lees came from Ireland, possibly from Limerick by way of Belfast. General Robert E. Lee's family came from England via the Randolphs of Virginia. Moreover, General Robert E. Lee was a direct descendant of King Robert the Bruce of Scotland. So unless my Lees were Robert E. Lee's poor Irish cousins, I could make no actual connection with him.

Mary Elizabeth Stillians Clay's mother was Catherine Lee, who was born in 1826 to Garrett Fitzgerald Lee and Ann Catherine (Anna Catherina) Bannister in East District, Monongalia Co., Virginia.[8] Garrett Fitzgerald Lee was born in 1771 in Ireland, and he relocated to Maryland ca. 1789. He may have arrived from Belfast on the ship *Brothers* that arrived in Wilmington, Delaware on June 30, 1789.[87]

Garrett Fitzgerald Lee settled in Frederick, Maryland and married Ann C. Bannister in the German Reformed Church in Frederick on January

---

87 Index of Passengers & Immigrants, Ireland from Belfast, 1789. Gale Group, Creator, *Passenger and Immigration Lists: 1996-2000 Cumulation* (Passenger and Immigration Lists Index Cumulated. Supplement. (Publisher: Gale—100 Edition) 2044.

3, 1790.[88] He next appears on the 1800 Census for Montgomery Co., Maryland.[89] From there they moved to Monongalia Co., where he and his wife spent the rest of their lives.

Garrett was a shoemaker by trade. His granddaughter, Mary F. Lee of Oklahoma, once wrote that Garrett had several brothers who relocated to America prior to his removal here but that he never located any of them after his arrival. He may have found one. A William Lee appears on the 1800 census for Montgomery Co., Maryland, District 1 with Garrett Lee.[90] It should also be noted that Garrett named his oldest son William. Also, an Abraham Lee, born about 1800, appears on the 1830 Census for Monongalia Co.[91] Abraham may have been a son of William Lee of Montgomery Co. And he may have been an older child of Garrett Lee, whose name has never been recorded.[9]

Garrett died in 1830 in Monongalia Co., Virginia, and his wife died in 1836[92]. Their children were:

William Lee;

David Lee;

Matilda Lee(who married a Monroe);

Garrett Lee, who was born in 1821;

Catherine Lee, who was born in 1826.[93]

---

88 Garrett Fitzgerald Lee and Ann C. Bannister. Frederick County, Maryland Marriages 1777-1804, Records of the German Reformed Church, Filmed at the Maryland Historical Society, Baltimore, Maryland.

89 Garrett and William Lee.. 1800 Census, District 1, Montgomery Co., Maryland. Ancestry.com, Provo, Utah. Accessed July 3, 2010. Available at http://www.ancestry.com.

90 Garrett and William Lee, 1800 Census, District 1, Montgomery Co., Maryland.

91 Garrett and Abraham Lee. 1830 Census, East District, Monongalia Co., Virginia. Ancestry.com, Provo, Utah. Accessed July 3, 2010. Available at http://www.ancestry.com.

92 Inman, Clay Family, 1992.

93 Inman, Clay Family, 1992.

The oldest child William Lee spent his life in West Virginia and died there in 1898. He appears on the 1860 Census for Clarksburg, Harrison Co., West Virginia with his wife Susan Lee and their children:

Mason Lee (age 23);

Margaret Lee (age 18);

Maryann Lee (age 14);

Herrod T. Lee (age 10)[94]

William followed in his father's footsteps by becoming a shoemaker. His younger brothers both became farmers. Through 1880, William appears on the Clarksburg records and may have moved to Morgantown by 1890 since his wife Susan died there in 1893. Records for the Oak Grove Cemetery, Morgantown, West Virginia show:

William Lee, b. December 1803; d. January 17, 1898;

Susan Lee, b. December 4, 1811; d. November 20, 1893.[95]

Matilda Lee (whose name often appears as "Malinda" on family history records) married David Marion Monroe of Hampshire Co., Virginia. David and Matilda Monroe appear on the 1850 Hampshire Co., Virginia Census in the home of Margaret Stump (age 49), where they are both described as laborers. It is interesting to note that Matilda, born in 1824, gave her birthplace as Maryland.[96] She would have been born in Montgomery or Frederick County. David Monroe was born in 1830 in Virginia. A 47-year old woman named Sarah Asbury is also listed in the residence as a laborer. Matilda appears to have died between the 1850 Census and sometime prior to 1880. David M. Monroe appears in the 1880 Spring Creek District, Wirt Co., West

94 William Lee. 1860 Census, Clarksburg, Harrison Co., West Virginia. Ancestry.com, Provo, Utah, Accessed July 3, 2010. Available at http://www.ancestry.com.
95 Oak Grove Cemetery, Morgantown, West Virginia, Record for William Lee (1803-1898). Find-a-Grave.com Website. Accessed September 1, 2010. Available at http://www.findagrave.com.
96 David M. Monroe. 1850 Census, Hampshire Co., Virginia. Ancestry.com, Provo, Utah. Accessed August 8, 2010. Available at http://www.ancestry.com.

Virginia Census as a brother-in-law in the Lorenzo Kidwell household.[97] Lorenzo's wife is listed as Eliza Ann Alexander, who was born
about 1847. (Lorenzo was born in 1829). The Kidwell children are
listed between the ages of 2 and 15. David is listed as a widower and a
laborer. His second wife would have been a Kidwell or Alexander and
died prior to the 1880 census.[10]

Garrett F. Lee, born 1821-1822, appears on the 1880 Census for Baker
Tp., Linn Co., Missouri.[98] He was the father of Mary Lee (cited earlier). Garrett's wife, Arminda Lee, was born in Indiana in 1840. Their
children were John W. Lee (age 13, born in Nebraska); Mary Lee
(age 9, born in Kansas); Manda Lee (age 4, born in Kansas). An older
daughter, Julia, (age 17, born in Nebraska), appears on the same record
with her husband Charles Morris (age 20, born in Missouri) and their
daughter Lizzie (age 1, born in Missouri). Garrett Lee had two marriages. He appears on the 1850 Census for Clinton Tp., Wayne Co.,
Ohio, where he is listed with a wife named Mary. Two children, Hely
and Annie Coleman, (ages 12 and 7) reside with them.[99] By 1860, 39
year-old G. F. Lee (single), born Virginia, appears on the Census for
Cass, Nebraska Territory, where he is listed as a laborer in the Thomas
Patterson household.[100] Sometime in 1860, Garrett married Arminda,
and their oldest daughter Eva was born that same year. The family
appears on the 1875 Censes for Cottage Grove Tp., Allen Co., Kansas,
where Eva is listed at age 15.[101] She disappears from the family by
1880, so had either married or died. The date of Garrett Lee's death

97 David M. Monroe. 1880 Census, Spring Creek District, Wirt Co., West
    Virginia.Ancestry.com, Provo, Utah. Accessed August 8, 2010. Available
    at http://www.ancestry.com.
98 Garret F. Lee. 1880 Census, Baker Tp., Linn Co., Missouri. Ancestry.
    com, Provo, Utah. Accessed July 3, 2010. Available at http://www.
    ancestry.com.
99 Garret F. Lee. 1850 Census, Clinton Tp., Wayne Co., Ohio. Ancestry.
    com, Provo, Utah. Accessed July 3, 2010. Available at http://www.
    ancestry.com.
100 Garret F. Lee. 1860 Census, Cass, Nebraska Territory. Ancestry.com,
    Provo, Utah. Accessed July 3, 2010. Available at http://www.ancestry.
    com.
101 Garret F. Lee. 1875 Census, Cottage Grove Tp., Allen Co., Kansas.
    Ancestry.com, Provo, Utah. Accessed July 3, 2010. Available at http://
    www.ancestry.com.

is unknown. His daughter, Mary, later moved to Oklahoma and was still alive in 1943. In all probability, the Garrett Lee family maintained contact with the Levi Clay family of Adair, Iowa. (Garrett was Mary Elizabeth Stillians Clay's uncle; his daughter, Mary, would have been a first cousin. Mary Lee maintained contact with Adelia Viola Clay Inman --daughter of Levi and Mary Clay -- into the 1940s.)

David Lee (born 1825 in Virginia) appears on the 1870 Census for Amanda Tp., Allen Co., Ohio with his wife Mary A. (b. 1833) and their children:

Elizabeth E. Lee (age 22);

James L. Lee (age 16);

Charles M. Lee (age 12);

Madison L. Lee (age 9)[102]

Mary E. Moorman (age 17), Jacob A. Moorman (age 14), John A. Moorman (age 9) and Mahala J. Moorman (age 5) appear in the same household with them. David's first wife was Mahala Moorman, and they appear on the 1850 Census for Amanda Tp., Allen Co., Ohio with their children: Elizabeth Lee (age 2) and William Lee (age 0).[103] The 1860 Census for the same location lists only the full name of the head of the household (David Lee) followed by initials of the rest of the family:

M Lee (age 33);

E. E. Lee (age 13);

W. H. Lee (age 11);

J. F. Lee (age 9);

J. T. Lee (age 7);

---

102 David Lee, 1870 Census, Amanda Tp., Allen Co., Ohio. Ancestry.com, Provo, Utah. Accessed July 8, 2010. Available at http://www.ancestry. com.
103 David Lee, 1850 Census, Amanda Tp., Allen Co., Ohio. Ancestry.com, Provo, Utah. Accessed July 8, 2010. Available at http://www.ancestry. com.

S. M. Lee (age 5);

C. M. Lee (age 2)[104]

A number of Moorman (Morman) families appear on the same census record with David Lee. Presumably, his second wife was a widow with four children from one of those families. She may have been married to one of Mahala's brothers.

David and Garrett Lee relocated to Ohio in the mid-to-late 1840s. David remained in Allen County while Garrett moved first to Wayne County and then to the Nebraska Territory after his wife's death.

Catherine Lee resided with her mother after her father's death, and her mother died in 1836. It is unknown what happened to Catherine and her siblings immediately after their mother's death. Garrett would have been 15. Matilda would have been 12. David would have been 11. Catherine would have been 10. In all likelihood, they may have lived with the older brother William, who would have been 33. And as noted, two of her brothers moved to Ohio sometime in the 1840s. Matilda married. Catherine, on the other hand, pursued a different direction.

A redhead, she has been delicately described as a "professional dancer prior to her marriage"[105] Given the period of time—1836-1848—and the location—Monongalia Co., Virginia, Catherine probably danced in a carnival or a circus. Perhaps she ran away from William Lee's household after witnessing the departure of her brothers and sister. And here's another interesting twist. Early in my research, I learned about a line of the Stillians family that no one liked to talk about because it consisted of a "terrible bunch of circus performers and carnival workers!" I found a photograph album of these people in my grandmother's collection—something I have nicknamed *The Wild Bunch!* Perhaps Catherine encountered this line prior to meeting William Stillians.

104 David Lee, 1860 Census, Amanda Tp., Allen Co., Ohio. Ancestry.com, Provo, Utah. Accessed July 8, 2010. Available at http://www.ancestry.com.

105 Mrs. Lula Splawn, daughter of Levi and Mary (Stillians) Clay, Unsent letter, 1957.

The children of William Stillians and Catherine Lee follow:

Mary Elizabeth Stillians, b. June 30, 1849; d. September 17, 1915, Adair, Iowa; m. Levi Clay February 7, 1869, Rockford, Illinois;[106]

Agnes M. Stillians, b. 1851, Pennsylvania; d. September 21, 1870, unmarried at age 18;[107]

Sarah Jane Stillians, b. May 3, 1852, Jamestown, Mercer Co., Pennsylvania; d. ca. 1910, Los Angeles, California; m. William Tift, ca. 1873, Woodbine, Jo Daviess Co., Illinois;[108]

Catherine Lee Stillians died at age 25 in childbirth with her third child Sarah Jane on May 3, 1852 in Jamestown, Mercer Co., Pennsylvania. Her death required a housekeeper and nanny for the three children, and that's when Rachel Dilley entered the household. William Stillians married Rachel Dilley (sometimes spelled Dillie, Dille, or Dilly) on August 22, 1852 in Mercer Co., Pennsylvania.

Rachel was born 1834/1835 in Pennsylvania, but I have yet to identify her parents. However, records of the Presbyterian Cemetery in Mercer County could provide the answer:

Joseph Dilley, Sr., died April 3, 1868, 77 years 23 days;

Mary Dilley, wife of Joseph, died Sept. 2, 1860—age 74 years 5 mos. 8 days;

Jane Dilley, wife of Thompson, died Oct. 4, 1849, 76 years.[109]

The Dille/Dilley families were in Washington Co., Pennsylvania as long as the Stillings/Stillians families and settled in Morris Tp. The 1784 Tax Lists for Amwell Tp., Washington Co., Pennsylvania identi-

---

106 Splawn Letter, 1957.
107 William Stillians. 1860 and 1870 Census, Woodbine, Jo Daviess Co., Illinois.
108 1885 Iowa Census, Manning, Carroll Co., Iowa—the William Tift Family.
109 Presbyterian Cemetery, Tombstone Inscriptions, Mercer Co., Pennsylvania. Micofilmed by the Pennsylvania Historical Society, Harrisburg, Pennsylvania. (Date Unknown).

fies Price Dille, John Dille, Samuel Dille, Isaac Dille and Caleb Dille.[110] Between 1776 and 1780, Caleb Dille, David Dille, Sr., David Dille, Jr., Israel Dille, and John Dille all signed the Westilvania Petition in Washington Co.[111] The Westilvania Petition demanded statehood for Western Pennsylvania since residents in that area were tired of being shuffled between Pennsylvania, Maryland and Virginia! Agitators were finally told that if they didn't stop protesting, they would be cited for treason. That's why many of them moved to Kentucky. Isaac Dilley and Samuel Dilley both appear on the 1790 Census for Washington Co.[112]

William and Rachel Dilley Stillians' children were:

William Stillians, b. June 5, 1854; d. Sept. 16, 1865;

John Stillians, b. Feb. 27, 1857;

Albert Spencer Stillians, b. Oct. 18, 1860; d. Jan. 18, 1901;

Charles Wesley Stillians, b. Oct. 8, 1862;

Henrietta Stillians, b. Nov. 4, 1865; d. Nov. 14, 1885;

Lou or Levi Fosnot Stillians, b. in Iowa Jan. 15, 1872; d. Jan. 8, 1938;

George Stillians, b. May 27, 1875; d. April 7, 1878. (George's middle name was Howard).[113]

By 1860, the William Stillians family settled in Woodbine, Jo Daviess Co., Illinois, where they appear on the 1860 and 1870 census records. In 1870, the family relocated to Bear Grove Tp., Guthrie Co., Iowa and by 1895 (or shortly thereafter), William Stillians and Rachel Dilley Stillians divorced. They both continued to reside in Bear Grove Tp., Guthrie Co., Iowa, but by 1900, William is found on the 1900 Census of Lu Verne Tp., Kossuth Co., Iowa, where he is listed

110 1784 Tax Lists, Amwell Tp., Washington Co., Pennsylvania, compiled by Bell.

111 *Washington Co., Pennsylvania Names on Petitions, 1776-1780*, compiled by Bell.

112 *1790 Census, Morris Tp., Washington Co., Pennsylvania*, compiled by Bell

113 Inman, Clay Family, 1992.

as "divorced."[114] Rachel last appears on the 1900 Census for Stuart, Adair Co., Iowa in the household of A. Stillians, where she is listed as "widowed."[115] Rachel may have died shortly after that census record. I have not located her date of death or burial site.

William Stillians died at North Branch, Bear Grove Tp., Guthrie Co., Iowa October 13, 1907. He is buried in the Sunny Hill Cemetery in Adair, Iowa. One of his granddaughters, Mary May Tift, is buried beside him. She was the only daughter of Sarah Jane Stillians Tift and her husband William. She was born February 15, 1875, and she died May 21, 1893. While going through my grandmother's photo collection, I found a picture of Mary Stillians Clay sitting beside her grave. The picture was taken after the death of William because his grave also appears in the photo. The inscription at the top of his tombstone once read: *In my Father's house are many mansions.*

114 William Stillians. 1900 Census, Lu Verne Tp., Kossuth Co., Iowa, Ancestry.com, Provo, Utah. Accessed July 18, 2010. Available at http://www.ancestry.com.
115 Rachel Stillians. 1900 Census, Stuart, Adair, Iowa, Ancestry.com, Provo, Utah. Accessed July 18, 2010. Available at http://www.ancestry.com.

Chapter 6: On to Adair

In 1865, Levi Clay left Jo Daviess Co., Illinois for Carroll Co., Illinois, where his brother, Alfred, lived, and he stayed there for two years.[116] In December 1867, about a month after his mother's death, he moved to Floyd Co., Iowa and spent a year in the town of Marble Rock, where he worked as a mason.[117] In 1869, he returned to Illinois and married Mary Elizabeth Stillians in Rockford on February 7.[118] He then returned to Marble Rock with his bride, and they lived there for several years.

While in Floyd County, Levi worked for Alonzo Inman, and the Clays lived on the upper floor of the Alonzo Inman farmhouse.[119] My grandmother, Adelia Viola Clay, was born there November 22, 1869. Alonzo Inman and Carrie Waiste Inman's son Loren Waiste Inman was born the following year on July 28, 1870. The two infants slept together in the same crib. Twenty-three years later, the two infants married on April 4, 1893. They are my paternal grandparents.

The Clays then moved to Bear Grove Tp., Guthrie Co., Iowa for two or three years and afterwards, moved on to Panora, Iowa.[120] In February 1873, the Clays moved to Casey, Iowa for a short time. Then they settled in Adair, Iowa March 15, 1873, where Levi signed on with the section.[121] The Rock Island Railroad was established in Adair in

---

116 Inman, Clay Family, 1992
117 Inman, Clay Family, 1992
118 Inman, Clay Family, 1992
119 Inman, Clay Family, 1992
120 Inman, Clay Family, 1992
121 Inman, Clay Family, 1992

1868, and the area was first known as Summit Cut. The Clays arrived shortly after the laying of the C. R. I & P Railway tracks, the second family to arrive.

The children of Levi and Mary Clay were:

Adelia Viola Clay, b. November 22, 1869, Floyd Co., Iowa, d. June 14, 1951, Cedar Rapids, Linn Co., Iowa; m. Loren Waiste Inman April 4, 1893, Floyd Co., Iowa;

Catherine Louisa Clay, b. May 6, 1872; d. April 4, 1874; buried at Bear Grove, near North Branch, Iowa;

Mary Jane Clay, b. in Adair, Iowa, Dec. 18, 1875; d. Jan. 22, 1917; m. Walter McCray June 30, 1901. (She is commonly referred to as Jennie);

Frances Elizabeth Eldora Clay, b. in Adair, Iowa, June 2, 1877; d. at Boring, Ore., Oct. 12, 1948; m. (1) Harry A. Robinson, Adair, Iowa, Jan. 1, 1896; (2) David Ricker, Omaha, Nebraska, May 1920;

Ida Artha Josephine Clay, b. Aug. 22, 1882, Adair, Iowa; d. Feb. 13, 1957, Adair, Iowa; m. Newt Parkinson, Adair, Iowa, June 7, 1916;

Lydia Lowella Lorena Clay, b. Aug. 22, 1882, Adair, Iowa; d. April 4, 1968 and is buried in Gresham, Oregon; m (1) John W. Baker, Dec. 25, 1901; (2) Berry A. Splawn, Jan. 24, 1939;

William Levi Woodward Clay, b. May 29, 1884, Adair, Iowa; d. Oct. 6, 1884; Adair, Iowa;

Clyde Emanuel Clay, b. Nov. 14, 1884, Adair, Iowa; d. Sept. 1955, California; m. Ethyl Crowell Dec. 25, 1906. (She burned to death in a stove fire in Adair August 22, 1911 and is buried with the Clays at Sunny Hill Cemetery beside her sister-in-law Jennie.) The Clays had two children. Clyde next married a widow named Myma R. Grim, and eventually relocated to California, where he spent the rest of his career as a fireman;

Agnes Suffiah Lucile Clay, b. May 2, 1889, Adair, Iowa; d. March 26, 1976; m. Ray B. Wilkinson March 11, 1910.[122]

[Note: Detailed information about these people appears in a later chapter.]

122 Inman, Clay Family, 1992

Part 1: Photo Section

John Clay Grave, Grill Cemetery, Summit Co., Ohio, taken May 1996

*Mary Hoy Clay Barn, Berreman Tp., Joe Daviess Co.,
Illinois (ca.1860). Used with permission of Jeremy Clay*

James Kirkpatrick Grave, Glade Run Presbyterian Church Cemetery, Dayton, Indiana Co., Pennsylvania, taken Summer 1993. James Kirkpatrick appears in the John Stillings 1785 estate file, Washington Co., Pennsylvania. While Dayton is in Indiana County today, it was in Washington County in the late 1700s. More information about James Kirkpatrick is in the Chapter 4 section of the endnotes.

*Levi Clay, ca. 1869, Rockford, Illinois. Taken
about the time that he was married.*

*Mary Elizabeth Stillians and her sister, Sarah
Jane Stillians, Rockford, Illinois. Taken about the
time of Mary's marriage to Levi Clay*

Part 2: Beginnings: Origins of the Clay Co., Missouri James and Cole Families

The Samuel-James Family of Clay Co., Missouri. Photo is believed to have been taken ca. 1858. Jesse James is standing on the back row beside his future wife and first cousin Zerelda Mimms. Dr. Reuben Samuel and Jesse's mother Zerelda Cole James Simms Samuel are seated. Susan James, Jesse's sister, is one of the females. The identities of the rest of the people are unknown or disputed. They may have been members of the Mimms family since Reuben and Zerelda's first child wasn't born until December 1858.

Chapter 7: Platte Co., Missouri: In Search of the Brown Family

Late spring 1977

There is something about an old vacant country farmhouse that captures my attention and invites my speculation! The older the house, the better! I love to visualize the occupants: who they were—where they were from—their dreams and desires—and why they would build such a house on *this* particular property. Old houses conceal fascinating stories within their rafters. I want to dig out those tales and breathe life into them again. And that's the way I felt the spring of 1977 after several months of watching an old abandoned farmhouse in the field across from my bus stop.

We were living in Platte Co., Missouri, our second experience in that county. Howard graduated from Park College in 1967, and we lived above an old barber shop on Main Street in Parkville for almost three years before moving to Kentucky. Now we were back. We first lived just off North Oak Trafficway in North Kansas City for several years before settling into an apartment just north of the Parkville area. Kansas City had not consumed all of the farmland out north as yet, but it was beginning to do so. I worked for an attorney in downtown Kansas City, and it was during my first morning on the bus stop that I noticed the place across the road. It engaged my curiosity the first morning I saw it—an old two-story frame farmhouse with a collapsed porch roof, empty windows staring across the field, the front entrance gaping open, allowing the wind to sweep up the staircase and fill the second floor, a roof that had surrendered years ago along with the paint, and a windmill beside the house, whose blades squeaked in patterned rhythm as they turned in the wind. I became a student of that property while waiting for the bus. I studied everything about it: its structure, its grounds, the wildflowers that grew beside it, the cattle wandering about the field. I wanted to transfer that image to canvas. And each night for at least a month, I dreamed the same dream about that house: dancing, laughing people from long ago and music filling the air--tables covered with steaming dishes of food—horses and carriages in the yard—a definite scene of celebration. Some of the men were dressed in uniform, but that is a hazy part of the dream. Then came the day when I could permanently step out of that dream and finally begin my painting.

I remember my first day of freedom. I had quit my job in order to stay home with the kids and tend to projects of my own choosing. When I awakened that morning, I knew exactly where I was going and what I planned to do. The day was perfect. Brian and Debbie were in school most of the day and Howard was at work. So I could pursue my creative endeavor and not be disturbed. Eager to begin my project, I gathered my easel, brushes, palette, paints and canvas board, and headed up the road to the entrance of the apartment complex.

The house stared silently at me as I sat down on the grass and set up the table easel in front of me. I paused to study the house for a while, wondering why I had overlooked this place when we lived in the area previously. We often drove out north on Sunday afternoon jaunts and didn't notice it.

Well, I noticed it now! I thought. *And I'm going to give it the attention it deserves!*

"That old place has quite a history!"

I jumped when I heard the voice and turned to see a woman heading in my direction. She sat down on the grass beside me.

"Going to paint it, huh?" she asked.

"I hope so," I responded. Something she said piqued my curiosity.

"You say it has quite a history? How old is it?"

"Oh, it dates back before the Civil War."

I thought it was that old!

"The man who owned that place was named Brown. He owned all the land between here and Weatherby Lake."

"Quite wealthy!" I commented.

"Oh, he was! This was a beautiful place back in its day. Too bad they let it go to waste."

I squeezed a few blobs of paint on the palette.

"Where did the Browns come from?" I asked.

"Some place in the South. They were Confederates."

So that explains the uniforms! I thought, as I remembered my dream.

"In fact, Brown was a friend of Jesse James!" she informed me.

"Oh, really?"

"Yes—he kept fresh horses on the back of his property for the James Gang. They always changed horses there."

Everyone has a Jesse James story! I thought, after she left. I paused and smiled. Well, so did I! I was born in Iowa with *two* Jesse James stories in my family! I kept those stories private, however. It is one thing if someone else has a Jesse James story. But if *you* have one, then the listeners don't believe it. My stories concerned my maternal grandfather, William Franklin Spence, and my great paternal grandfather, Levi Clay.

Grandpa Spence was born in Jasper Co., Missouri in 1884 and passed away in 1973. Long before he married my grandmother, Oda Elizabeth Hopper, and while he was still a young man, Grandpa spent a lot of time traveling through the American West. One such journey took him to Clay Co., Missouri and to the Jesse James Farm near Kearney, where he was given a grand tour by a distinguished gentleman who greeted him at the gate. Years later in the 1940s, Grandpa went there again and on his second trip, he purchased a postcard bearing the photo of his earlier tour guide. He kept that photo in his secretary for years. I became curious one day and asked him about it.

"That is Frank James!" he told me. "He was the brother of Jesse James!"

"You met Frank James?" I asked.

"I went to the James Farm when I was a young fellow, and he took me through the whole place."

"Did you meet Jesse James?" I exclaimed.

That's when Grandpa roared, "Just how old do you think I am???!!!"

I chuckled when I remembered that conversation, and wondered whether Grandma still had that picture. They moved from the large house to a small one in 1960. Many things were thrown away. Grandpa was especially proud to have that picture. And I remember how interested he was in 1966 when I told him about our own excursion to the James Farm with a group of people. Frank James had long departed. But we were greeted by a member of the James Family, and she conducted our tour. She quickly discounted the J. Frank Dalton story when one member of our group asked about him.[123]

The second Jesse James story concerning my family was still a mystery that spring of 1977. I remember hearing it originally at the dinner table years ago when my father first told it: something about a train robbery somewhere—Jesse James robbing the train—and his grandfather, Levi Clay, chasing the James Gang all night as a member of the posse. We had just finished watching a television show about Jesse James, and Dad told the story of his grandfather while we were eating dinner that evening. I tucked that tale away under Things to Research Some Day, and didn't give it second thought until *The Cedar Rapids Gazette* ran a story about it in 1963![124] However, the details in that article did not give me the answers I was seeking.

123 J. Frank Dalton, Outlaws and Gunslingers Website. Accessed July 21, 2010. Available at http://www.theoutlaws.com/outlaws5c.htm.
124 "Train Robbing Started in Iowa by Jesse James in 1873", *The Cedar Rapids Gazette*, Section B, 1, August 18, 1963.

Oh well! I decided, as I started mixing paint. *I'll sort it all out—some day!*

* * *

Platte Co., Missouri was created from the Platte Purchase December 31, 1838.[125] Its neighboring county to the east, Clay Co., was established much earlier on January 22, 1822, having been carved from Ray Co., and named after Henry Clay.[126] Settlers streamed into the area mostly from the upper southern states of Virginia, Tennessee and Kentucky. In Clay Co., they settled along the Missouri River in an area that was eventually called Little Dixie. They brought their families, slaves and southern traditions, and they engaged in raising hemp and tobacco. The soil was particularly fertile in these areas, and the fertile land quickly became a draw.

A number of Brown families settled in both Clay and Platte Counties. Lee Tp. in Platte Co. is the home of the Brown Cemetery, which was abandoned long ago.[127] Concerning the Browns who are buried there and the family for which the cemetery was named, Louise Gaiser wrote:

The monument, "Sacred to the Memory of William Brown, who was born in Greenbriar County, West Virginia, February 5, 1805," still stands erect except for the decorative obelisk meant to be on top of the monument. We found it lying on the ground, but I felt certain satisfaction upon finding William Brown's tombstone, the only one, standing upright. It seemed to add stability to his character. He obtained the property, preempted by the Gordons, from the Gordons. He died January 10, 1893 being nearly 78 years of age. His son, Clark, following his father into the Great Beyond

125 Platte County, Missouri Facts, Discussion Forum, and Encyclopedia Article, Wikipedia. Accessed July 19, 2010. Available at http://www.absoluteastronomy.com/topics/Platte_County%2c_Missouri

126 Welcome to Clay County, Missouri, An MoGenWeb Project Page, US GenWeb Project, Rootsweb Website. Accessed June 16, 2010. Available at http://www.rootsweb.com.

127 Louise A.Gaiser. A Historical Sketch of Brown's Cemetery, January 2, 1963, Accessed September 17, 2010. USGenWeb Archives. Available at http://files.usgwarchives.org/mo/platte/cemeteries/brown.txt.

five years later, February 17, 1888, at the age of 52 years. [128]

A transcription of the tombstones follows:

BROWN FAMILY CEMETERY

Deed says both sides of county line 18'
East & West - 15' North & South

T51 - R33 - S27

Brown, Anchises G. --???--2/20/1869
(son of Rowland & --, Martin

Brown, Ruth Ann (Simpkins)--3/29/1818
- 3/4/1909 (wf. of A. G.)

(born Madison Co., Ohio)

Brown, Samuel--fought in the Civil War and a member
of the family said he was buried in this cemetery.

Brown family cemetery continued: T52 - R35 - S3

Alexander, Dudley--4/??/1887(son of John & Eliza)

Alexander, Andrew W.--7/11/1842 - 7/22/1860

Alexander, John--9/24/1809 - 3/4/1854 (wf.- Eliza A. Gordon)

Alexander, Mary Alice (Russell)--3/29/1852 -10/21/1888

(g-dtr. of Lucretia(Gordon)

Anderson, Alexander--79yrs. 2da.--9/27/1884

Brown, Clark   52yrs.--2/17/1888--(son of William)

Brown, William--2/5/1805 - 1/10/1883--
(born Greenbriar Co., W, Va.)

128 Gaiser, A Historical Sketch of Brown's Cemetery, http://files. usgwarchives.org/mo/plate/cemeteries/brown.txt.

Brown, Willie   12/5/1878 - 12/30/1882
(son of William & Susan)

Daniel, Allie E. (Gordon)--6/22/1837 - 4/22/1888(wf of Wm. E.)

Daniel, Shelby   2/20/1808 - 12/10/1862-
-(wf. Cynthia A. (Gordon)

(Aunt of Silas Gordon)

Daniel, William E.--4/?/1834-???/(son of Selby & Cynthia)

Gordon, Lucretia--1795 - 1/25/1864--(wf of Wm.)

Gordon, Wm--Will probated 10/14/1844

Klein, Peter--48yrs.--11/5/1877

Knope/Knopf

Knopf, Elizabeth--11/??/1802 - 4/20/1892
(born in Germany)(wf of Matthew)

Knopf, Matthew--2/24/1803 - 7/11/1867[129]

These Browns supported the Union, came from West Virginia, owned no slaves, and were not wealthy, so I continued my search. And shortly after resuming my search, I found another family of Browns that appeared more likely. This second Brown family dates back to another William Brown, who married Martha Bassett May 28, 1767 in Charles City Co., Virginia or Charleston, South Carolina.

William Brown's will was filed for probate April 1805 in Knox Co., Tennessee.[130] The children of William Brown and Martha Bassett were:

Rebecca b 1764 m Harrelson;
Mary m Fulton;
Agnes m Fulton;

129 Gaiser, A Historical Sketch of Brown's Cemetery, http://files. usgwarchives.org/mo/plate/cemeteries/brown.txt.
130 Clint Joyce and Cecil Houck. Brown Family History, Part 1, Roostweb Database Accessed June 30, 2010. Available at http://www.rootsweb. com.

Thomas b 1753 Augustus County, VA;
Alexander;
Robert;
William;
Felix Canada b 1761-70, and John .[131]

Of these children, Felix Canada Brown is important to this narrative
since records show that he settled in Platte Co., Missouri:

> *Felix Canada Brown was born between 1761 - 1770 in North
> Carolina. He was descended from Scotch Presbyterians promi-
> nent in colonial history and active in the revolutionary conflict.
> He married Jane Leeper (b 1767), the daughter of Gawen Leeper
> of South Carolina, whose ancestors were from North of Ireland.
> Gawen Leeper and his wife were both born in SC according to the
> 1850 Platte Co., MO census. Jane was listed as age 83 in 1850
> Platte Co., MO census living with James L. Brown. Felix and Jane
> had 12 children:*

> *William;*
> *Joseph;*
> *Felix "Fake";*
> *Elizabeth;*
> *Devine ;*
> *John (b 27 Apr 1797 Knox, TN - d 2 Oct 1842 Andrew, MO);*
> *Gideon / Guyan Leeper (1800 - 29 Oct 1858) m Matilda Patton;*
> *James L. Brown (1803 - bef 16 Dec 1870) m. Rebecca Weaver;*
> *9.*
> *10.*
> *Hugh Leeper (24 Jun 1810 -23 Jan 1888) m Clarissa Browning;*
> *Thomas A. (28 Jan 1812 -13 Jan 1901) m 1Margaret
> Blakeley 2Leanna Leonard, 3 Mary E. Deacon.[132]*

Concerning Gideon/Guyan Leeper Brown (1800-1858), son of Felix
Brown and Jane Leeper:

---

131 Joyce and Houck, Brown Family History, Part 1, Available at http://
    www.rootsweb.com.
132 Joyce and Houck, Brown Family History, Part 1, Available at http://
    www.rootsweb.com.

Gideon Leeper Brown, son of Felix C & Jane, was born in 1800 and died on October 29,1858. He came west with his father as a boy and located at Knoxville, Tenn. where he was reared to manhood. He married Matilda Patton, (b 18 Dec 1814 Strawberry Plains, Knox Co., TN) on January 20,1830. He removed from Tenn. in 1831 and became one of the pioneer planters of Jackson Co., MO. Subsequently he moved to Platte and Buchanan counties. He was a man of shrewd business judgment, energy and enterprise and was considered one of the most successful planters in the locality. In 1854 he visited what is now Kansas, at that time still known as Nebraska territory, and took up land about eight miles west of Leavenworth, but never removed to Kansas. In 1856 he sold the land and continued his activities in farming in Buchanan County, where he had many friends. He was actively interested in politics but never aspired to hold office. He was a Democrat, a large slave holder sympathized with the pro-slavery party. Gideon and Matilda had 7 children.[133]

Those children were:

John b 3 Dec 1832 d 3 March 1833;
Martha m Arthur H. Squires of Platte Co., MO;
Thomas L. b 25 Dec 1837;
Amanda b 23 Jan 1839 m Samuel Fulton 7 Jun 1855;
Margaret b 13 Mar 1841 d 27 Mar 1892;
Felix Canada b 13 Aug 1843 d 21 Aug 1927, Age 84;
Mary C. b 3 Dec 1845 d 9 Sept 1846;
Missouri Tennessee b 6 Jul 1848 m Henry Turner d 11 Mar 1935;
Cornelia Caroline b 26 Jun 1851 d 3 Mar 1898.[134]

The Brown Family History contains an interesting note concerning Gideon Leeper Brown:

In his will dated 12 Oct 1858 Gideon stipulated who would inherit specific slaves and that Matilda would inherit his estate except if she remarried, in which case it would go to Felix C. Brown.

---

133 Joyce and Houck, Brown Family History, Part 1, Available at http://www.rootsweb.com.
134 Joyce and Houck, Brown Family History, Part 1, Available at http://www.rootsweb.com.

Gideon died 29 Oct 1858 shortly after the date of this will and Matilda lived until 7 Feb 1902, at which time she died in Brown Hospital, Salt Creek Valley, Leavenworth KS at the home of her son Felix, who at that time owned the hospital, a home for the insane. She is buried in Mt. Muncie Hospital, Leavenworth, KS Sec 26, Lot 209, Grave 1 on the Felix Brown lot. There is no stone. She married James Pennington in 1860 so we assume the estate went to Felix at that time...

(8-7-6) Felix Canada Brown son of Gideon L & Matilda, was born 13 Aug 1843 in Buchanan, MO and died 21 Aug 1927. He was buried in Mt. Muncie Cemetery. He was reared upon his father's farm and at the age of nine years accompanied his father on a trip to the present state of Kansas and remembered the stirring times of the border warfare. Prior to the Civil war Felix C. Brown was engaged in over-land freighting on the Oregon trail. When only 14 years old, he was a teamster in the outfit of General Sydney Johnston on his expedition from Fort Leavenworth to Salt Lake City, just prior to the outbreak of the war. The party spent the winter at Fort Bridger and nearly starved to death for lack of provisions. Soon after this he began to freight from Leavenworth, for Russell Majors & Waddell, who held a contract to supply food to the Army at Forts Laramie, Bridger, Kearney, Bents and Union. He enlisted in the Confederate Army at the outbreak of the Civil War at age 18, joining a company of dragoons under Governor Jackson. After a short time he became a member of the First Missouri Light Artillery and was assigned to Colonel Gates regiment. He was wounded in a skirmish near Newtonia, MO and a battle at Jenkins Ferry but neither time seriously. He took part in all the battles west of the Mississippi River in which the department of the Mississippi participated with the exception of the battle of Elk Horn. After the surrender of General Lee and the downfall of the confederacy in April 1865, he returned to his native county. He farmed on the old homestead there for 7 years. In 1872 he settled in Atchison County for 8 years then returned to Missouri. From there he came to Leavenworth county to take charge of an asylum, known as the Maplewood Asylum, for a year. He engaged in the mercantile business in Leavenworth for four years, then in 1889 he erected a private sanitarium and asylum,

Elmwood Hospital. On February 15, 1866 he Married Jincy A. Blakely(1848-Oct 30,1938) Mr. Brown was a democrat taking active part in the affairs of Leavenworth City, County and State. For two years he served as trustee of Walnut Township, Atchison County. (Jincy's father, Felix Blakely died Dec 13,1915).[135]

This family of Browns fulfilled the criteria I established concerning the original owners of the old vacant house in Platte Co: (1) Southern background; (2) wealth; (3) ownership of slaves; (4) support of the Confederacy; (5) large land holdings; (6) one of the largest planters in the county; (7) Platte and Buchanan Co., Missouri ties. [The Buchanan County connection will be explained in a separate chapter.]

After thirty-three years and in Summer 2010, I finally found my Brown Family!

---

135 Joyce and Houck, Brown Family History, Part 1, Available at http://www.rootsweb.com.

Chapter 8: The Clay Co., Missouri James Families and their Relatives

When historians describe the father of Jesse James, they paint an image of a restless, driven man struggling with his own identity. Robert Sallee James was born July 17, 1818 to John James and Mary "Polly" Poor, daughter of Robert Poor and Elizabeth Mimms, in Logan Co., Kentucky. Robert's grandfather, William James, is believed to have been born about 1754 in Pembrokeshire, Wales. William James first settled in Montgomery Co., Pennsylvania, before relocating to Virginia, where he married Mary Hines July 15, 1774.[136] John James, Robert Sallee James' father, was the oldest child.[11] Robert Sallee James' aunts and uncles from his father's line include:

Nancy Ann James (b. Feb. 24, 1777); m. David Hodges, Dec. 21, 1799;

Mary James, m. Edward Lee, Dec. 22, 1796;

William James, Jr., (b. April 27, 1782; d. 1807);

Richard James, m. Mary G. Poor, Dec. 18, 1813;

Thomas James, (b. Dec. 14, 1783) m. Mary B. Davis, Sept. 3, 1834;

Martin James, (b. 1789; d. 1867) m. Elizabeth Key, Nov. 21, 1825.[137]

John James was both a farmer and a minister. He and his wife left Virginia in 1811 for Logan Co., Kentucky. Their children include:

136 Phillip W. Steele. *Jesse and Frank James: The Family History.* [Gretna: Pelican Publishing Co., 1997] 23.

137 Steele, *The Family History*, 24

Mary James (b. Sept. 28, 1809; d. July 23, 1877; m. John Mimms, a cousin, 1827);

William James (b. Sept. 11, 1811; d. Nov. 14, 1895; m. Mary Ann Varble, Dec. 2, 1843; Mary Ann Gibson Marsh, April 24, 1865)

John R. James (b. Feb. 15, 1815; d. Oct. 25, 1887; m. Amanda Polly Williams Sept. 1, 1836; Emily Bradley, 1872);

Elizabeth James (b. Nov. 25, 1816; d. Nov. 2, 1904; m. Tillman Howard West, 1837);

Robert Sallee James (b. July 17, 1818; d. August 18, 1850, California; m. Zerelda Cole, Kentucky, Dec. 28, 1841);

Nancy Gardner James (b. Sept. 13, 1821; d. 1875; m. George B. Hite, May 7, 1841);[12]

Thomas Martin James (b. April 8, 1823; d. Dec. 25, 1903; m. Susan S. Woodward, Goochland Co., Virginia);

Drury Woodson James (b. November 14, 1826; d. July 1, 1910, California; m. Mary Louisa Dunn, Sept. 15, 1861).[138]

Steele adds:

Mary James (who was to become mother-in-law to Jesse James) married John Mimms in 1827, and they had the following children: Robert, March 30, 1830; John Wilson, July 4, 1831; Drury Lilburn, May 9, 1833; David Woodson, August 23, 1835; Mary Elizabeth, October 18, 1837; Lucy Francis, July 14, 1829; George Tillman, November 6, 1841; Nancy Catherine, August 15, 1843; Zerelda Amanda, July 21, 1845; Thomas Martin, November 27, 1846; Sarah Ann, May 3, 1849; and Henry Clay, August 13, 1857. Their ninth child, Zerelda Amanda Mimms, married her first cousin Jesse Woodson James, at her sister Lucy Browder's home in Kearney, Missouri on April 24, 1874. Zee, as she was called, died November 13, 1900.[139]

The Woodson, Poor, West and Mimms families are important links to this narrative. First of all, Jesse James received his middle name

138 Steele, *The Family History*, 27-29.
139 Steele, *The Family History*, 29.

Woodson[13] from his great grandmother, Elizabeth Woodson, who married his great grandfather, Robert Poor in the 1700s.[140] Frank James often used the Woodson surname as an alias, while Jesse James used the surname Howard. Mary "Polly" Poor, daughter of Robert and Elizabeth Woodson Poor, married John M. James in 1807.[141] John M. James' brother Richard married Mary G. Poor, who may have been a sister of Mary "Polly." These families all lived close to one another, and there were several generations of intermarriages between second and third cousins within these groups. Additionally, Elizabeth James, the sister of Jesse James' grandfather, John James, married Tillman Howard West in 1837. The Wests reportedly settled in Jackson and Clay Cos., Missouri and were a grand aunt and uncle of Jesse, Frank and Susan James.[142]

Robert Sallee James was orphaned at the age of nine and went to live with his 18-year old married sister, Mary Mimms. He enrolled at Georgetown College, Kentucky in 1838, where he studied the liberal arts curriculum. This was during a period of time when a primary education was minimal and anything beyond that, unheard of. Robert graduated from the college in 1843. He later returned to complete a master's degree in 1847. A very devout man, Robert Sallee James embarked upon becoming a Baptist preacher!

While a student in Georgetown, Robert Sallee James met his future wife, Zerelda Elizabeth Cole, who was attending a convent school in the area at the time. She was only sixteen when they were married December 20, 1842. Her uncle, James M. Lindsay, (with whom she was living at the time) gave the county officials written permission for the marriage. And shortly after receiving his diploma from Georgetown, Robert Sallee James and his young bride relocated to Clay Co., Missouri and to the New Hope Baptist Church, which had only fifteen members.[143] It was here where Robert James discovered his "inner light."[144] Stiles explains:

---

140 Steele, *The Family History*, 77.
141 Steele, *The Family History*, 77.
142 Steele, *The Family History*, 31.
143 T. J. Stiles, *Jesse James: Last Rebel of the Civil War*. [New York: Alfred A. Knopf, 2002] 18.
144 Stiles, *Last Rebel of the Civil War*, 18.

Baptist congregations ordained their own preachers from among their membership; nothing more was required than a mutual agreement that a man had received a divine calling to speak the word of God. And the pious, charismatic, well-educated young fellow from Kentucky inspired immediate consensus among these 'very plain' people...

In other words, James combined his college education with the emotional passion of the Second Great Awakening, the wave of religious fervor that had swept the country since its beginnings in upstate New York in 1826. Here, within the log walls of this country church, people prayed in shouts and tears to a deity who offered redemption to all those willing to confess their sins and accept forgiveness. Though the cold Calvinist God of predestination was hardly dead in Southern Baptist theology, the preacher's call for repentance and conversion struck a chord of popular Arminianism—a widespread belief in one's own moral agency, a conviction that each person could choose to accept or reject salvation.[145]

News about his preaching spread quickly. In 1844, he organized his growing group into the North Liberty Baptist Association. Robert Sallee James was also instrumental in bringing a new Baptist college to the area—William Jewell College—which first opened its doors in 1850 and is still in operation today.

Amidst the scene of growth and prosperity, however, the question of slavery imposed a dilemma in the minds of many people. Those who were raised with slavery and who owned slaves were not disquieted by the dilemma. Hemp was the main crop in Clay County, and the farmers used slaves for the growing and harvesting of hemp. But many people began to see a contradiction between the teachings of Christ and the institution of slavery. Some people began questioning whether ordained ministers should even own slaves and suggested that if these ministers should continue to own slaves, they should give up their pulpits. That proposition presented a particular dilemma for Robert Sallee James: he grew up with slavery and he owned slaves! Stiles notes:

145 Stiles, *Last Rebel of the Civil War*, 18

As a border state, Missouri shared characteristics of both North and South; indeed, many residents considered it part of a third section, the border West. But slaveholding families such as the James clan—born in Kentucky, living in slave-dependent Clay County, shipping their hemp down the Mississippi—felt themselves to be a part of the seamless fabric of the South. In their eyes, Southern people, Southern agriculture, and Southern markets made the Missouri River valley "Little Dixie" indeed. And like most Southern commercial farmers, Robert began to buy slaves as he prospered, probably paying between $200 and $400 for each of the boys and girls who populated his spread by the end of the decade.[146]

By 1845, two circuit-riding evangelists named Chandler and Love rode into Clay County, exclaiming: "No slave holder had a right to an office in the church, or a place in the church!"[147] One congregant named Tabitha Gill wrote, "Chandler and Love almost broke up all the churches."[148] She believed that their goal was to establish a northern conference in the state but "large numbers of local Baptists opposed them, as did most others in the county. As across the South, the challenge of abolitionism drove slaveholders into a fierce defense of their institution."[149] Since Robert Sallee James was a slaveholder, he rejected the preaching of Chandler and Love. And the war with Mexico temporarily quieted the issue.

President James K. Polk took his oath of office just five days prior to the annexation of Texas by Congress in March 1845. Polk wanted to expand the national boundaries to Oregon, Texas and at least part of California. However, the annexation of Texas practically guaranteed a war with Mexico. In January 1846, Polk ordered Zachary Taylor to lead American troops to the disputed border. A month later, they were ambushed by Mexican forces. On May 13, Congress declared war. And on June 6, 1846, troops departed for war.[150]

---

146 Stiles, *Last Rebel of the Civil War*, 20.
147 Stiles, *Last Rebel of the Civil War*, 20
148 Stiles, *Last Rebel of the Civil War*, 21.
149 Stiles, *Last Rebel of the Civil War*, 21
150 Stiles, *Last Rebel of the Civil War.*, 22

Robert Sallee James held one more evangelical crusade in Clay Co.
before his restless spirit took hold of him. Word of the California
Gold Rush struck the local papers, creating a great deal of excitement.
When people returned with specimens, gold fever spread and before
long, Robert James sensed a call from God that he should preach in
the gold fields of California. He preached his farewell sermon to his
congregation and headed west. Tabitha Gill wrote:

> *Brother Robert James preached his farewell sermon to us at New
> Hope two weeks since and left for California the Wednesday af-
> ter....Brother James seemed very much affected at parting from us
> and said his object was not to get gold but to preach, and numbers
> think he was justifiable in going...Aaron made a golden calf to
> worship whilst Moses was on the mount...and priests and min-
> isters with their members may do the same in this day and have
> done it no doubt...We will miss him very much."[151]*

Robert Sallee James left his wife, Zerelda, sons Alexander Franklin
James and Jesse Woodson James, and his newborn daughter Susan
Lavenia James in Clay County when he headed west. Stiles suggests:

> *Three decades later, after this contented corner of Missouri had
> passed through biblical plagues and apocalyptic trials, locals
> would recall this moment with vivid but unreliable memories. 'To
> this day,' a newspaper would report, 'the old settlers about the
> James home say, and it has been a tradition, that the Rev. Robert
> James was driven from home by his wife.' Robert's brother would
> agree, saying the sharp-tongued Zerelda had bitterly resented her
> husband's peripatetic preaching.*

> *Perhaps. He was a restless, driven man, and once before he had
> seemed discontented with life in Missouri. The 1846 trip had made
> clear that he was comfortable taking long absences from his wife
> and children. The movement to California, however, was a force
> far larger than any domestic squabble, and the preacher's sense of
> calling loomed larger still. The 1850 migration from Clay County
> dwarfed even that of the previous year; some thirty men made the
> journey with Robert (including the abolitionist Huffaker.)[152]*

151 Stiles, *Last Rebel of the Civil War*, 24-25.
152 Stiles, *Last Rebel of the Civil War*, 25.

Stiles describes the sense of fatalism that hovered around Robert James as he left Clay County. Perhaps he had a feeling that he would not see his family again. On May 1, he wrote to Zerelda, "Pray for me...that if [we] no more meet in this world we can meet in Glory."[153] There was an outbreak of cholera in the camp. Steele believes he may have encountered some type of food poisoning or fever in a Placerville gold camp and died suddenly August 18, 1850. He was buried in an unmarked grave.[154]

According to Anderson Family Records at Ancestry.com, when Robert James traveled to California, he was accompanied by a friend named William C. Anderson. William C. Anderson was the father of Bloody Bill Anderson, Confederate bushwhacker during the Civil War. The Records state:

> In the 1850's William C Anderson, accompanied by Robert James, left their homes and families, to travel to California in search of gold. They temporarily settled in a gold camp at Hangtown, California. On August 18, 1850, Robert James died of fever; however, William Anderson stayed on their claim for almost a year after Robert James' death.

> Robert James place of death is given as the gold camp at Hangtown (now Placerville), California. He was only thirty-two years old, but his life was full of accomplishment. As the Liberty Tribune summed it up:

> He was a man much liked by all who enjoyed his acquaintance; and as a revivalist he had but few equals in this country. We think within the bounds of reason when we affirm that more additions have been made to the Baptist Church, in Clay County, under his preaching (length of time considered) than under that of any other person....Peace to his ashes.[155]

The children of Robert Sallee James and Zerelda Elizabeth Cole were:

---

153 Stiles, *Last Rebel of the Civil War*, 25.
154 Steele, *The Family History*, 39
155 "Wild Bill Thomason's Relationship to Anderson Boys and James Boys," Ancestry.com, Provo, Utah. Accessed July 25, 2010. Available at http://www.ancestry.com.

Alexander Franklin James (b. January 10, 1843, Logan Co., Kentucky; d. Feb. 15, 1915, Jackson Co., Missouri; m. Anna Ralston, June 1874;

Robert R. James (b. July 19, 1845; d. August 21, 1845);

Jesse Woodson James (b. Sept. 5, 1847, Clay Co., Missouri; d. April 3, 1882, St. Joseph, Missouri; m. Zerelda Amanda Mimms April 24, 1874);

Susan Lavenia James (b. Nov. 25, 1849, Clay Co., Missouri; d. March 3, 1889; m. Allen H. Parmer, Nov. 24, 1870).[156]

---

156 Steele, *The Family History*, 37-38.

Chapter 9: The Cole Family

The Black Horse Tavern on the old Frankfort-Lexington Road near Midway, Kentucky was often the scene of excitement. Free-flowing liquor and predictable results often gave the impression of a bawdy house and a topic for numerous preachers' hell, fire, and damnation sermons. It became a focal point for both the famous and infamous and a popular stop for many a campaigner on a political jaunt. The tavern was owned by Richard Cole, Sr., great-grandfather of Zerelda Cole James.

Zerelda's Cole line extends back to John and Susanna Cole of Pennsylvania. John relocated to Culpepper Co., Virginia, where he died in 1757, followed by his wife in 1761.[157] Some family records on Ancestry.com claim that this John Cole was born in 1691 in Baltimore, Maryland and died in Baltimore in 1750. These same records indicate that John's parents were John Cole (1669-1746) and Johanna Garrett (1675-1715), also of Baltimore,[158] but published sources seem to agree on the Pennsylvania/Culpepper Co., Virginia location. Zerelda's great-grandfather, Richard Cole, Sr., was the son of John and Susanna, having been born in Pennsylvania in 1729, and later settling near Midway, Kentucky. Richard's first wife was Ann Hubbard, whom he married in 1762. His second wife was Emsey Margaret James, and he married her in Woodford, Kentucky July 21, 1795.[159] The Pennsylvania-Virginia-Kentucky location invites an interesting speculation regarding the reason for the Coles' migration to the South in that their impulse may have been motivated by the Westilvania Movement. They may have

---

157 Steele, *The Family History*, 39.
158 Murphy Family Tree, Ancestry.com, Provo, Utah. Accessed June 12, 2010. Available at http://www.ancestry.com.
159 Steele, *The Family History*, 39.

been among those who left Pennsylvania rather than be denied separate statehood. Other records at Ancestry.com indicate that the Coles were from Somerset County, which is in the western part of the state.

There does not appear to be a connection between these Coles and the New England Cole families. There also does not appear to be a connection between these Coles and the Quaker Coles or Coales of Maryland. That line's progenitor, William Coale, was born in England in 1655 and died at West River Meeting, Ann Arundel Co., Maryland in 1678.[160] His descendants either remained in Maryland or moved farther west. There is also no connection between this Cole line and the family of Cole Younger. Some writers erroneously assumed this was true because of the Cole name.

Born on the Younger Farm at Lee's Summit, Missouri on January 15, 1844, Thomas Coleman Younger was the oldest of the four younger boys: Coleman, James, Robert, and John. The Younger family was probably the most prominent in Jackson County and most respected in the Lee's Summit community. The father of the four outlaws was Col. Henry W. Younger, who was a Union man, owned 3500 acres in Jackson and Cass Counties and a livery business in Harrisonville. He was murdered and robbed just south of Independence by a group of Federal soldiers from Kansas under the command of a captain by the name of Walley. Love describes the killing:

> *Colonel Younger had been to Independence, capital of Jackson County, where he had sold a drove of cattle from one of his big farms. Driving toward Harrisonville in a buggy, he was shot down about five miles south of Independence, July 20, 1862. The murderers turned his pockets inside out, stole $400, missed several thousand which Colonel Younger carried in a belt beneath his outer clothing, and left his body by the roadside.[161]*

Cole Younger's mother was a daughter of the Hon. Richard M. Fristoe of Jackson County, a man of high esteem who had served not only on the bench but in the Missouri Legislature as well. She died in 1870 after many years of semi-invalidism "due chiefly to the results of harsh

---

160 Harris/Cannon Connections. Ancestry.com, Provo, Utah. Accessed June
    15, 2010. Available at http://www.ancestry.com.
161 Love, *The Rise and Fall of Jesse James*, 53.

treatment at the hands of Kansas Jayhawkers and Red-Legs and the Jackson County Federal militia."[162] While part of this harshness resulted after Cole and his brothers became outlaws, much of it occurred earlier after her husband's murder. The Younger boys were deeply devoted to their mother and sought retribution. However, Love believes:

That the Younger family was mistreated most vilely in wartime and afterward is a fact fully authenticated. Mrs. Younger suffered unbelievably at the hands of the enemies of her sons; but that those sons went into outlawry after the war for "vengeance," as many a penny-a-liner has written, is an insult to their intelligence. They were men of more than ordinary mental endowment, and they knew full well that the robbing of banks and trains some years after the war could not be interpreted by any reasonable human being as an act of vengeance for wrongs their people had suffered.[163]

Zerelda Cole's great grandfather, Richard Cole, Sr., died at Midway, Kentucky November 21, 1814. His children were:

John Cole (married Nancy Hines);

Richard Cole, Jr., (b. April 23, 1763; m. Sally Yates; d. July 9, 1839);

Jesse Cole (m. Nancy Sparks; Elizabeth Roberts; Elizabeth Hyatt;

Rachael Cole (b. 1760; m. Willa Jett; d. 1840;

Betsey Cole (m. Mr. Snape);

Agnes Cole;

Sallie Cole (m. Benjamin Graves);

Alsey Alice Cole (b. June 20, 1769; m. Anthony Lindsay, Jr.; d. July 7, 1813);

Lucy Cole (m. Jonathan Cropper).[164]

---

162 Love, *The Rise and Fall of Jesse James*, 54
163 Love, *The Rise and Fall of Jesse James*, 58.
164 Steele, *The Family History*, 40-41.

Zerelda's grandparents were Richard Cole, Jr. and Sara "Salley"
Yates. A wealthy farmer, Richard Jr. took over the operation of the
Black Horse Tavern after his father's death.[165] Richard Cole, Jr.'s will
follows:

> *I Richard Cole, Of the County of Woodford and State of Kentucky
> at present of sound mind and memory but impressed with the un-
> certainty of life do make and ordain the following for my last will
> and testament, after the payments of my debts and such funeral
> expenses as my Executors may as their decision incur. I devise all
> the residue of my estate as follows To Wit:*

> *First, I devise to my beloved wife Sara Cole 220 acres of land on
> the north side of South Elkhorn fork of Elkhorn, which is to be
> constituted of the tract computed at 156 and ½ acres formerly
> purchased of Sir William of the representatives of Wm. Alexander,
> decd. And 25 acres which I purchased from Vansant and which
> one belonging to Henry Hardy and the residences to be laid off
> out of land I purchased from Lee, by a live oak to his south line.
> The houses all to be removed from the Hardy track and the brick
> house alone to be entitled. To be held and occupied by my said
> wife during her life, but without the commission of warrant, also
> thence slave less choice of my slaves for life and their horse, four
> cows, fifteen sheep, six hogs, two boars, with a remarkable supply
> of furniture and such farming hand tools and kitchen furniture as
> may desire to be selected by her from my stock and three hundred
> dollars in money, but "A" expressly declared that if my said wife
> Sara Cole shall marry again, this provision shall cease and all
> estate embraced by "A" shall be forfeited by her, to be disposed
> of as is herein provided relative to the family upon which I live.*

> *Second, to my daughter Mary Finnie and her children who may
> survive her, and the children of her children who may have died
> before her if there be any such. I devise all the residues of it, land
> I purchased of the heir of Hancock Lee lying mostly on the North
> side of the South Fork of Elkhorn and including all the land I own
> on the North side of the said creek not embraced by the devised
> aforesaid to be held by said daughter during her life and by said*

165 Steele, *The Family History*, 41.

children and their heirs forever, their grandchildren, however who may have survived their parents at her death and to take the share that would have been of their father or mother and also give to my said daughter Mary and her children as aforesaid slaves, Charlotte and Henry and their increase forever and accessories give to my daughter Mary Finnie, 1 Dog, 10 sheep, her hogs and $200.00 in money.

Third, the plantation on the North side, except one piece of ground, including the graves, if and with a convenience to say to it I require to be sold upon a credit of two years with a lien upon the proposed for the price and all residues of my estate. I require to be sold at credit of 12 months the proceeds to be devised between my daughter Elizabeth Martin and, Paine, and my son James Cole and Sara Ann Cole, the daughter of my deceased son Jesse and children of Fanny Bevin and Jesse Cole, son of my son James, and Zerilda Cole the daughter of my son James, in the following portions to wit. My Daughter Sarah and Elizabeth are to have full shares. James and his two children aforesaid are to have one share. Lloyd Cole and Sara Ann Cole to have one each and one third of a share. It being my especial desire that Lloyd be well educated out of his portion.

Fourth, It is moreover my desire that upon the death of my said wife, or upon her marriage, If she shall marry again that the land and slaves devised to my wife aforesaid upon the condition aforesaid, to be sold and the proceeds be distributed as above provided touching the land upon which I live.

Fifthly, It is my intention and desire that the shares of a portion of the money hereby devised shall not be paid over to the infants until they retain their full age respectful, but shall be put to interest and well secured. I do hereby appoint my friend Benjamine Harrison and Thomas Martin my Executors of this will, forsaking all others by me at any time made.

Witness my hand and seal this 15th day of December 1834.

Signed and Sealed, Richard Cole Jr.

Witness, I Hagan, Hancock Lee, Edward C. Hifter

Codicil; I now make an alteration in my will as reflects, Lloyd Cole; I have a trial with him and think he would be better off without property than with it. I therefore consider he shall not have the part mentioned above, I wish him to have three hundred dollars cash only, and I also wish my Nephew Thomas Jett to be one of my Executors in addition to the two mentioned above. July 12, 1837.

In the August 1839 Session of Court for the County of Woodford, the foregoing instrument of writing purported to be the last will and testament of Richard Cole Jr., deceased, was this day produced in court and proven by the oath of Hancock Lee one of the subtending officers thereunto and ordered to record and on testament of writing there under written purporting to be the codicil to the last will and testament of the said Richard Cole by oath of George Weir, Hancock Lee and Hancock W. Davis, and ordered to record.

Attest Herman Boulman[166]

Zerelda's parents were James Cole and Sara "Sallie" Lindsay (first cousins). Sallie was the daughter of Anthony Lindsay, Jr. and Alcey "Alice" and granddaughter of Anthony Lindsay, Sr. and Rachel Dorsey.[167] James and Alice Cole had two children:

Zerelda E. Cole (b. January 29, 1825, Woodford, Kentucky; m. Robert Sallee James, December 28, 1841; d. February 10, 1911);

Jesse Richard Cole (b. November 29, 1826; m. Louisa G. Maret, December 26, 1846; d. November 16, 1895, Clay Co., Missouri)[168]

James Cole died when he fell from a horse on February 27, 1827.[169] Sallie lived with her children in the Black Horse Tavern until her

---

166 Richard Cole, Jr. Last Will and Testament, Public Member Stories, Accessed August 5, 2010.
Ancestry.com, Provo, Utah. Available at http://www.ancestry.com.
167 The Genealogy of Virginia Ann Snowberger Hagan, Ancestry.com, Provo. Utah. Accessed June 17, 2010. Available at http://www.ancestry.com.
168 Steele, *The Family History*, 42.
169 Steele, *The Family History*, 42.

father-in-law's death in 1839.[170] She then married Robert Thomason, who was a widower with six children, and the Thomasons moved to Clay Co., Missouri. Zerelda remained in Kentucky and lived with her uncle, James M. Lindsay in Stamping Ground, Scott Co., Kentucky since she despised Robert Thomason.[171] However, after her marriage to Robert Sallee James and her immediate pregnancy with her oldest son, Alexander Franklin James, the young couple relocated to Clay Co., Missouri as well and moved in with the Thomason family.

The following story relates the influence of the Thomason family on the Anderson and James boys in Clay County:

> *A major influence on the James boys at this time, "Wild Bill" Thomason. Thomason was the brother of Robert Thomason, their mother Zerelda's stepfather. Wild Bill had served as a lieutenant in the Mexican War.*
>
> *William "Wild Bill" Thomason is the father to Martha J Boyle, wife of James M Anderson, of the lineage of the Anderson family. Mahala Thomason, who was also a member in the William C Anderson household in the 1850 US Federal Census, is Martha's mother, and Wild Bill's wife. It goes without saying, that Wild Bill had as much influence on the lives of young William "Bloody Bill" and James "Jim" Anderson, as he did on Jesse and Frank James.[172]*

"Wild Bill" Thomason may have had a direct influence on the James boys. But there was another influence they inherited.

---

170 Steele, *The Family History*, 42.
171 Steele, *The Family History*, 42.
172 "Wild Bill" Thomason's Relationship/Influence to the Anderson Boys and the James Boys", Public Member Stories, Ancestry.com, http://www.ancestry.com.

Chapter 10: The Dorsey Influence

Early in this research, I made a discovery that caused me to chuckle one afternoon. And my eyes traveled across the room toward Howard, wondering how I should break the news to him. After all, were it not for Howard, I would have never spent two days in Adair—would never have tramped through an untold number of cemeteries or state archives—would never have had the persistence to pursue such a project. My eyes then landed upon a picture I was holding of Frank James taken sometime during his later years. I held it up and said, "This is what Frank James looked like!"

Howard studied the picture a while before exclaiming, "Why—he looks like he could have been a member of *my* family!"

Smiling, I made the announcement.

"Well—you see--that's because—*he was!*"

Then, waiting a moment or two for my announcement to soak it, I added, "Now, don't go out and rob any banks or trains!"

* * *

The Dorsey family was one of the most powerful families in the State of Maryland. They were into everything, and they did everything. Zerelda Cole James' great-grandmother was Rachel Dorsey Lindsay (1737-1805), a descendant of Edward Dorsey (1619-1659), the Immigrant, through his son, Col. Edward Dorsey (1646-1705) of Anne Arundel, County. And Howard's great-grandmother was Mary E. Dorsey DeLashmutt (1852-1934)—wife of John M. DeLashmutt—and she was also an Edward Dorsey descendant through Col. Edward's brother, the Hon. John Dorsey (1650-1715). Zerelda's descent is claimed through Col. Edward's son, Nicholas Dorsey (1689-1717). Howard's descent is claimed through Edward Dorsey (1683-1701), one of John Dorsey's sons. Zerelda Cole James and Howard's third great grandfather, John Sellman Dorsey (1788-1859), were fifth cousins. Alexander Franklin James, Jesse James and Susan James were sixth cousins of Howard's great-great grandfather, Walter Dorsey (1820-1891)—a sheriff--making Howard and his brothers sixth cousins four times removed of the James brothers and sister.

When I first met Howard's family in 1962, his mother, Mildred Lee Warfield Beall (1917-2007), talked at great lengths about her Warfield and Polk ancestors. I noticed that she never mentioned the DeLashmutts or Dorseys, so I asked her about them one day. She laughed and responded, "Oh, I don't talk about them! They were a bunch of horse thieves!" (She did, however, visit the DeLaChaumette [DeLashmutt] ancestral home in France sometime in the 1990s. And she did once tell me that her grandmother, Mary E. Dorsey DeLashmutt, was very pretty). I don't know whether my mother-in-law knew that she was a sixth cousin three times removed of Jesse James. Her sister, Gertrude Warfield Stukes, was the family genealogist, so I have an idea they knew it. They just didn't talk about it!

The Anne Arundel Dorsey family progenitor was Edward the Immigrant. The Dorseys were originally thought to be descended from a cousin of William the Conqueror, Sir. Norman D'Arcie, and from the Lord D'Arcy family of Hornby Castle.[173] A recent DNA test dated November 2005 and updated March of 2006 proved no connection whatsoever between Edward Dorsey's line and the Hornby Castle D'Arcys. It is now believed that Edward's family probably came from Ireland.[174]

In 1659, Edward Dorsey, the Immigrant, drowned near the Isle of Kent,[175] and his land in Anne Arundel County passed down through a

173 Frederic Z. Saunders, "Edward Dorsey of Anne Arundel County, Maryland." Accessed July 20, 2010. Available at http://home.netcom. com/~fzsaund/dorsey.html.
174 Saunders, Edward Dorsey of Anne Arundel County, Maryland, http:// home.netcome/com/~fzsaund/dorsey.html.
175 Edward Dorsey, Archives of Maryland 41:314

number of generations. On August 25, 1664, the three sons of Edward Dorsey (Edward, Joshua and John) patented their father's survey of 400 acres as Hockley in the Hole, and on December 6, 1681, Edward and Joshua sold out their interest to their brother John.[176]

Col. Edward Dorsey (1646-1705) married Sarah Wyatt in November 1670. Their children were:

Edward Dorsey (1676-1705);

Sarah Dorsey (1677-1727);

Hannah Dorsey (1679-1704);

Samuel Dorsey (1682-1724);

Caleb Dorsey (1685-1742);

Joshua Dorsey (1686-1747);

JOHN DORSEY (1686-1764);

NICHOLAS DORSEY (1689-1717);

Benjamin Dorsey (1690-1717).[177]

Sarah Wyatt died in 1690 (probably in childbirth with Benjamin.) In 1693, Col Edward married Margaret Larkin or Lacon. Their children were:

Larkin (or Lacon) Dorsey (1694-1712)

Francis Dorsey (1696-1749)

Charles Dorsey (1698-1732)

Edward Dorsey (1700-)

Ann Dorsey (1702-1786)[178]

---

176 The Dorsey Family, Descendants of Edward Darcy-Dorsey of Virginia and Maryland for five generations, Accessed July 27, 2010. Ancestry. com, Provo, Utah. Available at http://www.ancestry.com

177 The Dorsey Family, http://www.ancestry.com.

178 Col. Edward Dorsey, Owings Stone Family: A Genealogy of 20,000+ Ancestors and Relatives, Accessed July 27, 2010. Available at: http://whois.domaintools.com/owingsstone.com.

Col. Edward Dorsey's will, dated 1704, sets out the following items:

> *The inventory of Edward Dorsey's estate lists dozens of items, in-cluding "12 new silver spoons, 5 old ones...silver hilted sword...1 looking glass..." and numerous other pieces of silver, furniture, feather beds and household equipment. The list also includes 2 servants and 13 slaves.*

> *Will extract:*
> *Dorsey, Edward, Balto. Co., 26th Oct., 1704; 31st Dec., 1705.*
> *To son Levin at 21 yrs. and hrs., 100 A., "Hockly" on main falls of Patapsco R., and personalty including boy William Jackson.*
> *To sons Charles, Levin, Francis and Edward and their hrs., all land on n. side Patapsco R., all "Taylors Forrest" if it be bought at testator's death.*
> *To dau. Ann, personalty.*
> *To son Joshua and hrs., 100 A., "Barnes Folly."*
> *To son Samuell, part of "Major's Choyce" and also that which he has received by deed of gift.*
> *To son Nicholas, 100 A., part of "Long Reach" at Elk Ridge and personalty at 16 yrs. Of age.*
> *To son Benjamin, 100 A., part of "Long Reach" and personalty at 16 yrs. of age.*
> *To son John, 148 A., residue of "Long Reach" at 16 yrs. of age.*
> *To dau. Sarah Petticoate and 3 child. of dau. Hannah Howard, personalty.*
> *Wife Margaret, extx. and residuary legatee.*
> *Test: Kathcrine Organ, John Huntsmen, John Dorsey and John Ball.*[179]

Col. Edward Dorsey was a prominent member of the Maryland Colony. A creek just north of Annapolis was named for him (Dorsey Creek) before 1659. The Owings Stone Family website states: "He was one of the first subscribers and contributed 2,000 pounds of tobacco to fund the founding of King William's School (now St. John's College).[180] The website further notes:

179 Col Edward Dorsey, Maryland Calendar of Wills: Volume 3
180 Col. Edward Dorsey, Owings Stone Family: A Genealogy of 20,000+ Ancestors and Relatives, http://.domaintools.com/owingsstone.com.

In 1694, along with Major John Hammond, Hon. John Dorsey, Captain Philip Howard, Major Nicholas Greenbury and John Bennett, he was on a committee to lay out a town common and streets for the town of Annapolis, then to be called Proctor.

Sir Thomas Lawrence wrote of Edward Dorsey that, "Edward Dorsey lives near Annapolis and builds houses there, those who have dealings with him say his honesty more often fails him than his wit." This did not keep him from being elected a member of His Majesty's Council and being appointed a member of the House of Burgesses on 21 Sept. 1694.[181]

Col. Edward Dorsey was both a lawyer and a builder. He was Captain of the Militia in 1686, Major in 1687, Field Officer of Calvert Co. in 1694 and a Colonel in 1702.[182] As "Major of the Horse," he joined Capt. Edward Burgess in asking for additional arms and ammunition for defense.[183] Additionally:

He owned and sold hundreds of acres of land in Maryland during his life time. He first established his home on a plantation that embraced a considerable portion of what is now the city of Annapolis. It was here that his first 8 children were born. On 12 June 1698, he was granted land in the western part of Anne Arundel Co./Baltimore Co. on the shore the Patapsco, now part of Howard Co., that he called Major's Choice. He and his family moved to Major's Choice before 1700. This property remained in the hands of his children for several generations. Charles Hammond, son of his daughter Ann, sold an acre to Charles White, Elizabeth Dorsey and Achsah Howard for the purpose of building a Methodist meeting house.

Edward Dorsey bought several lots in Annapolis and built a number of houses there. It was referred to as "Bloomsberry Square."[184]

And:

"From 1680 to 1705, Major Dorsey was in every movement looking to the development of the colony. From 1694 to 1696 he was

181 Owings Stone Family. http://whois.domaintools.com/owingstone.com.
182 Owings Stone Family Website.
183 Owings Stone Family Website.
184 Owings Stone Family Website.

Judge of the High Court of Chancery, during which time he was commissioned to hold the Great Seal. In 1694, he was a member of the House of Burgesses for Anne Arundel, and from 1697 to his death, in 1705, was a member from Baltimore County (now Howard).

"He was one of the subscribers and treasurer of the fund for building St. Anne's Church, and a free school for the province also received his aid.

"He signed the protestant address from Baltimore County to the King's most gracious majestie, upon the succession of King William III - an appeal on behalf of Charles Lord Baron of Baltimore, whose proprietary government had been wrested from the family through the influence of Captain John Coode. Though a Protestant, he was found in support of a government which left religious faith untouched."

He was a supporter of the House of Stuart and a member of the Jacobean Party. His home was often a meeting place for other supporters.[185]

He died at Major's Choice April 2, 1705.

* * *

In the Spring of 2006, Howard and I traveled to St. Joseph, Missouri to visit the house where Jesse James was killed. We walked through the house, reading all the postings, and we learned that Jesse James used the name Thomas Howard while he was living in St. Joseph. As we left the house, Howard remarked, "Now, why would he use the name *Howard*?"

The Howard surname winds through both the James and Dorsey lines, as well as my own husband's family. My Howard was named for his grandfather, Howard Warfield (1873-1953), husband of Gertrude Augusta DeLashmutt Warfield. Jesse James used the surname Howard on numerous occasions. More than likely, he attributed that to his uncle, Tillman Howard West, who married Elizabeth James, sister of

---

185 Owing Stone Family Website.

Robert Sallee James (Jesse's father.) Tillman Howard West received his middle name from his mother's Howard line. Tillman's father married Mary Mourning Howard. And his uncle, John West, married Mary Mourning's sister, Lavenia Jane Howard. No doubt, both Frank and Jesse James considered it an honor using relatives' names. Frank chose the Woodson name while Jesse chose Howard.

Some researchers have thought that Jesse James acquired the Howard name from Edward Dorsey, the Immigrant, which is unlikely since Jesse James would have had no knowledge about those early ancestors. According to Frederic Z. Saunders in "Edward Dorsey of Anne Arundel County, Maryland":

> *Edward DORSEY was married to Ann, her surname being unknown. Some researchers have inaccurately listed her as Ann, daughter of Matthew HOWARD, Sr. While Matthew HOWARD did have a daughter named Ann, there is record of her husband being James GRENEFFE. Also, there is evidence that Edward DORSEY's daughter Sarah married Matthew HOWARD, Jr., son of the previously mentioned Matthew HOWARD. If Edward DORSEY's wife were the daughter of Matthew HOWARD, that would mean that his daughter Sarah's marriage to Matthew HOWARD, Jr. would have been to her blood uncle, a relation that was strictly forbidden, then as now.*
>
> *The listing of Edward DORSEY's wife Ann as a HOWARD probably came about through some researcher's incorrect interpretation of his son Joshua DORSEY's will. In his will, Joshua made bequests to his "cousins" John, Samuel and Matthew HOWARD. Though not stated these were children of Matthew HOWARD, Jr. [who married Joshua's sister Sarah DORSEY]. "Cousin" in the 1600s was a term often used for nephew or nieces, and sometimes used to refer to grandchildren. That researcher being unfamiliar with usage of the term apparently interpreted that they were true first cousins, and incorrectly concluded that Edward DORSEY's wife Ann was a daughter of Matthew HOWARD, Sr.[186]*

---

186 Frederic Z. Saunders, "Edward Dorsey of Anne Arundel County, Maryland", http://home.netcom.com/~fzsaund/dorsey.html

Chapter 11: Awaking a Sleeping Giant

After the death of Robert Sallee James, Zerelda encountered the unpleasant status of widowhood. She underwent one auction, only to be forced to endure another auction of all of her farm equipment, which essentially took away her means to exist. Prospects were few for a single woman in that day and time, especially for a single woman with three small children. Only one option was available for her. She needed to find a husband and preferably, a wealthy one!

On September 30, 1852, Zerelda married a widower named Benjamin A. Simms, a well-known Clay County farmer. Problems erupted at the outset, however. While Simms was wealthy and Zerelda could probably have lived well in his household, he could not stand her three young children. Even though he had children from his previous marriage, Frank, Jesse and Susan annoyed him tremendously. He thought they were pampered and spoiled and also felt that Zerelda had spoiled them after their father's death. For her part, Zerelda would not allow him to touch them, something he apparently attempted to do from time to time. Simms finally delivered an ultimatum: send the children away and remain married to him, or keep the children and leave the house with them. Zerelda did not want to give up her new life of comfort and at the same time, she realized she could not keep the children with her. Tilman Howard West and Elizabeth took the children, but Zerelda could not endure her separation from them. Finally, after a few months of marriage, Zerelda separated from Simms, fearing that her children would not recognize her if they were kept away from her for very long. Simms died before the divorce proceedings were finalized, so Zerelda became a widow once again.

Zerelda married a third and final time on September 15, 1855. Her new husband was Dr. Reuben Samuel, and he became the only father that Frank, Jesse and Susan actually knew. Born in Kentucky in 1828 and five years younger than his new wife, Dr. Samuel was described as a pleasant man with an easy-going nature. One local merchant who bore the same surname and who was not related to the doctor said, "He is no kinsman of mine, thank God…yet I think he is an easy, good natured, good for nothing fellow who is completely under the control of his wife."[187] Dr. Samuel gave up his medical practice to tend to matters on the farm. Additionally, Zerelda had him sign a prenuptial agreement guaranteeing her full ownership of the farm and all related property in the event of his death.

The children of Dr. Reuben Samuel and Zerelda Cole James were:

> Sarah (Sallie) Louisa Samuel (b. Dec. 26, 1858; m. William Nicholson Nov. 28, 1878; d. Sept. 15, 1915);

> John Thomas Samuel (b. Dec. 25, 1861; m. Norma L. Maret July 22, 1885; d. March 15, 1932);

> Fannie Quantrill Samuel (b. Oct. 18, 1863; m. Joe C. Hall, Dec. 30, 1880; d. May 30, 1922);

> Archie Peyton Samuel (b. July 26, 1866; d. Jan. 26, 1875);

> Perry Samuel[14] (b. 1862; d. March 1, 1936.[188]

While matters calmed down for Zerelda and her family, the situation about them reached a new boiling point—a situation that would change their lives forever.

The period of the 1850s was a turbulent time in Clay and Jackson Counties, as well as in other border areas. Groups of "Jayhawkers" from Kansas and "Border Ruffians" from Missouri streamed back and forth across the countryside desecrating the land and retaliating against one another. The Kansas-Nebraska Act repealed the Missouri Compromise, an act that only aggravated hostilities. Southern planters began worrying about the future of their "peculiar institution"

187 Stiles, *Last Rebel of the Civil War*, 31.
188 Steele, *The Family History*, 65-67.

(slavery) since they were so dependent upon it. The anti-slavery Kansas Jayhawkers (some of them called "red legs" because of the red banners tied to their legs) were led by men such as James Lane, James Montgomery, Charles R. "Doc" Jennison, and John Brown (formerly of Summit Co., Ohio). The pro-slavery Boarder Ruffians on the Missouri side began naming their businesses and their children after the term. According to Stiles, "George S. Withers, a proslavery leader in Clay County even named his son Border Ruffian Withers."[189] Other Border Ruffians included Claiborne F. Jackson and Joseph O. Shelby. These two men organized armed squads to fight in Kansas.

The first killing was November 21, 1855, setting off a full year of warfare in Kansas. The federal arsenal at Liberty was stormed December 4, 1855 by approximately one hundred local men. On May 21, 1856, David Rice Atchison (an outspoken Missouri Democrat) joined 800 Border Ruffians to loot Lawrence. Thereafter, John Brown and his sons led a raid against proslavery settlers in Osawatomie, Kansas and killed five. According to Stiles:

> *Columns under Brown, Atchison, Jim Lane, and others criss-crossed the land. Atchison ordered the Missouri River closed to free-state migrants and goods during the summer of 1856. Armed squads of men stood guard along the waterfront in Platte, Clay, Lafayette and Jackson Counties; they stomped aboard each steamboat, interrogated the passengers, and hauled out anyone who seemed suspicious. "We give you no mere rumors," Atchison declared to the people of Missouri on August 16, 1856, "but a simple statement of undoubted facts. We say to you that war, organized, matured, is now being waged by the Abolitionists. And we call on all who are not prepared to see their friends butchered, to be driven themselves from their homes, to rally instantly to the rescue."[190]*

In Platte County, Col. George S. Park's *Parkville Industrial Luminary* was ordered destroyed, and on April 14, 1855, a crowd broke into the newspaper shop, destroyed the press, and threw it into the Missouri River. Proslavery extremists demanded complete loyalty from the

189 Stiles, *Last Rebel of the Civil War*, 51.
190 Stiles, *Last Rebel of the Civil War*, 51-52.

white community and if anyone challenged them, they were silenced. [George S. Park became one of the future founders of Park College— today, Park University.]

While these events were taking place in Missouri and Kansas, an- other crisis loomed with the collapse of the national Whig Party. Most Missouri Whigs moved into the American Party (also called the Know-Nothing Party), an organization in which secret signals or signs were adopted along with other symbols of recognition.

Hostilities continued to grow and on April 12, 1861, rebel troops fired on Fort Sumter in Charleston, South Carolina. This event is given as the official start of the Civil War; however, warfare in Missouri and Kansas had already been underway for a good five years. Eighteen- year-old Frank James went off to war. And Missouri was placed under martial law. According to Stiles:

> *Amateurism exacerbated the inherent brutality of martial law.*
> *The Union army consisted largely of men who had been civilians*
> *until April 1861, and most were new to all things military. With*
> *each month, more and more arrested civilians arrived from the*
> *country in St. Louis and other cities, often with little paperwork to*
> *define their crimes or the evidence against them. "Washington,"*
> *comments one historian, "never exercised much control over*
> *Missouri."[191]*

And controlling those Missourians was certainly a frustrating expe- rience for the Union forces. Bridge burners and track destroyers at- tacked all the way up and down the Missouri Pacific and Hannibal and St. Joseph Railroads. In desperation and after twenty-seven people died when a train tumbled off a track, Order No. 32 was issued stat- ing "Anyone caught in the act [of sabotage]…will be immediately shot."[192] And while the Union officials must have felt they succeeded in getting a handle on these people, they only separated the weak from the strong. The "bushwhackers" were born. As Stiles notes, "Nowhere would the bushwhackers be smarter, tougher, and angrier than in Jackson County, just across the river from Clay…[Jackson County] has been represented as conquered by Union troops 5 times, but no

191 Stiles, *Last Rebel of the Civil War*, 73.
192 Stiles, *Last Rebel of the Civil War*, 74.

sooner are the forces withdrawn from their midst than they rise up and commence anew their depredations and persecutions of the Union men, confiscating their property, shooting, hanging, or driving them from the country."[193]

Frank James served under General Sterling Price at this stage of the war and accompanied the troops to southwestern Missouri, where they fought at Wilson's Creek on August 10, 1861, a battle that resulted in a Confederate victory. Frank returned home shortly after the battle, where he no doubt boasted about his exploits and his opinions about the war. (Young Jesse was no doubt proud but at the same time a little jealous of his older brother). The Wilson's Creek victory was short-lived, however. On February 12, 1862, Price's dwindling army was forced to leave Missouri altogether and on March 7-8, the Confederates were defeated at Pea Ridge in Northwest Arkansas. Price resigned from the militia in order to accept a Confederate commission. The Missouri State Guard came to an end.

For Frank, this stage of the war was over. He lay in bed in Springfield, covered with measles. Eventually, he was taken prisoner by the Federals, and was eventually released after signing an oath that he would not fight again. Apparently, he did not sign his full name!

***

Young Jesse James and the boys he played with must have executed and re-executed "Old Brown" and "Old Lane" and other abolitionist leaders a thousand times during this period of turmoil. Zerelda was outspoken, so Jesse understood the family's position on the matter. In his book *The Rise and Fall of Jesse James*, Robertus Loves notes:

> *Border Missouri men and women hated Brown and Lane, to whom they ascribed in their impetuous fury much of their miseries. Border Missouri boyhood most naturally shared this feeling. It was difficult to find any boy who would undergo the ignominy of playing the character of Jim Lane or John Brown. However, boys who sought the ecstasy and honor of shooting or hanging Brown or Lane—in play, mind you—were able to obtain raw material for*

---

193 Stiles, *Last Rebel of the Civil War*, 75.

those characters by agreeing to reverse the cast and themselves submit to the disgrace the next time they played the exciting and satisfying game.

Thus it came about that General Lane, "the Grim Liberator," was shot or drowned or hanged many times over, in Missouri, by boys who resented his Free Soil activities, many years before he poked the muzzle of a revolver into his own mouth and killed himself when an about-to-be-disgraced Senator of the United States and that some years before John Brown was hanged in Virginia for his so-called treason to that state. The border boys had shot him full of holes or stretched his neck beneath many an overhanging limb. Incidental to these executions were much raiding and robbing done in play and yet not altogether guiltless of violent feelings.[194]

[Apparently, Jesse James had no record of terrorizing cats or committing mean acts as a child, something Love concluded after interviewing friends and neighbors of the James boys: "We find that in their boyhood, both Frank and Jesse were notably fond of animal pets. In the case of Jesse this tenderness toward dumb beasts continued until the day of his death; and there is nothing to indicate that Frank James ever mistreated an animal."[195] Reportedly, Jesse had a little dog that he was quite fond of, who was living in the house with his family in St. Joseph. After Jesse James was killed, the little dog ran in circles about him, clearly upset that his friend was gone. It appears that Jesse James had more patience with animals than he had with some humans.]

Life wasn't all play for the boys. Living on a farm required a lot of work and effort. The James boys worked in the fields and did their share, and Jesse reserved his moments of play for special occasions. Love says:

They were brought up to work, and work hard. On a Missouri farm three-quarters of a century ago such things as labor-saving devices were unknown. Farm work meant real work, sweat-o'-the-brow toil, back-wearying labor. From the time they were big enough to drive a horse and hold the handles of a plow, Frank

---

194 Robertus Love. *The Rise and Fall of Jesse James.* [Lincoln: University of Nebraska Press, 1990] 39-40.
195 Love, *The Rise and Fall of Jesse James*, 28.

and Jesse made "hands" on the old home farm. They planted, hoed, plowed, harvested. Wheat, corn, hay, garden truck, all were grown there. Horses to feed and curry, cows to care for and milk, hogs to call and corral, firewood to chop and split—the chores alone were enough, winter or summer, to keep the two growing lads in healthful exercise.[196]

The boys were raised in the Baptist Church and attended services every Sunday as well as through the week. Love believes that they never discarded their faith, and describes the following incident:

Jesse James remained thoroughly orthodox in his religious beliefs as long as he lived. This, perhaps, is a hard nut for you to crack, but, being a simple statement of fact, it goes down upon the record. A Baptist minister who preached at Kearney when Jesse James was a youthful member of the flock met the strayed reveler some years later, when he had become an outlaw.

"Jesse," said the old pastor, "why don't you stop these things you're doing?"

"If you'll tell me just how I can stop," Jesse replied, "I'll be glad enough to stop; but I don't intend to stop right under a rope."

"Well, anyhow, you ought not to forget your religion, Jesse. You were brought up religiously. Your father was a good man of God. I'm sorry you've forgotten your bringing-up, Jesse. Get back to your religion!"

The outlaw thrust his hand into his inside coat-pocket and drew forth a small book which he handed to the minister.

"It was a copy of the New Testament," said the venerable clergyman, in relating the incident shortly before this was written. "I looked through it and was astonished. Never in my life have I seen a Bible so marked up, showing such constant usage. I handed it back to Jesse James. He smiled, as usual, replaced the Testament in his pocket, and his eyes blinked fast."

Jesse James believed in a personal God and in a personal Devil— probably a considerable number of the latter! He accepted the

196 Love, *The Rise and Fall of Jesse James*, 38.

*orthodox Heaven and the orthodox Hell, his faith being implicitly
simple. He expected to go to Heaven when he died, for he believed
that he had lived the best life he possibly could live under all the
circumstances, and that, therefore, he was entitled to salvation.*[197]

While it has been said that he had a charming smile, it has also been
said that he never smiled for a photograph. The reason was simple:
he was missing a tooth and his teeth were discolored from the type of
tobacco men used at that time. Jesse James' wife once reported that
he did not drink and did not use tobacco. On the other hand, when
Howard and I were in St. Joseph in 2006, we noticed a plaque on the
museum wall explaining how tobacco had impacted his teeth:

*None of the known photos of outlaw Jesse James show him smil-
ing. Dr. John McDowell of the University of Colorado suggests
the reason was that Jesse was missing an upper front tooth. A
review of the skeletal remains showed he had lost an upper incisor
at some point during his adult life.*

*Jesse did have many gold fillings, indicating he was willing to pay
a price for the advanced dental care brought on by use of a low-
grade chewing tobacco.*[198]

After a nine-year courtship and when he was 27 years of age, Jesse
James married his first cousin, Zerelda (Zee) Amanda Mimms in
Kearney, Missouri at the home of Zee's sister, Lucy Mimms Bowder
on April 24, 1874. Their children were:

Jesse Edward James (b. Aug. 31, 1875, Nashville, Tennessee; m.
Stella McGowan, Jan. 24, 1900; d. March 26, 1951, California.)

Twins—Gould and Montgomery James (d. infancy).

Mary Susan James (b. June 17, 1879, Nashville, Tennessee; m.
Henry Lafayette Barr, March 6, 1901; d. Oct. 11, 1935, Kansas
City, Missouri).[199]

197 Love, *The Rise and Fall of Jesse James*, 35-36.
198 "Why Jesse Never Smiled for the Photographer," St. Joseph Jesse James
    Museum, St. Joseph, Missouri.
199 Steele, *The Family History*, 49.

Jesse James may have spent all of his life on a farm had it not been for an event that occurred in Clay County when he was 15 years old.

Chapter 12: The Missouri Guerillas

Frank James did not marry until after he and his brother were full-blown outlaws. On June 6, 1874, he married Anna Ralston of Kansas City. Frank and Anna only had one child:

> Robert Franklin James (b. Feb. 6, 1878; m (1) May Sullivan; (2) Mae Sanboth; d. Nov. 18, 1959, The James Farm, Kearney, Missouri.[200]

Shortly after signing his promise not to fight any more during the Civil War, Frank James joined the guerilla group led by William Clarke Quantrill.

William Clarke Quantrill

Quantrill, a dashing figure with the gift of gab, had a way of convincing everyone that he was merely righting all of the wrongs that were done to him as well as to others. He spoke of his eternal vengeance against Kansas. In this respect, Quantrill told quite a story.

He was born in Maryland, or so he said, and he had an older brother named Charley. One night, he and his brother were camped out on the prairie, when they were attacked by a group of Jayhawkers. Charley was slain; Quantrill was left for dead. According to Love:

> *Quantrill, so his story ran, vowed eternal vengeance against the Kansas people. He joined the company of Jayhawkers that had murdered his brother. From time to time he managed to get one or another of the men separated from the best. Bang!—a bullet entered the exact center of the unsuspecting fellow's forehead. In this manner Quantrill ran up, after several years of untiring effort, a*

---

200 Steele, *The Family History*, 46.

tally of all but two of the marauding band, each victim being shot exactly in the center of the forehead. Thirty to one![201]

He was a lightning rod to the men who joined him. They were all bitter about treatment they and their family members had received at the hands of the Jayhawkers as well as members of Union forces. Cole Younger joined Quantrill for that very reason.

Quantrill commanded a large group at the outset. His stories were far from the truth, however, on several counts. In the first place, he had no older brother named Charley, or younger brother by that name either. He was the oldest child in the family. Secondly, he was not born in Maryland, as he claimed. He was born at Canal Dover, Ohio, where he grew up under abolitionist influences. He relocated to Kansas when he was about 20 years of age, and taught one term of school in a country schoolhouse, as he had been a teacher in Ohio. According to Love,

> *...Mr. Connelley shows that at about the time when Quantrill pretended to have lost his beloved imaginary brother and to have begun killing the murderers by the counter-shot process, the Ohio youth was in a Kansas settlement stealing things from a colony of boyhood friends who had come out from Canal Dover at his solicitation.*[202]

Love continues:

> *The scourge and terror of the border undoubtedly inherited certain unconquerable tendencies toward a career of crimson violence. His father was an embezzler, his mother has been described snappily as a "hell-cat." One of his brothers became a thief and a low scoundrel. An uncle was one of the most spectacular criminals of the generation preceding the Civil War, being a confidence man and a forger, serving sentences in several state prisons; he married and deserted six women, and attempted to murder the woman who had been his first wife; he defrauded people right and left, and for offenses petty or serious he saw the insides of jails in St. Louis, Cincinnati, New Orleans and other cities. Quantrill's paternal grandfather was accused of sharp practices in horse-*

---

201 Love, *The Rise and Fall of Jesse James*, 18.
202 Love, *The Rise and Fall of Jesse James*, 19.

*trading and was a professional gambler; a brother of this pro-
genitor was a pirate. If we must offer "excuse" for Quantrill's
blood-thirstiness, let us look to his heredity. Every man is a sort of
modified sum total of his ancestors.*[203]

Quantrill's bloodiest act was his murderous rampage of Lawrence,
Kansas. Love writes:

*Galloping into Lawrence early on the morning of Aug. 21, 1863,
at the head of about 450 men, by far the largest force ever under
his command, Quantrill ordered every male citizen shot to death
and the houses of the people put to the torch. His order was carried out as far as was possible in a day's bulleting and burning.
The guerillas murdered 182 men that day. Part of this tally went
to the pistols of Cole Younger and Frank James, and not an in-
significant part of it to Bill Gregg's six-shooters. Jesse James was
not at Lawrence; he never served directly under Quantrill. Jim
Cummins was not at Lawrence. John and Robert Younger were
boys at home, too young to be in the war.*

*Jesse James, Jim Younger and Jim Cummins served under
Anderson and Todd. Bill Anderson possessed a cutthroat personality if ever any man has been so furnished. He was one of the
earliest of the guerillas and one of the fiercest. Before the war, he
was a cattle thief in Kansas. His men did more killing at Lawrence
than did the squad of any other of Quantrill's lieutenants. A year
or so later Bloody Bill was operating more or less independently
in Missouri, chiefly north of the Missouri river. In his guerilla
band were Jesse James, Frank James, Jim Younger, Jim Cummins
and some others who became outlaws after the war closed.*[204]

A number of Quantrill's followers grew dissatisfied with his leadership and rebelled. In the end, the Guerillas split into separate factions:
one led by William T. Anderson (Bloody Bill) and the other led by
George Todd. Quantrill took some of the men and went to Kentucky,
where he planned to work out a surrender—one that would be accepted. However, those who still believed him were convinced that

203 Love, *The Rise and Fall of Jesse James*, 20-21.
204 Love, *The Rise and Fall of Jesse James*, 21-22.

he planned to go to Washington, assassinate President Lincoln and become the hero of the war! Love describes the events that followed:

> *Quantrill was asleep in a hayloft on a farm in Spencer County, Kentucky, when the Federal guerilla outfit of Capt. Ed Terrill, a boy of nineteen with a record remarkably bad for one of his youthfulness, rode down upon him and his. The battle was swift and decisive. Quantrill received a wound which paralyzed his lower body. Twenty-seven days later he died in a hospital at Louisville. Before his death, he mentioned his mother and his sister, up in Ohio, as those to whom he wished to leave a considerable sum of cash which he had accumulated. But later he thought of Kate Clarke, a [thirteen-year-old] girl he had induced to ride away with him from her home in Jackson County, Missouri, and with whom he had lain in the brush up in Howard County, that state, most of the summer of 1864, letting Todd and Anderson carry on the guerilla warfare. Quantrill forgot mother and sister and bequeathed his money to his mistress. She opened in St. Louis a house of ill repute which was notorious for years following the end of the war.[205]*

William T. "Bloody Bill" Anderson

Once described by Jim Cummins as "the most desperate man I ever saw,"[206] William T. Anderson was born in 1840 in Randolph Co., Missouri to William C. Anderson and Martha Jane Thomason. He earned his nickname "Bloody Bill" because of the many men he killed in battle and the brutal way that he killed them. And he also seemed to go crazy in battle—apparently foaming at the mouth.

As has already been noted, according to the Anderson family records, his father William C. Anderson accompanied Robert Sallee James to California. Apparently, after Robert James death, William C. Anderson worked the claim for almost a year and then returned home.[207] The William C. Anderson family arrived in Randolph County, Missouri in 1840, and this was the same year that young William was

205 Love, *The Rise and Fall of Jesse James*, 24.
206 Love, *The Rise and Fall of Jesse James*,25.
207 "Wild Bill Thomason's Relationship to Anderson Boys and James Boys," Ancestry.com, http://www.ancestry.com

born.[208] They also appear on the 1840 Census for Liberty Tp., Marion Co., Missouri.[209] They appear on the 1850 Census for Salt Springs, Randolph Co., Missouri.[210] The family lived in Huntsville, Randolph Co., Missouri prior to their removal to Kansas in 1854.[211] By 1860, they were in Leavenworth, Kansas and in March 1862, William C. Anderson was shot and killed by an unknown assailant. His killer has never been identified, although some researchers credit the Jayhawkers while others suggest that William C. Anderson was a horse thief and was killed for that reason.

Unfortunately, Bloody Bill would become a major influence on the life of young Jesse James. Jesse was a fifteen-year old boy on the farm when a group of federal militia approached the property. Reuben Samuel met them, only to be informed that they didn't appreciate his family's sentiments. Furthermore, they knew Frank was riding with Quantrill. So they decided to teach him a lesson. Putting a noose around his neck, they pulled him up until his feet were off the ground. Then tying the rope about the tree, they appeared to settle in, watching the doctor slowly choke to death. Then tiring of the sport, they soon left. Zerelda saved her husband's life. She was also on her way down the road, and stayed well behind until the federal group departed. Then she rushed in to cut her husband down.

However, the Federals had not completely left the premises. They knew another son was on the property, and they decided to hang him as well. And they found young Jesse out in the field. Much to their disappointment, he turned out to be much smaller than they origi-nally pictured. Reportedly, one of the Federals said, "Don't let's hang him—this time...He's too young to go and fight like that tall wild devil Frank. But let's teach the cub a lesson, anyhow."[212]

As Jesse raced down the rows, one of the culprits followed him, whip-ping him across his back. When Jesse reached the site of the farm-

208 William C. Anderson, 1840 Census, Randolph Co., Missouri.
209 William C. Anderson, 1840 Census, Liberty Tp., Marion Co., Missouri
210 William C. Anderson, 1850 Census, Salt Springs, Randolph Co., Missouri
211 Robert L. Dyer, *Jesse James and the Civil War in Missouri* [Columbia: University of Missouri Press, 1994] 33.
212 Love, *The Rise and Fall of Jesse James,* 43.

house, the militia rode away, looking for someone else to terrorize. Love writes:

> *When Jesse reached the house, running hard, his eyes were blinking more rapidly than ever. As a child he had suffered granulated eyelids. Throughout the rest of his life he had the involuntary habit of blinking. They were large eyes, of a light blue shade...The blue eyes of Jesse James were dripping as well as blinking, when he reached the farmhouse. The boy was hurt both physically and spiritually. That rope lashing had been an insult as well as an injury. The proud old Kentucky pioneer blood of the Jameses and the Coles was outraged. Jesse James was crying both from physical pain and from humiliation.[213]*

And to young Jesse, there was only one way to right such a terrible wrong. Some of Quantrill's men were in the neighborhood. Jesse told these men that he wanted to join the Raiders, only to be humiliated again. Quantrill couldn't use blue-eyed babies, they said.[214]

Several days later, the regulators returned again, this time intending to kill Reuben Samuel and Jesse James. They believed the two were giving information to Quantrill. The doctor and Jesse were away at the time. So the regulators arrested Zerelda and Jesse's sister Susan on a disloyalty charge and took them to jail in St. Joseph, an incarceration lasting several weeks. Zerelda had the two little Samuel children who were quite small, and the regulators permitted her to take them with her.

Jesse James was still nursing his anger and indignation when his mother returned home. And if Quantrill didn't want him, he knew of another guerilla leader who would. According to Love:

> *Jim Cummins lived on a farm, his birthplace, a few miles from the Samuel homestead. Jim was about eight months older than Jesse James. The boys had played together from time to time. Jim was a thin stripling and Jesse a slight lad when the pair, with two other boys of the neighborhood, left home together and joined a guerilla force affiliating with the groups under George Todd and Bill*

213 Love, *The Rise and Fall of Jesse James*, 43-44.
214 Love, *The Rise and Fall of Jesse James*, 45.

Anderson. The squad the four boys joined was under immediate command of one Fletcher Taylor, who made a remarkable record as a fighter. As "Fletch" Taylor, his name is written readily in the annals of the Quantrillians, and as Charles F. Taylor after the war he made a fortune in the lead and zinc mines at Joplin, Missouri ... Jesse and Jim presently got under immediate wing of Bloody Bill Anderson, who said of Jesse at 16, "For a beardless boy, he is the best fighter in the command."[215]

Then an event occurred that probably did more than anything to put Bloody Bill over the edge. In August 1863, Bloody Bill's sister was arrested along with a number of other female relatives of the guerillas. They were housed in a dilapidated building on Grand Avenue in Kansas City, a place that was filled to capacity. One of the Federals moved a support beam in an effort to make more room. As a result, the building collapsed, and Bloody Bill's sister was among those killed. Dyer notes:

Some people say that is why Anderson became such a brutal and crazed killer. Many of the men and young boys who rode with the guerillas were there to get revenge for things Union soldiers had done to their families. Sometimes the guerillas scalped the men they killed. Sometimes they cut off fingers or ears. They did not often take prisoners.[216]

In an essay about William "Bloody Bill" Anderson, J. Mark Hord concurs:

Anderson, by now a leader of a guerilla band, is said to have been driven insane with a lust for revenge. It is said that, after the jail collapse, he would ride into battle weeping his sister's name and that he claimed that he would never spare a federal. From that time on, there was no return to the "civilized" warfare for Anderson.[217]

215 Love, *The Rise and Fall of Jesse James*, 47.
216 Dyer, *Jesse James and the Civil War in Missouri*, 35.
217 J. Mark Hord, William "Bloody Bill "Anderson. The Southron Guerilas. April 22, 2008. Accessed April 23, 2009. http://www.geocities.com/ mosouthron/partisans/Anderson.html?200822.

Anderson's thirst for blood was exemplified in the Centralia Massacre of late September 1864. Hord writes:

On 27 September, Anderson led his men into Centralia to col-
lect supplies and disrupt the railroad station. They found the rail
schedule and noticed a train was due, so they stayed in the sta-
tion in order to rob the train. Anderson's guerillas blocked the
rail forcing the train to stop. They boarded the train and began
robbing the passengers when they discovered 25 union soldiers
on furlough from General William Sherman's command in the
southeast. The soldiers were lined up beside the train, stripped
of their uniforms, and executed. The guerillas would often wear
stolen union uniforms in order to ambush federal patrols so they
took the uniforms and left town suspecting a federal force was
likely on the way.[218]

A company of about 150 union troops had been on Anderson's trail. They followed Anderson south of Centralia. Figuring they were be-hind them, Anderson's men lurked the federals into the field, where they surrounded them. By now, several guerilla leaders had joined forces to annihilate the federal patrol. Many were killed, and just as the federals had done to them, the guerillas granted no quarter to those who tried to surrender. Some victims were even scalped.

Anderson's final end came in a daring charge he led against the feder-als in late October in the little town of Albany, just north of Orrick. According to Hord, "Anderson rode right through the federal lines bullets whizzing around him but as he passed through the lines his horse slowed and he dropped to the ground. The other guerillas, real-izing their bold leader had been killed, scattered in all directions."[219] Hord continues:

The federal troops took Anderson's body to Richmond where a
series of ghoulish photographs were taken. He was buried in an
unmarked grave in Richmond and in the evening federal troops
were said to have been seen urinating on his grave. The federals
found flowers on the grave a few days later and rode their horses
over and over the grave in an attempt to hide it. Just a few years

---

218 Hord, William "Bloody Bill" Anderson, 3 and 4 of 5.
219 Hord, William "Bloody Bill" Anderson 5 of 5.

ago, a simple marker was placed on his grave in what is now called the Pioneer Cemetery in Richmond, Missouri.[220]

George Todd

Described as an illiterate man from Canada, George Todd was a stone-mason in Kansas City before the war. After Quantrill lost his command, George Todd succeeded to the command and kept up the attacks until he was killed by a Federal bullet in Independence. Concerning George Todd, Love notes:

> *George Todd was a man of commanding presence, a "noble figure" on horseback, utterly without fear of man or of God. His wrath in battle has been described as a thing terrible to behold. He killed men with great gusto, and mercy was not in his make-up.*[221]

Quantrill became active again after Todd's death and with thirty-three of his followers, crossed the Mississippi River on New Year's Day 1865 for Kentucky. Frank James and Jim Younger were part of this expedition. Jesse, on the other hand, went to Texas with George Shepherd and a group of seasoned guerillas. He had been wounded in battle and needed time to heal. But on his return to Missouri and while on an attempt to surrender, he received another bullet that almost ended his life.

---

220 Hord, William "Bloody Bill" Anderson 5 of 5.
221 Love, *The Rise and Fall of Jesse James*, 25.

Chapter 13: Vengeance is Mine!

When the Civil War ended, another war loomed on the horizon—one that would plague the country for many years. The soldiers all returned home. While many of them settled into a normal lifestyle, others cultivated a restlessness that would not give them peace. The James brothers fell into the second category.

The end of the Civil War found Jesse James recovering from a bullet wound received at Lexington, Missouri while attempting to surrender. His first cousin, Zerelda Mimms, nursed him back to health and during the course of her tender loving care, Jesse James decided that he loved her. Thus began a nine-year courtship until their marriage on April 24, 1874. Frank James married Annie Ralston June 6, 1874, and Susan James, the sister of Frank and Jesse, married Allen Parmer in Clay Co., Missouri on November 24, 1870. According to Steele:

> There is no record indicating an early association between the James family and the Parmer family of Liberty, in Clay County, Missouri, although Liberty was only a few miles from the James farm. The son of Isaac and Barbara Parmer, Allen Parmer, who was to become the husband of Susan James, was born on May 6, 1848. He was, therefore, nine months younger than Jesse James. Allen is referred to in many creditable books on Quantrill as being among the leaders of Quantrill's guerilla organization. With Frank James, he participated in the infamous Lawrence, Kansas raid, under Quantrill's command, and in other major guerilla skirmishes throughout the border country. Parmer was listed as one of the Quantrill party, again with Frank James, that surrendered at the war's end on September 26, 1865 at Samuels Station, Kentucky. Since Parmer was apparently closely associated with

Jesse and Frank James as a member of the guerilla forces, it is reasonable to assume that he first met Susan James through her brothers.[222]

Parmer's later involvement in the James Gang outlaw activities is up for debate. He was arrested in Texas and returned to Missouri to stand trial for the Glendale train robbery that occurred October 8, 1879. Witnesses could not identify him, so he was released. Steele believes that while Parmer may have sympathized with the James brothers and may have supported their activities, he did not directly participate in those activities. Steele states, "Susan, a leader in the Baptist church and a very religious, highly respected lady wherever she went, would not have approved of her husband becoming involved in outlaw activities."[223]

Allen and Susan Parmer moved to Boonsboro (today Cane Hill), Arkansas where they could be close to his parents. Thereafter, they relocated to Sherman, Texas where Susan taught school, and subsequently settled in Wichita Falls, Texas, and finally to Archer City, Texas, where Allen became foreman of the J. Stone Land and Cattle Co.[224]

The Parmers had the following children:

Robert Archie Parmer (b. 1872, Arkansas; d. July 9, 1883);

Flora Parmer (b. June 13, 1877; d. 1926; m. William Benson;

Zelma Parmer (b. Dec. 19, 1879; d. Feb. 6, 1972; m. George R. Edwards;

Allen Parmer, Jr., (b. 1882; d. 1885);

Susan Kate Parmer (b. Dec. 25, 1885; d. Oct. 6, 1903; never married;

Feta Parmer (b. Sept. 14, 1887; d. Aug. 20, 1978; m. Bert A. Rose);

A stillborn son (b. March 2, 1889).[225]

---

222 Steele, *The Family History*, 51.
223 Steele, *The Family History*, 53.
224 Steele, *The Family History*, 53.
225 Steele, *The Family History*, 53-54.

Susan died March 3, 1889 from the complications of childbirth. After her death, Allen Parmer married Sarah Katherine "Aunt Kitty" Ogden, who was a housekeeper from Lexington, Missouri. Allen Parmer died October 20, 1927 in Wichita Falls, Texas.

***

Liberty, Missouri is often listed as the first bank robbery committed by the Jesse James Gang on St. Valentine's Day, 1866. George "Jolly" Wymore and Jimmy Sandusky, two William Jewell College students, happened to be in the street when a terrifying rebel yell pierced the air. In later years as Judge James M. Sandusky, Jimmy Sandusky described the incident:

> *"I saw the robbery of the bank at Liberty in February, 1866. I was a small boy on my way to college, and was about half a block away when I saw several men sitting on their horses in the middle of the street in front of the bank. One of them fired and killed a student, George Wymore, about nineteen years old, standing on the corner of the street across from the bank.*

> *"In a short time other men came out of the bank, mounted their horses, and rode east on Franklin Street about three blocks, and then turned north and left town on the road leading from Liberty to what is now Excelsior Springs, and crossed the Missouri river that night at some point in Ray County...*

> *"I think there were about ten men in the robbery. No one was recognized. I do not remember that they were disguised in any way. I do not think there was more than suspicion as to who the parties were. There was a man from Gentry County examined before a magistrate and discharged."*[226]

Jesse James has been credited with a number of "firsts" and according to Love, this was the first time in America that "a bank was being robbed in broad daylight and in a time of peace."[227] Love further notes: "There were, as we know, two Birds and two bandits present."[228] And

226 Love, *The Rise and Fall of Jesse James*, 63.
227 Love, *The Rise and Fall of Jesse James*, 65.
228 Love, *The Rise and Fall of Jesse James*, 65.

under threat of having his head blown off, the senior Bird opened the bank vault. Love further notes that a major question arises with this robbery: whether or not Jesse James was even present. He was flat on his back in bed at home, recovering from the bullet he received at the end of the war. There is, however, one story that suggests that he was present and that he did participate in the events. For one thing, the robber in the vault knew the cashier's name, which would suggest that he wasn't a stranger, although it doesn't prove that he was Jesse James. For another, Jesse James was known for his quick wit. The robber said, "All birds should be caged...Get inside the vault, Mr. Bird and step lively!"[229]

While the town people accused the James brothers of committing the robbery, they were never officially charged. The brothers had perfect alibis. Frank James was in Kentucky at the time and was not anywhere near the Liberty Bank. Jesse was at his birthplace, still recovering from the bullet wound in his lung. Friends stated that Jesse James still had to lean over a vessel and drain the pus from his wound.[230]

The Frontier.com website lists a number of robberies reportedly committed by the James Gang.[231] Of these robberies, the Gallatin Robbery brought the gang the most notoriety. According to Settle:

If the James brothers did not yet have reputations as highwaymen, such questionable renown was theirs very soon after the robbery of the Daviess County Savings Bank at Gallatin, Missouri, on December 7, 1869. This crime produced tangible evidence on which to base charges against them, and from that time their names were associated with bandit raids in Missouri and elsewhere.

The robbery of the Gallatin bank was committed by two men. One of them entered alone and asked Captain John W. Sheets, cashier and principal owner of the bank, to change a $100 bill. Sheets turned to the safe for the money; the second bandit entered

229 Love, *The Rise and Fall of Jesse James*, 67.
230 Love, *The Rise and Fall of Jesse James*, 70.
231 Jesse James. FrontierTimes.com Website. Accessed September 17. 2010. Available at http://www.frontiertimes.com/outlaws/jesse.htm.

and, according to the contemporary newspapers, said, 'If you will write out a receipt, I will pay you that bill.' As the banker sat down and started writing, the man drew his gun and shot him through the head and heart before his body slumped to the floor...

...That the killers thought Sheets was someone else is a frequently repeated explanation. The bandits are said to have whispered something to each other just before one of them shot Sheets. According to this theory of mistaken identity, the robbers had suddenly decided that the man before them was Major S. P. Cox, whose troops had ended Bloody Bill Anderson's career in 1864. Sheets did resemble Cox, who also lived in Gallatin. Impulsively and with the motive of avenging Anderson's death, the bandit shot him. Contemporary reports, however, indicate that the killers recognized Sheets and thought he had in some way been a party to Cox's killing of Anderson. In describing the crime, McDowell the bank clerk said the outlaw remarked with an oath, as he fired, that Sheets and Cox had been the cause of the death of his brother Bill Anderson and that he was bound to have revenge. One of the robbers told Helm, the man whom they forced to guide them around Kidder, that they had killed Captain Sheets and a Mr. Cox in revenge for the death of a brother, thereby implicating Jim Anderson, brother of Bill, in the crime.[232]

The James Gang focused on banks in the early years of these robberies. However, the "iron horse" soon caught their attention, and they began planning a "first" that would bring them even greater notoriety. Their new interest would take them into Iowa—Yankee country— where they hoped to make a bigger statement.

---

232 William A. Settle, Jr. *Jesse James Was His Name*. [Lincoln: University of Nebraska Press, 1977] 40.

Part 2: Photo Section

Robert Sallee James, the father of Frank, Jesse and Susan James

The James Farm, Kearney, Missouri (2008)

*Why Jesse James Never Smiled for Pictures. On display at the
Jesse James House Museum, St. Joseph, Missouri (2006).*

*Painting titled "Dingus" by George Warfel on display
in the Jesse James House Museum, St. Joseph, Missouri
(2006). Jesse James accidentally shot off a finger. His com-
ment was "Well, if that isn't the dad-dingus thing!" He was
called Dingus by close associates from that point on.*

Jesse James (1875). Taken at Nebraska City, Nebraska.

Part 3: Collision Course

Jesse James Historical Site, Adair, Iowa (2006)

Chapter 14: From Summit Cut to Adair

Each move of the Levi Clay family took them further west. After leaving Marble Rock in Floyd Co., Iowa, the Clays relocated to Bear Grove Tp., Guthrie Co., Iowa, where they were joined by Levi's father-in-law William Stillians and his family. The Clays lived in Bear Grove for two or three years. The family next settled in Panora, Iowa until February 1873. From there, they settled in Casey before moving to Adair, Iowa March 15, 1873.[233] They were the second family to settle in Adair and the first family to build a house there. According to the *Adair News:*

> *The section house in Adair was built in 1868, as the headquarters for an engineer corps, then making the survey for the railroad, and was the first house in town. This was in two parts, each 18 x 30 feet in size. The first dwelling house in the town was erected in the summer of 1873, by Levi Clay, in west Adair (on the ground now occupied by the Wm. Sachau residence. "[234]*

Named for John Adair, a general during the War of 1812 and the sixth governor of Kentucky, Adair Co., Iowa was established in 1851. The town of Greenfield was laid out in 1856 and because of its central location, people in Greenfield fought to have the county seat moved to their community. In 1858, 91 people signed a petition, but 137 signatures from Summerset kept the county seat at that location.[235] Fontanelle was the county seat during the Civil War, but after the war ended, a new drive began hoping to move the county seat to Greenfield.

---

233 Inman, 1992.
234 *Adair News*, July 23, 1922. Reprinted Summer 1987 as The Adair News Special Edition.
235 Lucian M. Kilburn, Editor. *History of Adair County, Iowa and its People.* 2002.

The move was finally successful in 1874 when Greenfield supporters won out, not without confrontation however. When Fontanelle refused to turn over the records to Greenfield, an angry mob seized the records and hauled them off to the new county seat. Greenfield defied an order to return the records to Fontanelle by tearing up a judge's order. The town did move the records to Summerset until a final decision was made. And about a month later, a final decision officially moved the county seat to Greenfield.

Guthrie Co., Iowa, which is adjacent to Adair, had a similar battle over the location of its county seat, although not as feisty. Also organized in 1851, Guthrie County was named by the sheriff and later county judge Theophilus Bryan for his friend, Captain Edwin B. Guthrie, who commanded a group of Iowa volunteers in the Mexican War.[236] Panora, the oldest town in Guthrie County, was chosen as the original county seat. Problems arose when a courthouse could not be built in Panora, leading to a petition drive to move the county seat to Guthrie Center. That drive was temporarily silenced when a courthouse was finally built in Panora in 1859. After numerous petition drives and legal maneuvers, Guthrie Center was finally declared the county seat on April 7, 1860. A wagon train moved the records from Panora to Guthrie Center but in 1861, the people of Panora started another petition drive for return of the county seat. Their attempt was successful, and the records then journeyed back to Panora. Guthrie Center tried several times to regain control and finally in 1873, they won back the county seat. Once the records were all returned to Guthrie Center, the matter quieted down and Guthrie Center has retained the county seat ever since.

Although officially within the boundaries of Adair County, the town of Adair overlaps both Adair and Guthrie Counties. The portion in Guthrie County is part of the Des Moines-West Des Moines Metropolitan area.[237] When the Rock Island Railroad was built through the area in 1868, the area was known as Summit Cut, referring to the ridge that

236 Guthrie Co., Iowa Genealogical Page. Rootweb Website. Accessed September 17, 2010. Available at http://www.rootsweb.ancestry.com/~iaguthri/html/index.html.

237 Adair, Iowa. Wikipedia.com. Accessed June 20, 2010 Available at http://www.wikipedia.com

forms the watershed between the Missouri and Mississippi Rivers.[238] The town of Adair was incorporated August 20, 1872 and was given the same name as the county in which it primarily resides. It has been called the highest point in Iowa, as related from the following online journal:

> *Sunday July 18, 2004*
>
> *Casey to Adair IA*
>
> *Well, we made it to Adair, which - one resident told us - is the highest point in Iowa. There is a sign at a local park which says it's the Iowa high point on the old Rock Island RR. That's good enough for me, especially since I spent just about all of Sunday afternoon going up (and down) hills on the way from Casey to Adair.*
>
> *You see one hill and think, well this has to be the top. Then you reach the top and see more. That happened a lot.*
>
> *It reminded me of a particularly nasty stretch of Pennsylvania (in the Appalachians) where the hills weren't the highest, but there were sure a lot of them.*
>
> *The hills are tough, but they make it some of the prettiest country we've encountered. Adair, by the way is the site of the first train robbery in the west, or so they say. Jessie [sic] James no less.*
>
> *We should be in Omaha by Saturday.*[239]

The History of Adair and Guthrie Counties corroborates the highest point reference:

> *...Adair is located on the great water shed of the state, which is the highest point on the C. R. I & P. Ry. And the place selected seemed to be a natural point for a town, so one was laid out on land owned by George C. Tallman of Brooklyn, New York, during the summer of 1872, and the name of Adair given it. The plat of the town was filed for record in the office of the county recorder on the 20th day of August, 1872. Soon after the filing of the plat,*

---

238 Adair, Iowa, http://www.wikipedia.com
239 Hurley, Joe. Joe's Route 6 Journal, Casey to Adair IA.   Accessed September 17, 2010. Available at http://www.route6walk.com/.

the railroad built a station and Charles Stuart, a lumber yard. In 1873, the census of the town showed a population of 18 people, 15 section hands and Messrs. Arnold, Starr and Moran. In 1874 this had grown to 84 and 150 in 1875. The population in 1883 was estimated at 500.[240]

As with any new town, Adair was the site of a number of "firsts." The first store was established by Moody & Moran of Casey in the early fall of 1873. The pioneer dealer in agricultural implements was J. A. Ramsdell, who commenced business in 1874. The first drug store was opened by D. W. Moss in a building erected on a lot now occupied by the Powel Drug Co. The pioneer milliners of Adair were the Misses Donahey and Moss, who opened a millinery store in Adair in 1876. The pioneer shoemaker of Adair was J. H. Henryson, who came to Adair in 1873, and worked from his house. The first blacksmith shop in Adair was run by J. A. Beebe, who came to Adair in 1874, and built a shop on a lot just south of where L. R. Dickey now lives. The first physician was Dr. T. D. Lougher, who came to Adair in 1875. And in the spring of 1875, Heacock & Delaney erected a mill across from the depot.[241] And while the Levi Clay family was the second family to move to Adair, the section foreman and his wife were the first. According to the *History of Adair:*

A section house was built here in 1868 to be used as headquarters for an engineering corps making the survey for the main line of the Rock Island Railroad. It was the first building erected in Summit Township, in which Adair is located, and later was used to house Robert Grant, sent here in 1870 to maintain this section of the railroad which was built through here in 1868-69. He was accompanied by his wife, first woman to come to live here, and their children.[242]

After Levi Clay and his family moved into their home, others began following in their footsteps. In the fall of 1873, D. E. Bancroft and John Henryson each built houses and in the winter, H. P. Starr fol-

240 *The History of Adair and Guthrie Counties, 1884.* Portions Reprinted in The Adair News Special Edition, Summer 1987.
241 *The History of Adair and Guthrie Counties, 1884.* (1987 Reprint)
242 *The History of Adair and Guthrie Counties, 1884.* (1987 Reprint)

lowed suit. The county history notes that the Starr residence was "just east of the Methodist Church."[243]

More business structures followed including a general merchandise store owned by V. M. Lahman, and another building in 1874 built by F. D. Arnold. The town began to blossom; however, Adair was not the division station for the railroad. That title belonged to the town of Stuart in Guthrie County, an area that was first settled by a group of Quakers from Indiana and Ohio around 1850. According to the Stuart County Website:

> *Later Captain Charles Stuart, a veteran of the Civil War, purchased land near the present day Stuart. In 1868, Capt. Stuart purchased additional land that eventually was the original town of Stuart lying in Guthrie and Adair Counties. At the same time, the Rock Island Railroad was completed, with Captain Stuart and the railroad officials working closely to lay out the town and ensure that Stuart would be the site of the division station and machine shops. Captain Stuart was the manager and leader of the project. The plat of the town was filed for record on September 29, 1870. During these early years, prominent businessmen of the community invested money and land to ensure that the Rock Island Railroad would establish division headquarters in Stuart. The railroad wrote a contract the Stuart would be the division headquarters forever.*[244]

Mary Clay, wife of Levi, wrote letters to relatives and friends in Floyd County and sent pictures of the booming town of Adair. When the Clays first moved there, they lived on the second floor of one of the business buildings until their own home was completed. One letter suggested: "We hope you *frinds* will come out to see us."[245]

---

243 *The History of Adair and Guthrie Counties, 1884.* (1987 Reprint)
244 The Official Site of Stuart, Iowa. Accessed September 17, 2010. Available at http://www.stuartia.com/old/.
245 Mary Stillians Clay, Text of letter [addressee unknown], Summer 1873.

Chapter 15: First Peacetime Train Robbers: The Reno Gang

Peacetime train robbery was unheard of before the Civil War. The Jesse James Gang certainly didn't invent the crime. That "honor"—for lack of a better term—goes to the Reno Gang of Southern Indiana—who committed the first peacetime train robbery in the town of Seymour, Indiana October 6, 1866.

Like the James family, the Reno family's ancestral roots lay in Kentucky. In 1813 James Reno and his family left Kentucky for Indiana and settled near Rockford, just north of present-day Seymour. In 1835, their son Wilkinson Reno married Julia Ann (surname unknown), and they had the following children:

Frank Reno, born in 1837;

John Reno, born in 1838;

Simeon Reno ('Sim'), born in 1843;

Clinton Reno, born in 1847;

William Reno , born in 1848;

Laura Reno, born in 1851.[246]

The parents were strict Methodists and forced the children to read the Bible all day every Sunday. When the sons grew older, they discovered

---

246 The Reno Gang's Reign of Terror, HistoryNet.com Website. Accessed September 17, 2010. Available at http://www.historynet.com/reno-gangs-reign-of-terror.htm.

they didn't like school and they didn't like the strict requirements of their parents' religion, and so they rebelled. John Reno claimed in his autobiography that his older brother Frank bilked travelers who passed by their farm through crooked card games. At the age of 11, John left home after stealing a horse and headed for Louisville, Kentucky. He returned the following year and left once again after stealing some of his parents' money. By 1851, a series of strange occurrences erupted. According to the HistoryNet website:

> *Beginning in 1851, a series of mysterious fires began to break out in Rockford. Businesses and homes were set ablaze at night and sometimes even in broad daylight. During a seven-year period, almost the entire town was burned down, partially rebuilt and then burned again. No one ever discovered the identity of the arsonists, but popular rumor suggested that the Renos were involved. They had burned the town, the story went, so that they could buy the land at a reduced price and add to their holdings. These incinerations also helped the growing town of Seymour, founded in 1852 by Meedy W. Shields, a landowner who managed to convince the Ohio & Mississippi (O&M) Railroad to cross his property and intersect with the Jeffersonville, Madison & Indianapolis (JM&I) Railroad, thereby creating both a town and a railroad center.*[247]

The Renos were well-to-do for families of that period of time. The parents separated in 1858. Julia stayed on the farm while Wilkinson moved into Seymour. Julia died in 1868 and Wilkinson followed in 1877. John Reno later claimed that his parents' divorce led to his life of crime. However, the Reno brothers' criminal activities began long before the parents separated.

During the Civil War, the Renos discovered a new way of making money. They would enlist in the Union Army, collect the bonus money for signing up, and disappear. No one knows how often they did this, but some historians believe they did so numerous times under different names.

Frank and John returned to Seymour in 1864 and weren't in town very long before assembling a group of outlaws consisting of men they felt

---

247 The Reno Gang's Reign of Terror Website

they could trust. Simeon and William joined the gang and the nucleus was then formed. According to the OutlawHistory.com website:

> The Reno Gang was suspected in a number of crimes around Jackson County in 1865. Post office robberies took place in Dudleytown, Indiana and Seymour, Indiana. In addition, several burglaries of local businesses and a home invasion were reported. A hotel in Seymour, the Rader House, became a haven for the Reno Gang, and many travelers who stayed there were burglarized. The July 27, 1865, issue of the Seymour Times issued a warning to visitors of the area to 'be wary of thieves and assassins that infest the place.' On August 3, the same paper ran an editorial that condemned lawlessness in Jackson County and called for vigilante action to restore order. 'Nothing but Lynch law will save the reputation of this place and its citizens,' declared the paper.[248]

The gang grew in size after the Civil War with returning restless men who had nothing to do and who were not ready to settle down on the farm. While the Reno Gang had been operating in Jackson Co., Indiana, they soon expanded into other areas of the Midwest, and they began to focus on new ways to commit robberies. On November 17, 1867, for example, John Reno decided to strike an area outside Indiana:

> On November 17, 1867, several gang members raided the treasurer's office at the Daviess County Courthouse, in Gallatin, Missouri., and made off with some $23,618 in cash and bonds. John Reno was positively identified as one of the robbers. Frank Reno remained in Indiana and a number of local county treasurer offices were robbed. Frank was arrested and charged for a Clinton County, Indiana robbery but was acquitted of the charges.

Their biggest act was to commit the first peacetime train robbery in the United States. OutlawHistory.com relates the following:

> On the evening of October 6, 1866, an Ohio & Mississippi train left the Seymour, Indiana depot. By most accounts, John Reno, Sim

248 Reno Gang—OutlawHistory.com Website. Accessed September 17, 2010. Available at http://www.outlawhistory.com.

Reno, and Frank Sparks were aboard the train when it departed. Once the train had traveled a few miles from town, the men made their way from the coach car, across the platform to the Adams Express Company car, and forced their way inside. Messenger Elam Miller gave up his keys to the outlaws. The men opened the small local depot safe, which contained the packages picked up at the various stations en route. They obtained, according to Jackson County Court records, 'one safe the value of Thirty Dollars, Three Canvas Bags of the value of One Dollar Each, Ten Thousand Dollars in Gold Coin and Thirty Three Dollars in Bank Notes.' They attempted to open a larger safe, containing valuables shipped from St. Louis, but were unable to do so. The men rolled the large safe to the door of the express car.

One of the gang then pulled the bell rope to signal the engineer to stop the train. As the train slowed, the gang rolled the large safe out the door and also stepped off the train. The men hurried to where they had dropped the safe and met with other Reno Gang members who were holding their getaway horses. Try as they might, the gang could not pry open the larger safe, which some stated held $35,000 in gold.

Train Agents, alerted to the robbery, quickly traveled to where the Gang was last seen. The agents found the abandoned safe but no sign of the outlaws. A passenger on the train, George Kinney, was a witness to the robbery and told officers that he could identify at least two of the 'holdups,' both suspects being members of the Reno Gang.

John Reno, Sim Reno, and Frank Sparks were arrested for the train robbery on October 11, 1866. The men soon made bail and were released. Robbery witness George Kinney was fatally shot when he answered a late-night knock at his door. Officers soon realized that without their eyewitness, the case they had against the Reno Gang would never hold up in court. The charges were soon dropped.[249]

---

249 The Reno Gang—Outlawhistory.com website.

Jackson Co., Indiana lawmen were unable to curtail criminal activities in that county. After the December 29, 1866 murder and rape and robbery of Marian Cutlor, who lived alone in the western end of Jackson, and the release of the Reno Gang from jail, local residents decided to take matters into their own hands by forming vigilante committees. They hanged the men who were accused of the rape and murder. And they attempted to seize two men who were being held in jail for performing a copycat train robbery.

Altogether, the Reno Gang robbed four trains in addition to committing other robberies. They attempted to rob a fifth train on July 9, 1868, but the Pinkertons were waiting for them. While some of the gang members escaped, the Pinkertons apprehended three members. And on July 10, 1868, while being transported, the prisoners were taken from the train by vigilantes and were hanged on a nearby tree. Three other members were subsequently captured—Henry Jerrell, Frank Sparks, and John Moore—and they were all hanged from the same tree. The site became known as Hangman Crossing, Indiana.[250]

William and Simeon Reno were captured July 27, 1868 in Indianapolis. Frank Reno and Charlie Anderson were apprehended in Windsor, Ontario. All captured gang members were incarcerated at the New Albany, Indiana jail. The vigilantes won out, however, as is noted in the following account:

> On the night of December 11, about 65 hooded men traveled by train to New Albany. The men marched four abreast from the station to the Floyd County Jail where, just after midnight, the men forced their way into the jail and the sheriff's home. After they beat the sheriff and shot him in the arm for refusing to turn over the keys, his wife surrendered them to the mob. Frank Reno was the first to be dragged from his cell to be lynched. He was followed by brothers William and Simeon. Another gang member, Charlie Anderson, was the fourth and last to be murdered, at around 4:30 a.m on December 12. It was rumored that the vigilantes were part of the group known as the Scarlet Mask Society or Jackson County Vigilance Committee. No one was ever charged, named or

250 Reno Gang. Wikipedia.com website. Accessed September 17, 2010. Available at http://en.wikipedia.org/wiki/Reno_Gang.

officially investigated in any of the lynchings. Many local newspapers, such as the New Albany Weekly Ledger, stated that "Judge Lynch" had spoken.[251]

HistoryNet provides a detailed account:

The vigilantes hurried to the iron door that led to the cellblock and there encountered another jailer, Thomas Matthews. After these men on a mission threatened to hang him with the prisoners, Matthews opened the door. One by one, the doors to the individual cells were opened and the terrified prisoners extracted. Frank Reno was first on the death list. A preknotted noose or halter was placed over his head, then secured to an iron pillar near the stairwell leading to the second-floor cells. The oldest Reno brother was then pushed from the landing. William, the youngest of the brothers, was next, and he was hanged beside Frank. When the vigilantes entered the cell of Sim Reno, he fought madly, but they overpowered him and strung him up in the southwest corner of the jail, his feet barely grazing the ground. It took him almost half an hour to strangle to death. Last was Charlie Anderson, who had to be hanged twice, as the first rope broke. The grisly action unfolded quickly, and the vigilantes left the jail by 5 a.m., taking one of the commissioners as a hostage. They reboarded the train at the foot of State Street and returned to Jeffersonville, then back to Seymour. The bodies of the three Reno brothers were turned over to their sister, Laura, and Frank Reno's widow, Sarah, and they were buried in Seymour.[252]

John Reno was the only brother gang member to survive. His brother, Clinton, and sister Laura were not involved in the criminal activities. John had been arrested and charged with the Treasury heist in Gallatin, Missouri and was sentenced to prison. According to the HistoryNet website:

John Reno was sentenced to 25 years at the Missouri State Penitentiary in Jefferson City. He had been the leader and brains of the Reno Gang, but older brother Frank and the others carried

251 Arville L. Funk. *A Sketchbook of Indiana History*. Rochester, Indiana [Christian Book Press, 1969—revised 1983], 106.
252 Reno Gang's Reign of Terror. HistoryNet.com.

on without him. John would get out of prison in February 1878 and return to Seymour. By then, all his criminal brothers were dead. Seven years later he would be sentenced to three years in the Indiana State Prison at Michigan City for passing counterfeit bills. John Reno would die at his home in Seymour on January 31, 1895.[253]

---

253 Reno Gang's Reign of Terror, Historynet.com website.

Chapter 16: The World's First Robbery of a Moving Train

Exactly how much Jesse and Frank James knew about the Reno Gang and their activities is open for debate. Contrary to some assessments that the James brothers were illiterate, both boys were well read and no doubt kept up on newspaper accounts. And exactly how much the Renos influenced Jesse and Frank is also open for debate. The idea of robbing a train certainly would have appealed to them, only they did not want to be captured, nor did they desire to dangle from a rope.

Jesse James' previous experience with trains took place during the Civil War. He was in Centralia when Bloody Bill Anderson and his men murdered unarmed Union soldiers who were heading home on furlough. And after the war, he no doubt watched the trains grow in size and number. He knew about the powerful interests behind the railroads, and he no doubt resented their capability of gobbling up farm land, oftentimes cheating the landowners in the process. There was another matter about trains that would have piqued his interest: huge gold shipments were being transported on those tracks.

Interest in train robbery quieted down after the destruction of the Reno Gang. Other would-be robbers decided against giving it a try. During the Reno reign of terror, two men attempted a copy-cat heist, only to be captured. They barely escaped the hands of the vigilantes in the aftermath. Perhaps Jesse James was an observer at that time, although he no doubt began toying with the idea—wondering how he could succeed when others failed. Then he heard about a $75,000 gold shipment scheduled to be traveling across Iowa on the Chicago, Rock Island and Pacific Railway the third week in July, 1873. Jesse immediately thought the shipment would consist of gold coins.

This would not be the gang's first sojourn into Iowa. On June 3, 1871, four men robbed the Ocobock Brothers Bank at Corydon, Iowa and made off with $6,000. According to Settle:

> *The robbery was committed with little hazard to anyone, for nearly every man in town was at the Methodist Church to hear the noted orator Henry Clay Dean discuss the merits of a proposed railroad for Corydon. The bandits, on entering the bank, found the cashier alone, quietly forced him to give them the money, tied him securely, then rode to the meeting at the church, where their leader interrupted the speaker to announce that the bank had been robbed. The crowd, judging the interruption a hoax to break up the speaking, was slow to believe the leader's announcement, and the brigands rode out of town, unchallenged. Several minutes elapsed before the townsmen realized the situation and sent a posse in pursuit of the bandits.[254]*

Later descriptions of the bandits identified them as Jesse and Frank James, Cole Younger and Clell Miller, who was also from Kearney. Jesse denied that he had anything to do with the robbery in a letter published in *The Kansas City Times.* Clell Miller was the only one who stood trial for the robbery and he was acquitted when Missouri witnesses swore that he was in another location at the time of the robbery. (Missourians protected the James boys and the members of their gang since they perceived them as modern-day Robin Hoods.) And on July 21, 1873, Robin Hood and his Merry Men galloped into Adair, Iowa for what would be described as the world's first robbery of a moving train and the first train robbery in the West. Adair was an isolated stretch of the Rock Island Railroad, and the train carrying the gold shipment would be moving across the tracks there. Evidence supports the belief that the seven bandits started from Jackson Co., Missouri on July 12, heading for Iowa.[255]

Another aspect made this location appealing. A sharp curve in the track meant that the train would have to slow down. As Stiles notes, the location

---

254 William A. Settle, Jr. *Jesse James Was His Name,* 43.
255 Love, *The Rise and Fall of Jesse James,* 126

...sat only two hundred yards from a bridge, in a shallow cut—a dug-out depression—which would allow them to easily control the occupants from the banks above; it was far from any house or settlement, the nearest being the Adair signal station, some four miles away. It was there that they had begun their work, breaking into a handcar house to steal a crowbar and a hammer. They bent over the tracks, using the tools to pry out a pair of spikes on the northern side. Then they ran a rope through the holes in the rail and hid themselves some fifty feet away. And waited. Waiting was an art they had each learned in the Sni and Fishing River bottoms, and practiced many times in the years since. No technology would ever eliminate the tedium of their work.[256]

Citizens of Adair knew a group of strangers arrived earlier in the day. Reportedly, Jesse James previously sent Cole Younger and Frank James to Omaha to verify the actual date the gold shipment would pass through Adair. Jesse James, Jim and Tom Younger, Clell Miller and Bill Chadwell waited for them at Council Bluffs, Iowa, a town that became the headquarters for the enterprise. Once the information was obtained, the robbers headed into Adair, posing as a group of land buyers. The afternoon of the robbery, they stopped at the section house in Adair and bought some pies and other food from Mrs. Robert Grant, wife of the section foreman. According to *The Adair News:*

Mrs. Grant did not know until sometime later that she had served a meal that would put her into the history of the world on July 21, 1873. She was 40 years old at the time of the James Gang visit and she lived to the age of 105. She vividly remembered the very shy and polite young man who knocked at her door and requested pie and homemade bread. He offered to pay well for the food. Mrs. Grant was not aware of the intent of the visitors, as they had told the Grants they were in the area to purchase prairie to settle on.[257]

In the days preceding the robbery, the James Gang stayed south of town at the Sisson farm. *The Adair News* states:

---

256 Stiles, *Last Rebel of the Civil War*, 233.
257 *The Adair News Special Edition*, Summer 1987.

Jesse and the gang were guests of the Sissons and were happy to
board in their large barn. Each morning the gang would eat their
early morning meal in the Sisson home and then leave the farm,
returning at dusk for the night. Carrie Sisson was a young girl at
the time of the James visit and she too, remembered until her death
of the "famous" guests.[258]

The gang bought new rope at one of the local hardware stores the day
of the robbery. Then they broke into the handcar house, stole a spike-
bar and hammer "with which they pried off a fish-plate connecting
two rails and pulled out the spikes."[259] The rope was then "tied on the
west end of the disconnected north rail. The rope was passed under
the south rail and led to a hole they had cut in the bank in which to
hide."[260]

The chug of the steam engine could be heard about 8:30 that evening,
and the gang knew it was the 5:00 express train from Omaha. The train
approached the Turkey Creek Bridge from the west pulling a coal-
filled tender, two baggage cars, a smoking car, two more passenger
cars, the ladies car and two Pullman sleepers. The bandits expected
to find the gold shipment in that second baggage car. Stiles describes
the scene:

They watched the train slow sharply as it approached the curve,
its speed slackening to just twenty miles an hour. As it drew close,
they yanked on the cord, displacing the rail. Immediately the ax-
les groaned as the engine went into reverse and the air brakes
clamped tight. With the train screeching toward the fatal break in
the track, the Missourians opened fire, spattering the locomotive
with bullets. Then the locomotive slipped off the rails and toppled
over. In a roaring crash, the tender upended, spilling its load of
coal; the first baggage car jackknifed, crashing onto its side; the
next baggage car and the smoking car popped off the rails. Out

258 *The Adair News Special Edition*, Summer 1987.
259 The Great Train Robbery Near Adair July 21, 1873, *The Adair News*
    Special Edition, Summer 1987.
260 The Great Train Robbery Near Adair July 21, 1873, *The Adair News*
    Special Edition, Summer 1987.

of the wreck the fireman appeared, dragging the inert form of the engineer.[261]

While some accounts state seven bandits were present, the general consensus is that there were actually six. Two of the bandits stood guard outside, "one walking along each bank, shooting and cursing."[262] Passengers who ventured to peer from windows were ordered to stay down out of sight or they would be shot. Two of the bandits jumped inside to keep an eye on the passengers. The remaining bandits stepped inside the second baggage car.

What is little known about this train robbery is that twenty- eight Chinese students from upper-level families in China were aboard that train. They had arrived from Hong Kong and were heading to the Chinese Educational Mission at Springfield, Massachusetts, where they intended to remain for ten or fifteen years. The youngest members were ten, and they ranged in ages up to fifteen. It took 32 days for them to cross the Pacific Ocean, five more days to travel from San Francisco to Adair, and they anticipated three more days of travel to the East Coast. According to *The Adair News:*

> *This party went east over the Chicago, Rock Island and Pacific road, and General Agent, S. S. Stevens was on hand, doing all in his power to make the Celestials comfortable. The splendid palace car, City of Leavenworth, was placed at their disposal and a special agent detailed to accompany them, with instructions to see that their every want was supplied. Their baggage occupied an entire car.[263]*

The Chinese lay prone during the entire attack and did not venture to look out the windows. They were probably the calmest group on the train during the robbery.

A description of the robbers appearing Saturday, July 25, 1873 in *The Council Bluffs Nonpareil* follows:

---

261 Stiles, *Last Rebel of the Civil War,* 233-234.
262 Stiles, *Last Rebel of the Civil War,* 234.
263 Chinese Students on Train from Upper-Crust Families. (Taken from the *Council Bluffs Nonpareil* July 22, 1873) *The Adair News Special Edition,* Summer 1987.

The man that seemed to be the leader is described as follows: He is about five feet seven or eight inches high, has light hair, blue eyes, heavy sandy whiskers, board shoulders, straight and tolerably short nose, a little turned up, tolerably high broad forehead, intelligent looking, and looked like a tolerable well educated man, and did not look like a working man, from 36 to 40 years old.

The second man was tall and slender, light complected, rather delicate looking, had a high forehead, not very broad, light brown hair, very long, and light whiskers, inclined to be sandy, he was near six feet high, long slender hands, and did not look as though he had ever done any work in his life, his nose is a little Roman, he had blue eyes, he looked like a man who was well educated, was very polite, and not inclined to talk much, he was from 36 to 40 years old, he was dressed in light clothes.

The third man was rather slender built, five feet nine or ten inches high, hair cut very short, his hair was a little sandy, through [sic] it could be considered light brown, nose Grecian, not very refined, but rather sarcastic, hard and bad countenance, brown eyes, looked like an intemperate man, he wore a dark wool hat with stiff rim, and dark clothes. He was from 35 to 38 years old.

The fourth man was dark complected, dark hair, no whiskers, he had a broad and tolerably high forehead, five feet seven or eight inches high, heavy set, straight, and rather intelligent looking countenance, black eyes, and straight Grecian nose, he was 34 to 38 years old, dressed in light pants and vest, dark coat, and light wool hat.

The fifth man had a fair complexion, blue eyes, light brown hair, with chin whiskers, a little sandy, he is five feet and nine or ten inches high, large and portly, but not very fleshy, broad shoulders, and intelligent looking, had a large roman nose, and is from 36 to 38 years old, he was dressed in light clothes, and made quite a pleasant appearance.

The description was given by Mr. and Mrs. Stuckey, who live on the northeast quarter of section 20, township 70, range 37,

*Ringgold County, where these men ate dinner on July 22ⁿᵈ. No
other particulars have been received here today.*[264]

As Stiles notes, "Eyewitness accounts are rarely completely accurate, but the descriptions that emerged leave no doubt that the James
Brothers and Cole Younger walked the cars that night."[265]

Stiles continues:

*When the crash occurred, the occupants of the express car—
Assistant Superintendent H. F. Royce, register clerk O.P.
Killingsworth, and express messenger John Burgess—piled into
one another, leaving Royce with a bloody nose. As they disen-
tangled themselves, they saw two masked men in the door, one of
whom promptly yanked off his disguise. "The one whose face was
uncovered was of sandy complexion, full whiskered, and wore a
broad brimmed hat," Burgess said. His recollection matched that
of a couple who saw the gang without masks a day later. "The
man who seemed to be the leader," they reported, had "light hair,
blue eyes, heavy sandy whiskers, broad shoulders and a straight,
tolerably short nose, a little turned up; a tolerably high, broad
forehead, intelligent looking, looked like a tolerably well educated
man and did not look like a working man." This was a precise a
description of Jesse James as anyone could ever hope for. They
went on to identify Frank James, who "looked like a man well
educated , and very polite, not inclined to talk much," as well as
Cole Younger, "large and portly, but not very fleshy, board shoulders, form straight, is intelligent looking with large Roman nose,
and…made quite a pleasant appearance.*[266]

Jesse James pulled off his mask during the robbery. He pointed his gun
at John Burgess and said, "If you don't open the safe or give me the
key, I'll blow your brains out."[267] Burgess gave him the key and Jesse

264 Description Given of Five of the Train Robbers, (Taken from *the Council
Bluffs Nonpareil* July 25, 1873), The *Adair News Special Edition*,
Summer 1987.
265 Stiles, *Last Rebel of the Civil War*, 234.
266 Stiles, *Last Rebel of the Civil War*, 234.
267 Stiles, *Last Rebel of the Civil War*, 234.

opened the heavy door—and no doubt paused. He "found $1,672.57, along with another bag for Wells, Fargo & Co., the express firm. He demanded to know where the rest of it was, only to be told by Burgess that this was it—this and "numerous bags jumbled on the floor—three and a half tons of precious-metal bullion, on its way from Western mines to the gold market in New York."[268] According to the Annual Report to the President, Directors and Stockholders of the Chicago, Rock Island, and Pacific Railroad Company, April 1, 1874: "Gold and silver remained legal tender, and could be taken in refined bullion form to a U.S. mint, where it would be turned into coin (though the federal government stopped minting silver in 1873.) Large shipments of bullion were regularly made from the West to New York, where it was sold for greenbacks in the gold market. The Rock Island shipped 8,138,879 pounds of bullion east in the year ending March 31, 1874."[269]

The total take would prove to be $2,337, far less than what Jesse James had expected."[270] What mattered at that moment was that the gang was there—the gold shipment was too heavy to haul away—and the gang had to make the most out of their endeavor and get back to Missouri.

Two of the bandits moved through the cars, taking money and jewelry from the passengers. While that was taking place, the conductor, William Smith, darted ahead of them, looking for a gun. He was willing to take on the bandits. According to Stiles:

> In the rear he met the fireman Dennis Foley, who had been shoved back onto the train. "Billy," Foley said sadly, "Jack is dead." Engineer John Rafferty's quick reflexes, he explained, had saved everyone—he had reversed power and closed the brakes as soon as he saw the rail move, but after the locomotive toppled over, Foley found Rafferty lying on top of him, dead. His neck had snapped in the crash.[271]

---

268 Stiles, *Last Rebel of the Civil War*, 234.
269 Annual Report, Chicago, Rock Island and Pacific Railroad Company, April 1, 1874, qtd. In Stiles, *Last Rebel of the Civil War,* 234-235.
270 Stiles, *Last Rebel of the Civil War*, 234.
271 Stiles, *Last Rebel of the Civil War*, 235.

The robbery took all of ten minutes. The bandits plundered the express safe and with money and jewelry taken from the passengers, they leaped onto their horses and galloped off into the night.

***

As an employee of the railroad, Levi Clay was working in the area of the train robbery that night. When he saw the train topple and heard the gunfire, he knew immediately what was at stake. Then he saw the masked men.

It is unknown whether Levi Clay and Jesse James made actual eye contact with one another. If so, it would have been for one brief moment, and it would have happened after Jesse pulled the mask from his face. Jesse James may have ordered Levi Clay with a threat: "Get down and stay down or I'll blow your head off!" Levi Clay would have complied with that command—briefly. When Jesse James entered the baggage car, Levi Clay then slipped away from the scene under the cover of darkness.

He needed to get help immediately. The closest place for that was the town of Casey, located four miles away. According to *The Adair News:*

> *Levi Clay, employed by the railroad in Adair, which was then not quite a year old, walked to Casey where the alarm was sent by a telegrapher to Des Moines and Omaha, and soon the news was spread all over the nation. A train loaded with armed men left Council Bluffs for Adair and dropped small detachments of men along the route where saddled horses were waiting.*

> *The trail of the outlaws was traced into Missouri where they split up and were sheltered by friends. Later the governor of Missouri offered a $10,000 reward for the capture of Jesse James, dead or alive.* [272]

---

272 The Great Train Robbery Near Adair July 21, 1873, *The Adair News Special Edition, Summer 1987.*

After telegraphing for help, Levi Clay joined one of the armed groups and chased the James gang all the way back to Missouri. According to my father, Gordon Loren Inman, "He spent the rest of the night chasing the Jesse James Gang!"[273]

---

273 Gordon Loren Inman, Personal Remembrances, 1953-1955.

Chapter 17: Sounding the Alarm

Jesse James may not have obtained what he originally wanted during the robbery, but his name quickly spread everywhere, making him a household discussion. An article from *The Des Moines Register*, dated July 23, 1939, establishes this fact, although some of the details are not accurate:

Jesse James robbed his first train in Iowa

The outlaw made his own peculiar contributions to society by inventing the train stickup and the daylight bank robbery.

His first train holdup was the Rock Island at Adair, Iowa, in July 1873. That was the first train ever to be wrecked and robbed in the United States.

At this time, James was already becoming noted for his bank crackings and stage coach robberies. Tall tales of this two-gun man were already making him a legend.

Jesse James, a preacher's son, grew up about like any other Missouri kid. He and his brother, Frank, went to Sunday School, and were known as good boys. But young Jesse could drop a red headed woodpecker at 50 paces.

He became an outlaw when he was 16. The Civil War was on and members of his family were known as southern sympathizers.

A band of Union soldiers hunting the notorious guerilla, William C. Quantrill, invaded the home.

When nobody would talk, they hanged Jesse's stepfather to a tree until he was almost dead, then beat Jesse on the back with a knotted rope.

Jesse was not one to take it. "Ma!" he yelled. "I'll join Quantrill!" And he did.

During the war Jesse James got his "education" under Quantrill, one of the bloodiest Americans who ever lived. He and Frank took part in Centralia, Mo., massacre, when the Quantrill band wiped out 226 Union soldiers in one day. Jesse survived 22 would, including two great holes in his lungs.

But when the war was over, he gave himself up and went home to Clay County, Missouri, to cure his lungs, get married and join the Baptist Church. After that there was a race in Jesse's life between God and the devil.

But there was blood on his hands and the law would not let him alone.

One night detectives came to his house to arrest him. Jesse arose from his bed where he still lay with his lung wound and fired at them through the front door. The detectives fled from the front of the house while Jesse ran out the back.

Now Jesse and Frank took up with their band of desperadoes.

Jesse James became the fabled outlaw of the dime novels, "both man and hoss" who lived in a cave in the mountains with a snake and a wolf and a bear.

When Jesse went abroad he always wore two Colt .45 revolvers, three cartridge belts and carried a rifle inside an umbrella—said the legends.

He planned the Rock Island robbery when it was said the train carried $75,000 in gold from Cheyenne. Members of the gang waited in Council Bluffs and Omaha to give him the tipoff.

Jesse was then 26, tall and wiry with a blond stubby beard and shifty blue eyes.

On a hot July night the James boys and five of their gang rode their horses through the rolling country of southwestern Iowa to the scene of the holdup.

Raiding a station house for tools, they unbolted a rail an tied a rope to it. At 8:30 the train rounded the curve headed for Adair. The outlaws jerked the rail out of place.

The engineer reversed his lever—too late. The engine jumped into the gap, turned over, killing the engineer, while the coaches piled up.

The gang rode yelling and shooting to the baggage car. The guard at the point of a gun, opened the safe for the bandits.

They did not find the $75,000 in gold—just $2000 in currency and some silver bullion--and began sticking up the passengers. They yelled and cursed and shot at the conductor. Women and children shrieked, cried, and fainted.

Thirty Chinese students headed for eastern universities were in the cars, their queues almost on end from fright.

With a few extra oaths and shots the James boys mounted their steeds and rode into the night. Soon the wires were hot with the news of the first American train robbery.[274]

When people opened their July 22, 1873 newspapers, headlines rang everywhere, announcing the robbery. *The Daily Iowa State Register* announced that the train due in Des Moines at 10:30 the night before did not arrive on time. According to the Register: "...about 11 o'clock the news spread over the city that it had been attacked, ditched and sacked by a masked gang of robbers, half-way between Anita and Adair, 61 miles west of Des Moines."[275] According to the article, the first dispatch was received about 10:30 from superintendent Royce

---

274 Kent Pellett, First Train Robbery of the West, orig. published July 23, 1939, *The Des Moines Register*, Reprinted, Knights of Pythias, Anita, Iowa, 224-225

275 Rock Island Train Wrecked & Robbed Near Adair July 21, *Daily Iowa State Register*, Tuesday Morning, July 22, 1873, reprinted in *The Adair News Special Edition*, Summer 1987.

"who fortunately happened to be on the train sent from Casey."[276] The article later noted:

> *John Rafferty, the murdered engineer, was a resident of East Des Moines. He was aged about 35, was married, and his wife and three children had the dreadful news sent them at midnight last night. His comrades speak of the dead man as a man of bravery and noble heart...No other person besides the engineer was killed. Comparatively few of the passengers are injured; none, it is reported, seriously...*[277]

By July 23, 1873, newspaper accounts were more specific. According to the Daily Iowa State Register:

> *The aim appeared to be to keep all the passengers in the car, and to drive the train men in there, too. One passenger, a Chicago man, stepped out of the car and appealed to the robbers not to shoot the women and children. They swore with frightful oaths that they were "no damn common robbers" and only took from the rich to give to the poor. At the same time they commanded him to return to the car, enforcing the command by letting off several loads of a revolver at him. One of the scoundrels stated that they were grangers...*[278]

The Missouri press also became involved in the speculation about the identity of the robbers. On August 7, 1873, *The Carthage Banner* of Carthage Missouri, reprinted a story from *The St. Louis Times*, dated July 25, 1873:

> *Information was received yesterday at the police headquarters which taken with facts before known, leave not the shadow of a doubt but that several members of the party who robbed the train on the Chicago, Rock Island and Pacific Railroad near Adair, Iowa, on Monday night, were the gang who robbed the Ste.*

276 Rock Island Train Wrecked & Robbed Near Adair July 21, *Daily Iowa State Register*.

277 Rock Island Train Wrecked & Robbed Near Adair July 21, *Daily Iowa State Register*.

278 Full Particular of the 1873 Train Robbery Near Adair, org. printed in the *Daily Iowa State Register*, Wednesday Morning, July 23, 1873. Reprinted in *The Adair News Special Edition*, Summer 1987.

Genevieve Bank last May, and have been connected with other villainies of a similar character, perpetrated during the past three or four years.

The members of the band were almost without exception engaged on one side or the other in the Southwest during the civil contest, and know the wilds and ..... of the Osage country, and all Missouri, foot by foot.

Osage township, Jackson county, is the rendezvous for several of them, and when not on the war path they range around in the east part of Jackson, the west part of Clay, and the wilder portion of Ray and Lafayette counties. They have homes there where their families live and cultivate small farms. All about them are relatives and friends who, although they would not be guilty of such deeds, will shield the perpetrators of them to the last...

The last job in Iowa was characterized by the same daring haste, and they are riding toward their homes in Missouri with a good prospect of eluding all pursuit. Once back in their native wilds and "a regiment can't catch them," to borrow the words of the chief of police.[279]

The day following the Adair train robbery, five members of the James gang stopped for dinner at a farmhouse in Ringgold County, Iowa just above the Missouri line. According to Love, "They talked politics, agriculture—and religion. One of the visitors was described thus by the host whom they had entertained with their sprightly talk:

"Seemed to be kind of leader; five feet seven or eight inches tall, light hair, blue eyes, heavy sandy whiskers, broad shoulders, short nose, a little turned up; high, broad forehead; looked to be a well-educated man not used to work; age, thirty-six to forty."[280]

Love goes on to note that this was a fairly accurate description of Jesse James:

---

279 The Iowa Robbers Identified as the Band who went through the Ste. Genevieve Bank and other Villainies. Orig. pub. In the *St. Louis Times*, 25 July 1873. Reprinted in *The Carthage Banner*, August 7, 1873.

280 Love, *The Rise and Fall of Jesse James*, 128.

*Jesse was not quite twenty-six at the time. He was not well-edu-
cated, save in outlawry, but to a simple farmer a young man of
Jesse's experience in travel and in general contact with the world
might have seemed so. The farmer's descriptions of the other four
seemed applicable to Frank James, Clell Miller and two of the
Youngers. However, that supplies no proof. Personal descriptions
frequently are misleading.*[281]

The St. Louis Times identified one of the robbers as Arthur McCoy:

*The fourth man was about thirty-five years old, five feet seven
inches high; had dark hair, moustache and whiskers; wore a light
grey coat and pants, grey hat, fine boots; his left arm and hand
crippled. He was riding a gray horse of about fourteen and one-
half hands high, smoothly shod.*

*This last man described was one of the railroad robbers. His name
is Arthur McCoy, and will be remembered by some of the readers
of the Times. Before the war he was a painter in this city and lived
on Morgan street. He was mixed up in an express robbery on the
plains three or four years ago, but slipped away and was hidden
away in a little place near Ste. Genevieve for a year and a half.
Then he disappeared and was not seen until he came with the
gang on the bank expedition. He was the one who held the pistol
to the head of the Cashier of the bank, and he also made himself
conspicuous enough in the railroad robbery on Monday in Adair
for the express messenger to get a good description of him.*

*McCoy, after leaving Ste. Genevieve, got a place in Montgomery
county about three miles south of Florence, on the Ste. Louis,
Kansas City & Northern Railroad and ten miles of Hermann, on
the Missouri Pacific. He was in St. Louis a few weeks ago, but by
the barest accident escaped falling into the hands of the police
slipped off and joined the band for this northern trip.*

*Other members of the gang who are known to the police by name
are Jesse James, Frank James and Bill Shepard. The first two
named are understood to answer to the two descriptions first
given. Altogether the gang is composed of what the Kansas City*

281 Love, *The Rise and Fall of Jesse James*, 128-129.

Times upon one occasion called "the chivalry of highway robbery." Thus far these operations have been entirely successful and thus far they bid fair to elude the pursuers in Iowa. Once across the line and in Mercer county, they can ride back leisurely to Osage township and take a rest.[282]

By July 29, 1873, the Council Bluffs Nonpareil announced the identity of the robbers:

From a detective who had been in pursuit of the robbers of Chicago, Rock Island and Pacific road, the St. Joseph Herald gets these statements:

Two of the gang are the James boys, of Clay County, Mo., the same party which robbed the Chariton and Clarendon banks, one of them is of the Rambo party which attempted to rob the Chillicothe bank, and the other two are supposed to belong to Pattonsburg, or Chillicothe.

The James brothers crossed the Hannibal and St. Joseph railroad at Kidder last Friday morning before daylight on their way south, evidently going to their mother's house. In the evening they stopped at the farm house of Mr. Bacon and wanted to stay all night. He refused, but told them of a house further on where they could stop. They rode on and passed over the ridge, but not seeing them ride over the ridge beyond he became uneasy and slept very little during the night.

Next morning he arose and immediately went in the direction they did and soon found where they had lain in the brush, and also where they had pocketed their horses. He followed the tracks of their horses some distance in a southerly direction towards Clay County and returned home. He says all the members of the party had fine horses, but they were much jaded and looked as though they had traveled a long distance with little care or food. When the riders jumped off, the horses began to eat smartweed with apparent relish.

This Jesse James is known to be the chief of a gang of robbers which is a terror from their headquarters in Clay County to

282 Love, *The Rise and Fall of Jesse James,* 128-129.

*Sherman Tex. Indeed, when it is known that they have commit-
ted any depredations, everyone gives up further effort to capture
them.*

*The two other suspected parties, which belong to the same gang,
and who separated from the James brothers at a more northerly
point, crossed the Rock Island branch Saturday morning at 11:00
near Jamesport and went in the direction of Pattonsburg. Special
detectives are in front of them awaiting their appearance and others were not more than an hour behind them at the last accounts,
and in all probability will be captured.*[283]

After the dust settled, it is interesting to note that the railroads did little
or nothing to protect their trains. According to Stiles:

*...After the Iowa raid in 1873, the Rock Island had posted a
reward, put rifle-carrying guards on its trains, and let it go at
that. The Iron Mountain line did even less after Gads Hill. But
Dinsmore was a hardheaded businessman. He would have seen
that robbers had, in fact, cost the railroad companies almost
nothing. The Rock Island had repaired its tracks and restored its
derailed locomotive—one of 108 it operated in Iowa—the night
of the robbery; it didn't even mention the incident in its annual
report. The Iron Mountain had suffered even less annoyance, certainly nothing to compare with the $156,700 it earned that month.
The American Railroad Journal and other industry publications
never even bothered to discuss the robberies. Nor did the U. S.
Post Office make any effort to pursue the outlaws, despite the ri-
fling of registered mail at Gads Hill (and press reports to the contrary), Dinsmore, however, saw clearly that the Missouri bandits
did not rob railroads—they robbed express companies. If anyone
was going to put up the money to catch them, it would have to be
the Adams Express.*[284]

Enter Allan Pinkerton of the Pinkerton Detective Agency—and a new
phase in the life of Jesse James.

---

283 Railroad Robbers Identified as Members of James Gang. Originally
published in the *Council Bluffs Nonpareil*, July 29, 1873. Reprinted in
The Adair News Special Edition, Summer 1987.
284 Stiles, *Last Rebel of the Civil War*, 250-251.

Part 3: Photo Section

Construction of Early Adair, Summer 1873

Another view of early Adair, Summer 1873

Site of the train robbery, May 2002

Part of the original track, Adair, Iowa, May 2002

*The oldest house in Adair, May 2002. This was origi-
nally the Section House, built in 1868. The James
Gang ate there just before robbing the train.*

Monument in an Adair park, Adair, Iowa (1999)

Part 4: Jesse, By Jehovah!

Jesse James House Museum, St. Joseph, Missouri, March 2006

Chapter 18: A Time and a Season

After the Adair train robbery, the Pinkertons spent the rest of the 1870s tracking down members of the James gang. What aggravated the Pinkertons was the amount of time spent looking for the outlaws and the fact that not a single James or Younger was captured or killed. Some of the associates had fallen, but the names of James and Younger were absent from the list. This fact would change after the robbery at Gads Hill. First target? John Younger. According to Love:

> *The Pinkertons knew that the Youngers had relatives in St. Clair County, Missouri, about two hundred miles northwest of Gadshill. A rural watering-place called Monegaw Springs had been for some years an occasional resort and refuge for the Youngers. Acting on the theory that one or more of these brothers had taken part in the Iron Mountain train holdup, Allen and Wright proceeded to St. Clair County. They stopped first at Osceola, the county seat, the very town, by the way, the burning of which by Gen. Jim Lane of Kansas early in the Civil War was alleged by some of the guerillas to be the chief occasion of Quantrill's day of sacking and slaughter in the Kansan city of Lawrence.*[285]

The Pinkertons enlisted Edwin B. Daniels, a former sheriff of the county, at Osceola. Daniels took the Pinkertons into the wild country—an area with which he was well familiar—and the three detectives posed as cattle buyers. Love continues the narrative:

> *...Near the Springs lived a farmer bearing the odd name of Theodoric Snuffer; he was related to the Younger family. Some distance beyond was the home of a widow named Simms.*

---

285 Love, *The Rise and Fall of Jesse James,* 137-138.

"I know the Youngers by sight," said Wright to his companions, "and I reckon they know me; I served in the Confederate army, where I met some of the boys. I'll not stop at Snuffer's, therefore, but will ride on ahead."

Allen and Daniels stopped in front of Snuffer's and inquired the way to the Widow Simm's house. Snuffer directed them, and they rode on. In the Snuffer farmhouse at the time were James and John Younger, who kept themselves hidden from the ostensible cattlemen. They heard all of the conversation and watched from a window as the Pinkertons rode away.

At a fork in the road they observed that Allen and Daniels took the wrong direction. So they were not going to the widow's, after all! The Youngers mounted their horses and followed. About a mile beyond Snuffer's they caught up with the detectives. The hour was about 2:30 P.M. on the 16th of March, 1874. Daniels and Allen rode side by side. Wright was in sight not far ahead.

John Younger carried a double-barrel shotgun. Jim had two revolvers. John cocked both barrels of his gun and ordered Allen and Daniels to halt. Wright, up the road, drew rein, turned in his saddle and leveled a pistol at one of the Youngers. Apparently he changed his mind, for instead of firing he put spurs to his horse and dashed away. The Youngers ordered him to halt, but he kept going. One of them fired, shooting Wright's hat from his head...[286]

A few words were exchanged, followed by bullets. Allen fired at John Younger. According to Love:

Allen's shot was followed immediately by one from each of the Youngers. The detective's left arm, which held the reins, dropped to his side. His horse took fright and jumped into the bushes beside the road. One of the Youngers rode past Allen and fired twice at him. The horse brushed against a sapling and knocked Allen out of his saddle. He staggered across the road and fell, having received a fatal wound.

---

286 Love, *The Rise and Fall of Jesse James*, 138-139.

Almost simultaneously John Younger fell out of his saddle, dead. At the end of the battle Daniels also lay dead in the road, a big bullet having struck him in the middle of the neck, crushing his bones.[287]

John Younger was dead at age 24. Actually, he had very little to do with the outlaw activities, for he was not identified in any of the robberies. Love states that he had a bad record in Texas, however, where he lived just outside Dallas. His older brothers, Coleman and James often sought refuge there. Cole Younger later wrote a letter, defending not only his brother, but himself as well. The letter was addressed to Lycurgus Jones, a brother-in-law of the Youngers, who lived in Cass Co., Missouri. This letter was published November 26, 1874 in the Pleasant Hill, Missouri *Review:*

"Poor John! He has been hunted down and shot like a wild beast, and never was a boy more innocent. But there is a day coming when the secrets of all hearts will be laid open skirts be white as the driven snow, while those of his accusers will be doubly dark."[288]

***

It was only a matter of time before the James family would be attacked. The attack was set into motion when a Pinkerton detective arrived in Independence, Missouri, and turned up dead on the road leading to the Blue Mills ferry on the Missouri River in early 1874. A young college student named Will Wallace, worked as a lawyer and reporter for the *Kansas City Times* and the Independence *Sentinel.* He heard about the excitement and went out to investigate the scene. Love provides the narrative:

...A man about thirty years of age had been shot to death and left lying in the road. He was dressed roughly, like a farmhand. But his hands were soft and smooth; no callouses, nothing to indicate that he had done any kind of manual labor. To the contrary, the

287 Love, *The Rise and Fall of Jesse James*, 140-141.
288 Love, *The Rise and Fall of Jesse James*, 143-144.

*bullet victim appeared to have been in such circumstances that
he was able to take excellent care of his person. But the old jeans
pants and coat, the old blue-check shirt, the old slouch hat—why
such apparel?*

*Will Wallace turned up the right sleeve of the shirt and found,
a few inches above the wrist, the initials "J. W. W." neatly tat-
tooed. These facts and such other scant information as he picked
up he reported to his newspapers. It was all in the day's work
for Wallace, who could not be aware that he was reporting the
beginning of a murder mystery, intimately relating to the career of
the Missouri outlaws, which time never can solve completely; nor
that he, as prosecuting attorney of Jackson County, was to become
some years later the active and successful Nemesis of the James
Boys' Band, so called throughout the country.*[289]

"J. W. W." turned out to be the late John W. Witcher, a Pinkerton detective from Chicago, whose sole determination was to go to the farm
in Kearney, where he planned to disguise himself as a farm laborer and
capture the outlaws. He outlined his plan, and the Pinkertons approved
it. But he underestimated his targets. Love states, "The considerable
error committed by the unfortunate young detective lay in his assump-
tion that Frank and Jesse James were, after all, just a couple of rural
bad men of average mental caliber, and that he could fool them with
comparative ease."[290]

Witcher first spoke with the president of the Commercial Bank in
Liberty, and outlined his plan. The bank president forewarned him:

*"Young man, you'd better not try it. It won't be safe for you. You
do not know those James boys as we know them, here in Clay
County...You don't know what you're up against. I do; I know the
resources of those James boys; they are not in any sense to be
looked upon as ordinary criminals. You are not going out after
a pair of city crooks, mind you. No—you are about to undertake
the capture of two of the keenest-minded young men in America.
Those boys are not asleep, I warn you! They never sleep, in the*

289 Love, *The Rise and Fall of Jesse James*, 145-146
290 Love, *The Rise and Fall of Jesse James*, 146.

sense of being confident of security. If they happen to be at home, or either of them, your life won't be worth fifteen cents if you go out there disguised as a farmhand; they'll see clean through you. I repeat, you can't fool Frank or Jesse James."²⁹¹

Witcher was determined, however. He took the afternoon train for Kearney and four miles from the Samuels farm. According to Love:

> *In the meantime the Pinkerton man had been shadowed by a very private detective who lived in Clay County and was a particular friend of the Jameses. This unofficial sleuth mounted a swift horse and rode to the Samuel farm, where Jesse James was visiting his mother. He told Jesse all about the young stranger who was using such open-work detective methods.²⁹²*

Love's narrative provides the rest of the story:

> *Leaving the train at Kearney, Witcher walked out the road toward the farm. It was late in the afternoon, almost dusk, when suddenly he was challenged by a man who stepped from the bushes with a big six-shooter in his right hand.*
>
> *"Who are you, and where are you bound for?"*
>
> *"I'm out looking for work on a farm" Witcher replied. "Can you tell me where I might be able to find a job in these parts?"*
>
> *"You don't want any job—you've got one already, with that damn Pinkerton outfit," said the man with the drawn weapon, smiling sardonically.*
>
> *"I don't know what you're talking about," the detective said. "I'm a poor man out of work, and—"*
>
> *"And you're looking for the James boys, hey? Well, here take a look at one of 'em—Jesse James!"*
>
> *Witcher winced, but kept up his pretense. Jesse James signaled. Two other men stepped into the road.*

291 Love, *The Rise and Fall of Jesse James*, 147.
292 Love, *The Rise and Fall of Jesse James*, 148.

"Search him," Jesse ordered.

One of the men extracted Witcher's weapon from its place of concealment. Jesse's eyes blinked angrily.

"A farmhand with a loaded weapon on his chest!" he snarled. "Let me see your hands."

Jesse felt one of Witcher's palms—soft and smooth.

"A hell of a farm laborer you are! A poor man, hey? You put some of Mr. Pinkerton's money in the bank at Liberty, didn't you? And you left your fine clothes at the hotel. Where are you from—Chicago?"

"I'm from Indiana," responded Witcher, who was a native of the Hoosier state. "Now I can't see why you don't let me pass on, for I'm not trying to harm you are anybody."

The three men consulted briefly.

"Better finish him, right here," suggested one.

Witcher began to plead for his life. He told his captors that he had a young wife at home, and for her sake he begged them not to kill him. Jesse James, who was going to take unto himself a young wife within a few weeks, is said to have been touched by his method of appeal. Such was the statement made by members of his band about eight years later, whose confessions provide the raw material for this record of the meeting on the road out of Kearney.

"Well, don't let's do it here, anyhow—not on my side," Jesse is supposed to have said. "My side" meant the Clay County side of the Missouri river.

Late that night the elderly man who operated the ferry at Blue Mills was awakened by some men on horseback; the hour was about 2 A.M. The party wanted to be ferried across the Missouri. The ferryman noticed that one of the four men was bound, hands tied behind, feet secured by a cord under the horse's belly.

"Who's this fellow—why's he tied up this way?"

The old ferryman then spoke directly to the bound man, who made no reply, though he gave his questioner an appealing look in the dim flare of the lantern.

"Gagged, by golly!" exclaimed the ferryman. "You-all must be afeard this here hossthief'll holler and skeer your hosses."

The party was ferried across. The rest of the episode, so far as facts are known, has been told earlier...Frank James, according to the stories told by members of the later James Boys' Band who confessed to Prosecuting Attorney Will Wallace in 1883, was not of the trio that captured and killed Detective Witcher. The two companions of Jesse James on that night remain anonymous; various alleged identities have been applied to them without proof of any.[293]

After losing three men in one month, the Pinkertons became all the more determined to put the James-Younger Gang out of commission. They had another man in the field who used the name Jack Ladd and who had hired out as a farmhand on Daniel Askew's farm, which was close to the farm where the James boys grew up. He no doubt came from a farming background, for he worked hard each day and appeared in church each Sunday. He used the dialect of the countryside and was popular among all the farmers in the area. He also became acquainted with Dr. and Mrs. Samuel and with Jesse and Frank James on a limited basis. The James boys did not suspect Ladd of being connected with the Pinkertons.

Word soon spread about the area that Frank and Jesse James would be visiting the Samuel home. Jack Ladd reported seeing both Frank and Jesse at the home on the 20th and 21st of January, 1875.[294] Ladd thought they would be staying there for a week or so. Love reports:

That night the Pinkerton operatives, accompanied by several men supposed to be residents of Clay or Jackson, surrounded the Samuel farmhouse, arriving about midnight. All the occupants of

293 Love, *The Rise and Fall of Jesse James*, 148-150.
294 Love, *The Rise and Fall of Jesse James*, 151.

the house were in bed, asleep. Neither Frank nor Jesse was there. With Dr. and Mrs. Samuel and the three Samuel children were an old negro woman and a small negro boy.

Archie Payton Samuel, half-brother to the James boys, was just eight and a half years old, the baby of the family. Jesse and Frank, who always liked children, were very fond of little Archie. Though they had been hiding out most of the time since he was born, they had played and romped with him many a time on their visits home...

Four men of the investing party approached the house, each bearing a big ball of cotton waste soaked with kerosene and turpentine. They forced open the shutter of a kitchen window and were raising the sash when the old colored aunty, sleeping in that room, was awakened by the noise. She gave a shrill shriek, awakening the whole family.[295]

All members of the Samuel family rushed inside the kitchen. As they worked frantically to get the burning object to the door, another fireball was lobbed through the window. According to Dr. Samuel, the second fireball was not like the first. He described it as a bombshell, much heavier than the first. Working together, the family members maneuvered it toward the hearth, and that's when the shell exploded, killing Archie and tearing off the lower portion of Zerelda's right forearm.

Clay County newspapers called the bomb-throwing incident "the crime of the century." None of the newspaper accounts were favorable to the Pinkertons. The agency lost much of its support from locals because of its attack on the Samuel family. In March, "a Clay County grand jury investigated the bombing and found indictments for the murder of Archie Samuel against Robert J. Kin, Allan K. Pinkerton, Jack Ladd, and five other persons whose names were unknown to the jurors."[296] Charges against these people were subsequently dismissed. According to Settle:

In the weeks following the fireball explosion the build-up of a move to grant amnesty to the James and Younger brothers be-

295 Love, *The Rise and Fall of Jesse James*, 151-152
296 Settle, *Jesse James Was His Name*, 80.

came evident. A long article in the Chicago Times of February 24, written by a special correspondent at Jefferson City, Missouri, presaged the introduction of a resolution offering amnesty. It presented a one-sided history of the Jameses and Youngers and argued that Radicals and Jayhawkers had prevented their settling down to peaceable lives after the war, that they had not committed the crimes charged to them, and that the mobbing and murdering of former bushwhackers made it unsafe for them to present themselves for trial.[297]

The Amnesty Bill was subsequently defeated. As for Jesse and Frank James, they wanted revenge against those who attacked their family. On April 12, 1875, three shots rang out at the Askew place. In *The Secrets of Jesse James*, George Turner notes:

Askew was found dead with three bullet holes in his body. He had been bushwhacked as he returned from the spring with a bucket of water. The identity of the assailant(s) never was ascertained.

Allan Pinkerton, head of the detective agency, was fortunate to escape a similar fate, if a story told by Jesse's friend, George Hite, is true.

"Jesse went to Chicago to kill Allan Pinkerton and stayed there for four months but he never had a chance to do it like he wanted to," Hite said to reporters after Jesse's death. "That was after the Pinkertons made a raid on his mother's house, blew off her arm and killed his stepbrother. He said he could have killed the younger one but didn't care to. 'I want him to know who did it,' he said. 'It wouldn't do me no good if I couldn't tell him about it before he died. I had a dozen chances to kill him when he didn't know it. I wanted to give him a fair chance but, the opportunity never came.' Jesse left Chicago without doing it, but I heard him often say: 'I know that God will someday deliver Allan Pinkerton into my hands.'"[298]

---

297 Settle, *Jesse James Was His Name*, 80.
298 George Turner, *The Secrets of Jesse James* [Baxter Lane Co., Amarillo, TX, 1975] 24.

Chapter 19: The Best Laid Plans

The Northfield, Minnesota bank robbery was the beginning of the end for the James-Younger Gang, and it became their Gettysburg and their Waterloo.[299] About the middle of August, 1876, the gang moved upon Minnesota consisting of the two Jameses, the three Youngers, Clell Miller, Samuel Wells (alias Charlie Pitts) and William Stiles (alias Bill Chadwell). Stiles had relatives in Minnesota and had also worked there. So he was familiar with the lay of the land. Once inside Minnesota, they split into small groups or scouting parties.

The outlaws lacked a definite plan when they first entered Minnesota. They originally thought Mankato would be an excellent target. However, someone in the town reportedly recognized Jesse James and reported it to the police. And that's when everyone started looking for him. And that is also when the Missourians rode out of Mankato.

Stiles was familiar with the First National Bank of Northfield, which was located in the northeastern part of that county. Love describes the town as "…a pleasant little place of about 3000 people, about 40 miles east and slightly north of Mankato, in the midst of a rich farming country."[300] Love notes:

> The outfit had determined to raid and rob a bank somewhere in southern Minnesota, the Bill Chadwell country, but no particular institution of finance had been selected when the eight left Missouri for the North, where, incidentally, three of them were to remain as corpses quick-prepared, one was to die in prison, a fifth was to take his own life after serving twenty-five years, and

299 Love, *The Rise and Fall of Jesse James*, 189.
300 Love, *The Rise and Fall of Jesse James*, 195

a sixth was to be permitted to quit Minnesota only after a quarter of a century's perfect behavior record in the state penitentiary.[301]

The outlaws pretended to be cattle and horse buyers, grain dealers, or real estate speculators, or civil engineers looking out prospective railroad routes. No one questioned their motives, and they were taken for what they pretended to be. And on Thursday, September 7, 1876, the gang committed the crime that would end their career. Love provides the narrative:

On that afternoon the outlaws rode into Northfield in three groups, having met for final consultation in a piece of woods about five miles to the westward. At that meeting each man was given to know precisely what part he was expected to take in the Northfield job—emergencies, of course, not being lost from the reckoning. The octet divided into three sections. Three men were to enter the bank and get the money—if they could; two were to sit their horses on Division Street, opposite the bank, and keep too-curious people away; three were to occupy posts on Bridge Square as a rear guard, the gang intending to make its get-away by crossing the bridge over Cannon river.

The three who were to rob the bank rode across the bridge about 2 o'clock, crossed the square, dismounted in front of the bank and threw their reins over hitching-posts. These men were Sam Wells, Bob Younger and, it is believed, Jesse James. They walked in a leisurely way to the street corner and sat down upon some dry-goods boxes in front of a store. Nonchalantly, in appearance, they began whittling the pine boxes.

In a short time Cole Younger and Clell Miller rode up Division Street. The three whittlers pocketed their knives, arose, walked slowly to the bank entrance and went inside. Leaving his horse unhitched, Clell Miller walked to the door of the bank, which the other three had left open. He closed the door and sauntered back and forth on the sidewalk, keeping an eye on the door.

Cole Younger's saddle-girth seemed to be troubling him; anyhow, he got off his horse, in the middle of the street, and pretended to be

301 Love, *The Rise and Fall of Jesse James*, 191.

tightening the girth. He was an excellent actor, but this particular bit of acting failed to go down with the Northfield male element, which already had begun to suspect that the play was a bad one.

One of the spectators who didn't like the prologue was Henry M. Wheeler, a youth of twenty-two who was at home on vacation from Ann Arbor, where he was a senior medical student in the University of Michigan. Henry's father conducted a drugstore on the east side of Division Street. The college student had been sitting under an awning in front of the pharmacy when the horsemen rode up. He arose and walked along until he was opposite the bank and the bandits.

Another spectator who was not impressed with the genuineness of the acting was J. S. Allen, a hardware merchant. When he saw the three strangers enter the bank he tried to follow. Clell Miller seized him by the scruff of the neck and ordered him to stand back, get away, go inside somewhere else.

"And if you speak a word," said Miller, fingering a large revolver, "I'll kill you!"

Nevertheless, Allen jerked loose, ran around the corner to his store, and shouted so loudly that he was heard all up and down the square:

"Get your guns, boys! Get your guns! Those fellows are robbing the bank!"

Henry Wheeler, who had heard a pistol shot from inside the bank, also was shouting loud alarms. Cole Younger and Miller remounted and ordered young Wheeler to "get inside," firing a shot or two over his head to frighten him. The future physician and surgeon was not of the frightening breed. Nor did he get so excited as to lose presence of mind.

Whilst Younger and Miller were riding up and down, yelling for everybody to get in, and firing right and left, the three bandits from the bridge side were dashing into the square and beginning tactics similarly violent. Wheeler dashed into the drugstore to get his gun. He was a huntsman and kept a competent fowling piece.

Suddenly he recollected that he had left the weapon at home, some blocks away. He ran on through the store and into the Dampier Hotel, where he found an old army carbine, a relic of Federal use against Southerners of the Sixties, including possibly some of the ex-guerrillas now invading Northfield.[302]

Clell Miller was killed, as were Bill Stiles and Charlie Pitts. Pitts' body was given to a medical school in St. Paul, where his mummified remains wound up in a private museum.

Inside the bank, the three bandits encountered another problem. The safe was set on time-lock and could not be opened. According to Love:

Sam Wells rushed to the vault and stepped inside. Joseph Lee Heywood arose, walked rapidly to the vault and tried to shut Wells inside. Before he could slam the heavy door shut he was seized by both Wells and the leader of the robbing squad.

"Unless you open that safe at once you'll be shot dead!" cried the leader.

"I can't open it—the time lock is on."

"You're lying!"

Repeatedly they demanded that Heywood open the safe. They pulled him back and forth about the big room, cursing him.

"Murder! Murder!" Heywood shouted.

The leader struck him on the head with a heavy revolver. Heywood sank to the floor.

"Let's cut his damn throat!" cried Sam Wells, who opened his pocket knife and made a slight cut in the neck of the fallen man. At least a semi-cutthroat was Wells of Jackson County! Then the pair caught Haywood under the armpits and dragged him back to the door of the vault, again insisting that he open the safe.

From time to time the desperate men turned to Wilcox and Bunker, ordering each in turn to unlock the safe. Both replied that they could not unlock it.

302 Love, *The Rise and Fall of Jesse James*, 197-200.

Heywood lay upon the floor near the vault, hardly conscious. Wells bent low and fired inside the bank. This was done in the hope of inducing Heywood to unlock the safe. The bullet passed through a tin box in the vault, containing valuables left by a special depositor.[303]

Heywood was eventually shot through the head and killed by the last of the fleeing bandits. Love notes that this was not an act of self-defense but of cold-blooded murder since Heywood was not armed. All the outlaws were able to get from the bank was a small amount of change. They missed the $3,000 in paper money that was secured in a drawer, very close to the robber's hands.

Turner continues the narrative:

Young Henry Wheeler was still sniping at the bandits from the second floor of the Dampier House. One Elias Stacey had entered the fray, firing from a second floor window of the Scriver Block with a shotgun loaded with .06 shot. He peppered Cole Younger and some of the others and blasted Bill Chadwell in the face. Half-blinded, his face a red horror, Chadwell rode like a madman, aimlessly firing his revolver.

A bullet caught Cole Younger in the shoulder; the marksman who stood in the open, was the hardware merchant, Manning. Cole charged toward Manning, who drove him back with a withering fusillade of rifle fire. The other hardware merchant, Allen, was serving out rifles and ammunition to other citizens.

As Jesse and Frank exited the bank, one of them turned and glared at Heywood, who was struggling to his feet. The outlaw described by Wilcox as the shorter of the two—it would have to be Jesse—callously put a bullet through the injured man's head.

Manning drew a bead on the rampaging Chadwell and shot him squarely through the heart. As Bob Younger tried to ride out, his horse was shot out from under him. Using the iron stairway of the Scriver Block as a shield, Bob started to take a shot at Manning. Wheeler took in the situation and shot Bob through the right

303 Love, *The Rise and Fall of Jesse James*, 202-203

elbow. Grabbing up his pistol with his other hand, Bob tried to carry on the fight.

More citizens had turned out, some of them throwing rocks at the bandits. Frank James caught a bullet above the right knee as he was mounting up.

As the crossfire worsened, it became obvious that the good people of Northfield had the upper hand. Cole Younger had received more wounds and was bleeding all over. Bob Younger's shattered elbow left him virtually helpless. Jim Younger had been hit several times and his jaw was shattered and hemorrhaging. With wild cries the outlaws lit out of town, Bob Younger riding double with Cole.[304]

When the gang reached a place they considered safe to hide at the moment, it became apparent that Jim Younger was so badly injured that he was slowing them down. Then Jesse James made a suggestion that would split the old comrades permanently. According to Turner, Jesse said, "Jim Younger…was holding them back. There was nothing they could do to help Jim except to put him out of his misery or leave him to fend for himself. The rest of the band wouldn't consider such an idea. Cole Younger, though he remained friends with Frank for the rest of Frank's life, hated Jesse from that moment on."[305]

Jesse and Frank rode on while the three Youngers remained behind, where they were eventually apprehended. And the results of that expedition? According to Turner:

Charlie Pitts lay dead with five bullet holes in his chest. Jim Younger appeared near death with five wounds. Cole had been shot eleven times. Bob sustained two wounds. The clothes of the survivors were soaked with blood. Cole blinked at Vought with the good eye (the other was swollen shut) and said, "Hello…I didn't expect to run across you out here." As Vought looked down at Charlie Pitts, Cole told him, "That's your other guest."[306]

Bob Younger would die of tuberculosis in prison. After serving twenty-five years, Cole and Jim Younger were released. Turner relates:

---

304 Turner, *The Secrets of Jesse James*, 31-32
305 Turner, *The Secrets of Jesse James*, 32.
306 Turner, *The Secrets of Jesse James*, 36

Cole was a model citizen during his later years, serving part of the time as a minister. The brothers worked as tombstone salesmen for the N. P. Peterson Granite Co. of St. Paul and Stillwell, but Jim later gave up the job because of ill health.

Jim worked as an insurance man for a while, but was declared ineligible to write policies because he was a former convict. The same argument was used against him by the parents of a girl reporter from St. Paul to whom he became engaged in 1902. Deeply in love, Jim found himself unable to face life alone. On Sunday afternoon, October 19, 1902, he shot himself through the head in his room at the Reardon Hotel in St. Paul.

Cole saved considerable money from his travels with a wild west show co-starring his pal, Frank James, and the Lew Nichols Carnival. He retired and lived at Lee's Summit with his niece, Nora Hall, in a house he had given her. He outlived all the other members of the James-Younger gang, dying at age 72 on February 21, 1916. The youngsters of the community were sorrowed by the passing of the beloved old tale-teller they knew as Uncle Cole. He had survived 26 bullet wounds (17 chunks of lead remained in his body); only time, it seems could take the measure of Cole Younger.[307]

---

307 Turner, *The Secrets of Jesse James*, 42-43

Chapter 20: Life on the Run

History does not record exactly how the James brothers made their way back to Missouri. They could have crossed into the Dakotas and traveled through Nebraska. They may have found a safe route through Iowa. We can only speculate about the mind of Jesse James at that period of time. The robbery was not successful. Many of his comrades were dead. The Youngers would no longer be part of his life. The demons were no doubt chasing him as well. Turner describes some of the inner conflict: "The religious side of his nature surely told him that the Pit yawned for him, just as the rationalization that he was in the right must have suffered with the knowledge that so many hands were turned against him."[308]

After they made it back to Kansas City and were reunited with their families, they realized that they needed a change of scenery. Too many people knew about them as well as their whereabouts, and it was simply too dangerous to stay in Clay County. Close friends and family members helped them relocate:

All their belongings were loaded into two wagons and Jesse, Zee, Frank and Little Jesse Edwards soon shook the dust of Missouri. Dr. Samuel's son, John, and one Tyler Burns drove the wagons as far as Kentucky, so that Frank and Jesse could remain on horseback and ride clear of towns the wagons passed through. Then the two loyal friends bade the fugitives goodbye.[309]

One important point should be noted here about the James Gang. They did not sleep in caves or use caves as their official hideout! Some tourist trap cave sites have posted signs over the years proclaiming *Jesse*

308 Turner, *The Secrets of Jesse James*, 44.
309 Turner, *The Secrets of Jesse James*, 44

James Slept Here! or *Visit the Jesse James Hideout!* When the gang fled the scene of the Adair train robbery, they slept in a grove of trees. Oftentimes, they stayed in people's homes, or slept in their barns.

Jesse and Frank split up with Frank heading toward Nashville and Jesse settling in the town of Waverly, Humphreys County, Tennessee, where he rented the Banks Link farm under the name Dave Howard. Zee was pregnant at the time and seemed to relish the peaceful farm life the family had settled into. They may have spent the rest of their lives here, only a series of misfortunes befell them. Zee gave birth to twins, both boys, who were dead within the week. Jesse bought a herd of cattle from Mark Cooley on a $900 credit and after two years, it became apparent that he could not pay off the loan. Jesse and Cooley became involved in a heated argument, after which Jesse announced to Zee that they were moving! They next moved to Nashville, where Frank was living under the name of B. J. Woodson. According to Turner:

> *Nursed back to health by a friendly farm couple and the farmer's sister, Frank worked at the Josiah Walton farm until harvest time. Then he drove a four mule team for the Indiana Lumber Company for a time, made wooden buckets for the Prewitt-Spur Lumber Company, worked at another farm and at last rented the Felix Smith farm. During his stay at Nashville his wife presented him with his son, Robert Franklin James.*
>
> *Frank did well with the farm, raising prize-winning Poland China hogs and participating in the local horse races. Mr. Woodson was a popular man around Nashville, a friend of the mayor, the sheriff and other leading citizens—despite the fact that part of his disguise was that he pretended to be a Northern gentleman. Young Robert was kept in disguise as well, being dressed as a girl called Mary, just in case Frank had to go on the run again. Two things about Frank struck people as being peculiar: he liked to quote Shakespeare and he always had a saddled mount nearby.[310]*

The Howards joined the Woodsons in Nashville and shared the same residence at the Smith farm. Mr. Howard and the locals got along well together. They also admired his new race horse, Jim Malone. Mr.

310 Turner, *The Secrets of Jesse James*, 45

Woodson had a race horse called Jewel Maxey. It was also in Nashville where little Mary "Howard" was born on July 17, 1879.

Shortly after Mary was born, Jesse boarded a train for Kansas City and from there traveled to Las Vegas, New Mexico. He decided to go into the cattle ranching business. Turner notes: "There is a story to the effect that while staying at the Old Adobe Hotel, he became acquainted with young firebrand Billy the Kid, but it's probably just a story."[311]

Jesse could not scrape up the money in order to buy a ranch and cattle, and so he decided to return to his old "profession." Turner describes this decision:

> *Frank preferred life as he was living it; he wanted no more of the lawless life. Jesse meantime had reestablished contact with Dick Liddil, Jim Cummins and Bill Ryan. Only Ryan was particularly to Jesse's liking, and he wasn't quite sober enough much of the time. With this motley shadow of the old gang, Jesse set out for Missouri and a dangerous enterprise.*

> *Just at twilight, on October 7, 1879, the new James gang made their return to Missouri official. The little Chicago & Alton railroad station at Glendale, twenty-two miles out of Kansas City, was thoroughly hoorawed by six horsemen who shot up the place and locked the employees in a store room. When the now-famed Glendale train arrived it was flagged down and the robbers boarded her. The express car messenger was pistol-whipped and relieved of the $35,000 in his charge. Passengers were invited to contribute their valuables to the grain sack.*

> *The bandits with Jesse were Dick Liddil, Bill Ryan, Ed Miller (kid brother of the late Clell), Jesse's cousin Wood Hite and a farm boy named Tucker Basham. The latter, new to the business, couldn't keep his mouth shut about the big money he'd made so easily and soon fell into the hands of the law. Basham confessed and named his associates to William Wallace, prosecuting attorney of Jackson County.*[312]

This was the same William Wallace who investigated the murder of

---

311 Turner, *The Secrets of Jesse James*, 45-46
312 Turner, *The Secrets of Jesse James*, 46

the Pinkerton detective, John W. Witcher, some years previously.

Everything began to unravel. Bill Ryan got drunk in Nashville, Tennessee and was arrested with some of the money obtained during the Glendale robbery. Ryan was returned to Missouri and indicted. Turner notes: "Wallace was assured by almost everybody that he could never convict members of the James gang in Jackson County, but the spunky prosecutor was determined to see both men "up the river.""[313] After that, everything became quiet for a year and a half until March of 1881. According to Turner:

> The James brothers, along with Ryan, Liddil and Miller showed up near Muscle Shoals, [Alabama] where they relieved the passengers and strong box of a stage coach of about $1,400. On July 10 the same group held up the Davis & Sexton Bank of Riverton, Iowa, escaping with about $5,000.

> Five days later, Passenger Train Number Two of the Chicago, Rock Island and Pacific left Kansas City en route to Davenport, Iowa. Three men dressed in black boarded the train at Cameron, a station sixty-four miles out of Kansas City, and settled down in the smoking car. Some of the passengers noted that the men's heavy beards appeared to be false.

> At 8:30 p.m., as Number Two approached Winston, Missouri, seventy-one miles from Cameron, the three bearded men leaped to their feet, shouting, "Hands up!" and firing their revolvers for effect. Then, very deliberately, one of them aimed at the conductor, William Westphal, and fired. The conductor turned to flee and other shots were fired at him. He ran up the aisle and out onto the forward platform, then toppled out into the shadows.[314]

The robbers were furious when they found only $600 in the safe, and they demanded to know where the rest of the money was hidden. Charles Murray, a messenger for the United States Express Company, swore that the rest of the money was in silver bullion. The bandit leader seemed to toy with the idea of killing Murray, but knocked him down instead. The conductor, William Westphal, and Frank McMillan,

313 Turner, *The Secrets of Jesse James*, 46.
314 Turner, *The Secrets of Jesse James*, 47.

a stonemason from Kansas City, were both killed, and for a while, Westphal's killing did not make sense. According to Turner:

> *Later it was learned that Westphal was the conductor of the special train that took the Pinkerton men to the Samuel farm on the "Night of Blood." It is generally believed that the men who fired upon Westphal were the James brothers. One of the unsolved mysteries of the case is whether Westphal's participation in the affair at the Samuel place was known to Frank and Jesse, and, if so, whether they knew the identity of the man they murdered.*[315]

Then an announcement was made that would signal the beginning of the end for Jesse James. According to Turner:

> *On July 28, 1881, Thomas Crittendon, governor of Missouri, called a press conference and told reporters of the latest move to fulfill his campaign pledge "to destroy outlawry in this state whose head and front is the James gang." Although he was empowered by the laws of the state to offer only a maximum reward of $300, he had met with representatives of several railroad companies and made arrangements to offer a much greater incentive to bring the James gang to justice. With the financial assistance of the railroads, the state now authorized "a reward of $5,000 for the capture of Frank and Jesse James and $5000 for the conviction of each."*
>
> *The James brothers, hiding out in Kentucky, doubtless were shaken by the news. No longer could they trust anybody. There were almost certain to be betrayed for such a princely sum.*[316]

---

315 Turner, *The Secrets of Jesse James*, 48
316 Turner, *The Secrets of Jesse James*, 48.

Chapter 21: The Killing of Jesse James

Sprawling on the banks of the Missouri River, the town of St. Joseph claims its status of county seat of Buchanan County, some portions of it extending across the county line into Andrew County along the northern edge. Before the Civil War, the town was the hot bed of confederate activities and in 1861, a full-fledged riot took place there. Originally, St. Joseph was to have been the beginning point of the Transcontinental Railway, but because of Confederate activities there, the new location point was moved to Omaha, Nebraska. According to the St. Joseph History Website:

> *Joseph Robidoux established the Blacksnake Hills trading post with the Indians in 1826. Robidoux's trading post soon became a fur-trading empire stretching to the southern Rocky Mountains. The Platte Purchase joined his land to the state of Missouri in 1837. Ideally situated, Robidoux's trading post became the City of St. Joseph in 1843 and remained relatively small until the discovery of gold in California in 1848 which greatly altered and accelerated westward migration. St. Joseph became the head water for the journey west as hundreds of thousands of settlers arrived by steamboat and hundreds of wagon trains lined the streets waiting to be ferried across the Missouri River. The covered wagons, oxen, and supplies purchased by the emigrants established the economic foundation of the City.*[317]

St. Joseph, Missouri was the eastern terminus of the Pony Express and after 1865, the city returned to normal with the end of the Civil War. In the 1870s, St. Joseph became a leading wholesale center for distribu-

---

317 The City of St. Joseph, Missouri Website, Accessed September 5, 2010. Available at http://www.ci.st-joseph.mo.us/history/history.cfm

tion to the West. The 1880s and 1890s are often called The Golden Age of Prosperity in St. Joseph, and existing mansions will testify to that. Meat packing was a prime industry there, and the stockyards opened in St. Joseph in 1887. The website goes on to state:

> *In 1886, the Chicago Times reported that "St. Joseph is a modern wonder--a city of 60,000 inhabitants, eleven railroads, 70 passenger trains each day, 170 factories, thirteen miles of the best paved streets, the largest stockyards west of Chicago, a wholesale trade as large as that of Kansas City and Omaha combined..." One count of the U.S. Census had the City's population in 1900 at 102,000.[318]*

In the fall of 1881, the Thomas Howard family arrived in St. Joseph and settled into a house at 23rd and Lafayette Street. [This same family was previously the J. D. Howard family in Kansas City.] And now in St. Joseph, Thomas Howard next moved his family to a house at 1318 Lafayette street, a place he liked because of its high location. He could see in all directions from the house and would be able to notice anyone attempting to creep up on him. Concerning Thomas Howard, Love notes:

> *Mr. Howard was a regular customer of August Brokaw, a druggist on lower Sixth Street. He became a warm favorite there. He bought cigars to give to his friends—including the Fords. Nearly every day he would sit in the drug store and tell stories—clean ones, stories with points. He told Brokaw he was a railroad man out of a job. The druggist promised to get him a railroad job! Undoubtedly Mr. Howard laughed, upsleeve, at this. After all, and after a fashion, Jesse enjoyed life. Major Edwards wrote, comparing the two brothers: "Jesse laughed at many things, Frank laughed not at all. Jesse was light-hearted, reckless, devil-may-care; Frank was sober, sedate, a splendid man always for ambush or scouting parties. Both were undaunted."*
>
> *Mr. Howard liked to play billiards. Late one night, after a game in a St. Joseph billiard hall, another player remarked to him that*

318 The City of St. Joseph, Missouri Website, Accessed September 5, 2010. Available at http://www.ci.st-joseph.mo.us/history/history.cfm.

*he was afraid to go home alone—he might be held up and robbed.
Mr. Howard volunteered to escort the fearsome citizen home. At
the man's door he called out a cheery good night.*

*Under caption of "Worthy of Notice", the Gazette said on April
6, 1882: "It is positively known that Jesse James attended the
Sunday services at the Presbyterian church, opposite the World's
Hotel, repeatedly. Last Sunday, he was seen with his entire family
at the Union Depot, viewing the improvements.*[319]

In describing Thomas Howard, Turner states:

*Thomas Howard was known as a cattle buyer, but in truth he
could barely afford the $14-a-month rent for the so-called House
on the Hill, which was a well-known landmark in the booming
town. It is probable that Jesse entertained thoughts of entering
some kind of business and trying to forget the past. The Howards
attended church regularly, becoming members of the St. Joseph
Presbyterian Church. At one point he made arrangements to rent
a farm near Pawnee, Nebraska, but he never completed the deal,
probably for lack of funds.*[320]

Jesse James no doubt felt comfortable in assuming the identity of
Thomas Howard and in hiding out in St. Joseph. The town had a firm
basis in the South. In addition, a number of old friends resided in the
area, including members of the Brown family, who supplied him with
fresh horses in Platte County. He may well have been in contact with
those people. The Browns were in Buchanan County initially, according to the family records, and then moved out to Andrew County on
the north end of St. Joseph. Jesse James lived and died in Buchanan
County.

Charles and Robert Ford were not related to Jesse James, though they
posed as cousins of Thomas Howard. They were the grandsons of
Austin Ford (1790-1841), who was born in Fauquier Co., Virginia and
Jane Allison (b. 1817 or 1818). Their children were:

James Thomas Ford (born 1820);

319 Love, *The Rise and Fall of Jesse James*, 366-367
320 Turner, *The Secrets of Jesse James*, 50

John W. Ford;

Lucella Ford;

Charles Ford (born 1828);

Elizabeth Ford;

Mary Jane Ford;

William H. Ford;

Arthur F. Ford (d. 1885);

Robert A. Ford (born March 13, 1840)[321]

In 1840, Austin Ford took his family from Virginia to Clark Co., Missouri, and it was there he managed a large farm for a man by the name of Lee. In July 1841, Ford was killed by a blow to the head from Lee. John Wesley Ford then became the head of the household.

Charles and Robert Ford were the sons of James Thomas Ford and Mary Ann Bruin. According to Steele:

James moved to Missouri along with his father, Austin, and their family. James T. Ford returned to Virginia shortly after his father died and there became a tenant farmer for John A. Washington at Mt. Vernon. In 1843, James T. and his wife returned to Clark County, Missouri where the following children were born:

Georgia Ford (b. 1844)

John T. Ford (b. 1846)

Elias Capline Ford

Martha and Amanda Ford (twins—born 1855)

Charles Wilson Ford (born July 9, 1857)

Wilber Ford (b. 1860)

Robert Newton Ford (b. Jan. 31, 1862)[322]

---

321 Steele, *The Family History*, 95-96.
322 Steele, *The Family History*, 98-99.

The family returned to Mt. Vernon shortly after the birth of Robert Newton Ford. And then they again moved back to Missouri, settling this time in Clay County. James Thomas Ford was a well-known student of the Bible, and he pastored a church near their home.

The Ford brothers joined Jesse James at the end of Jesse's outlaw career. Charles was the first to join, and he brought his brother, Bob, into the gang. Turner notes that Zerelda Samuel did not trust Bob, and she warned Jesse about him.:

> *Jesse's mother scrutinized the Ford brothers carefully. Charlie was a weakling but put up a good front. Both boys were handsome, especially young Bob, who had a clean-cut look. Mrs. Samuel didn't trust Bob, however, and said as much to her son.*
>
> *In the evening the three rode out. Mrs. Samuel's brow was wrinkled with worry.*
>
> *"Mother, if I never see you here again I'll see you in Heaven," Jesse said as he rode away."[323]*

– an almost prophetic statement as though Jesse James knew what would happen. Settle provides further detail:

> *Charles and Robert Ford, newly recruited, youthful members of the band, had been staying with Jesse and his family for several days. Charles had helped rob the Chicago and Alton train in September, 1881, but Bob had not yet participated in a robbery; plans were being made for the robbery of a bank in Platte City [Missouri] on April 4. Bob, however, had been in contact with Crittenden, Timberlake and Craig for several weeks and through his older brother had gained Jesse's confidence. After breakfast on the morning of Monday, April 3, the three men went into the living room. Jesse removed his guns, laid them on a bed, and stepped up on a chair to straighten and dust a picture. Catching him thus off guard, Bob quickly drew his pistol and shot his host in the back of the head. Jesse fell lifeless to the floor.*
>
> *Zee rushed into the room and, on seeing her husband lying dead, gave way to unrestrained grief and anger. As quickly as they*

---

323 Turner, *The Secrets of Jesse James*, 51-52.

*could escape the house, the Ford brothers telegraphed Governor
Crittenden, Timberlake and Craig that they had killed their man
and gave themselves up to the St. Joseph authorities. When towns-
people appeared at the house, Zee first maintained that the dead
man was 'Thomas Howard,' but she soon broke down and revealed
that he was indeed Jesse James. St. Joseph forgot the heated city
election of the day, and the curious swarmed to the little house to
view the murdered outlaw's body.*[324]

Newspapers worldwide spread the story. *The Carthage Banner,*
Carthage, Missouri April 6, 1882 story follows:

Jesse James Killed

Bob Ford is Said to be the Slayer of the Desperado

Talk of Lynching Little[Liddil] and Bugler

*Independence, Mo: April 3—Police Commissioner Craig has just
received authentic information that Jesse James was killed near
St. Joseph, at 12 o'clock today. No particulars.*

Murdered by his Pal

*Independence, Mo, April 3—From all that can be learned Jesse
James was murdered by Rob. Ford, one of his gang, with whom
the authorities had entered into an arrangement, through Little,
to do the work. The town is wild with excitement. There is a probability that Bugler, now on trial, will be lynched. If Little is found
he will be lynched to a certainty.*

Jesse's Mother Identifies the body

*St. Joseph, Mo., April 4—At the Coroner's inquest Mrs. Samuels,
mother of Jesse James, identified that it was her son Jesse.
Considerable excitement was created by her denunciation of the
treachery of Dick Little.*[325]

[In a separate article, same edition]

---

324 Settle, *Jesse James was his Name,* 117.
325 Jesse James Killed, *The Carthage Banner,* Carthage, MO, Thursday,
April 6, 1882.

Jesse James

The man who has been the store talk and has so long been a terror to good peace loving citizens of the Southwest, is reported to have been shot yesterday near St. Joe. If so, it will be a welcome relief to law abiding citizens and the traveling public, whose lives have so often been jeopardized under the leadership of this desperado.[326]

While Jesse James was dead, the James legend was just beginning. Some people refused to believe that Jesse James had been killed. Some claimed to have seen him; some claimed to be him; others claimed to be actual descendants of the *real* Jesse James. Settle describes some of these situations:

Scarcely a year had passed, however, before a Clay County farmer was reported to have seen Jesse James.

The identification of the man who was shot in the James's front room was positive enough to leave little doubt that the body buried in Mrs. Samuel's yard was Jesse James's. But numerous claimants have said since, that they were Jesse. Nor are the pretenders limited to impersonation of Jesse. Even while Frank James was living, a berry picker in Washington "revealed" that he was Frank James. Then there was the man who lived as Joe Vaughan in Wayton County, Arkansas. Vaughan died on February 26, 1925, and in the fall of 1926, Sarah E. Snow, who said she was a daughter of Frank James, alias Joe Vaughan, published what was allegedly a manuscript left by her father, telling the story of his life and setting forth his claims to being Frank James. Burton Rascoe called the book "maudlin, illiterate, vague, confused, pathetic." It is all of that.[327]

Jesse James had one funeral and two burials—three if you count the recent exhumation in 1995 and subsequent reburial. Love describes the scene of the first burial:

When the cortege reached the Samuel farmhouse a considerable number of country folk had gathered there. All were quiet and re-

326 Jesse James, *The Carthage Banner*, Carthage, MO, Thursday, April 6, 1882.
327 Settle, *Jesse James Was His Name*, 169

spectful, as befitted the solemn occasion. Jesse James was buried in a corner of the yard, on the premises where he was born, where his mother could look from her windows upon the mound at the foot of a big coffee-bean tree. Mrs. Samuel planted flowers upon the grave, and for twenty years she tended them with affectionate care. A tall white marble monument was erected there, on which the mother had this inscription carved:

In Loving Remembrance of My Beloved Son

JESSE W. JAMES

Died April 3, 1882

Aged 34 Years, 6 Months, 28 Days

Murdered by a Traitor and Coward Whose

Name is Not Worthy to Appear Here.

The writer, Robertus Love attended the second burial on June 29, 1902 and describes the proceedings:

"And they laid Jesse James in his grave," for the second and, doubtless, the last time.

Not as a bandit, but as a brother in arms, as a soldier, as a guerilla rough rider of the border warfare, as a fighter in the lost cause, a squad of Quantrill's men who rode and shot with the boy Jesse James in the last two years of the Civil War, bore his bones this Sunday afternoon to his new grave between those of his wife and his little half-brother.

"Not a sound was heard, not a funeral note," not a word was spoken at the grave during the twenty minutes required for carrying the coffin from the hearse, lowering it into the earth, shoveling in the clay and rounding off the mound.

Yes, there was one sound—just for a moment or two—the sobbing of Jesse's mother.

It was a burial in silence. A preacher, in white necktie, stood in the crowd, but merely as a spectator. There was no religious ceremony, either at the farmhouse or at the cemetery.

Frank James, who had stood uncovered at the head of the grave beside his aged mother, Mrs. Zerelda Samuel, and young Jesse James, his nephew, turned away as the last spadeful of sod was tossed upon the mound saying:

"Well, boys. That's all we can do."...

Disinterment of the remains this morning revealed the fact that somebody—either the great state of Missouri or an undertaker— had deceived the James family at the first burial twenty years ago. It was represented at that time that the coffin in which the body was shipped from St. Joseph was an enduring metallic casket, costing $500, and that the body had been embalmed. When the old coffin was lifted out of the grave it fell apart, and there was nothing inside but the skeleton in clothing.

This was indeed a dreary day for a disinterment and reburial. From early morning until noon the rain poured...

As the coffin bottom was being turned around above the ground, the skull again fell off and dropped to the bottom of the grave. Zip Pollock jumped down and picked it up, placing it once more upon the old coffin bottom. At this juncture John Samuel picked up the skull and began to turn it over in his hands, closely examining it.

"What are you looking for, John?" asked old Zach Laffoon.

"Bob Ford's bullet hole," replied the bandit's half-brother; "and here it is."

There it was, a little more than an inch behind the left ear, and as large as a quarter. A small piece of the skull above it had broken in; otherwise the hole would have been round...

But there are said to be persons in Clay County who still refuse to believe that the real Jesse James is dead. To such doubters as these a postal card received this morning by the city marshal of Kearney—the town has 700 people and a city marshal—furnished new proof, but to the rest it is a ghastly joke. It was mailed in a Kansas town and signed "Original Jesse James." The writer said:

"I will not be buried in Carny next Sunday. I am not dead. I was not shot by Bobie Ford. Tom Howard was shot by Bobie Ford, but I wasn't there, so you can't bury me."[328]

Unfortunately, this type of claim still exists!

***

After learning of his brother's death, Frank James surrendered. The following is Turner's description:

On October 5, 1882, Governor Crittendon received the noted newspaperman, Major John N. Edwards, in his office at Jefferson City. It was in honor of Edwards that Jesse James had named is son Jesse Edwards. With Edwards was a tall, silent man known as B. F. Winfrey. After being introduced to a number of state officials, Edwards said, "Governor, allow me to introduce an old friend of mine, Frank James."

The governor and the outlaw shook hands. Then Frank handed over his revolver, saying, "I want to hand over to you something no man except myself has touched in twenty-one years. I've taken the cartridges out so you can handle it safely." The governor stared at the weapon and at an old leather belt Frank disclosed when he opened his coat. Its buckle bore the U.S. Army insignia. The truth began to penetrate Crittendon's mind.

"Yes, that's a Union belt," Frank said. "I got it off a dead Federal soldier in Centralia...We had killed him." Crittendon, half dazed, had Frank held overnight while a decision was pondered as to what charges were to be made. He could find only one charge outstanding: robbery and murder at Independence. The ensuing trial was a sensation with an all-star cast, including Dick Liddil and the Ford brothers...

The jury found the "prince of robbers" Not Guilty. An Alabama Jury decided likewise in the matter of the Muscle Shoals robbery of a United States paymaster. Another trial was pending at

---

328 Love, *The Rise and Fall of Jesse James*, 376

Boonville, Missouri, regarding the robbery of the Otterville train.
The case never came to trial and was dropped officially in 1885.
No more indictments were brought and Frank had nothing to fear
but poverty—lawyers and other expenses had wiped him out.[329]

Zerelda James, Jesse James' wife, died November 30, 1900 at age
55. Two years later, Reuben Samuel decided that Jesse's remains
should be removed to the family plot in the Mount Olivet Cemetery
at Kearney, Missouri. Dr. Samuel's health steadily declined, and he
eventually became a ward of the Missouri State Hospital, St. Joseph,
where he died March 1, 1908.

Jesse James' children, Jesse Edwards James and Mary James lived full
lives. According to Steele:

> Jesse Edwards was raised by his mother in Kansas City after his
> father's assassination. He attended law school and practiced there.
> He later moved to los Angeles, California. He married Stella
> McGowan on January 24, 1900 in Kansas City, Missouri, and they
> had the following children:
>
> Lucille Martha James (b. Dec. 21, 1900; m. Frank Lewis, Sept. 1,
> 1931; d. June 17, 1988)
>
> Josephine Francis James (b. April 20, 1902; m. Ronald Ross, Sept.
> 2, 1925; d. March 31, 1964)
>
> Jessie Estelle James (b. Aug. 27, 1906; m. Mervyn Baumel, May
> 23, 1931; d. Feb. 2, 1987)
>
> Ethel Rose James (b. July 10, 1908; m. Calvin T. Owens, Oct. 16,
> 1937)[330]

Steele also notes: "James R. Ross, son of Josephine and Ronald Ross
and grandson of Jesse Edwards James, presently serves as the superior
court judge in Orange County, California."[331]

Mary Susan James was only three years old when her father was
killed. She was born in Nashville, Tennessee on June 17, 1879. She

---

329 Turner, *The Secrets of Jesse James*, 63-64.
330 Steele, *The Family History,* 56.
331 Steele, *The Family History*, 57.

was raised by her mother in Kansas City and married Henry Lafayette Barr on March 6, 1901. The Barrs had the following children:

Lawrence H. Barr (b. Oct. 16, 1902; m. Thelma Duncan; d. Feb. 25, 1984

Forster Ray Barr (b. Oct. 11, 1904; m. Gertie Essary; d. June 23, 1977)

Chester A. Barr (b. May 27, 1907; m. Beatrice Holloway (divorced); d. March 22, 1984)

Henrietta Barr (b. March 14, 1913; d. October 10, 1913)[332]

Steele provides an interesting story about the Barrs:

Lawrence Barr attended his last James family reunion on the James Farm in 1983. This writer had occasion to meet Mr. Barr at that reunion and to discuss this James family project with him. He admitted that until his later years he had always been somewhat ashamed of being the grandson of the outlaw Jesse James and kept what family history he knew to himself. He realized late in life, however, that the folk hero status of Jesse James made preserving the James family history important, and before his death in 1984 he contributed greatly to the family history recorded here. Since his death, his wife, Thelma Barr, has continued to serve as an honorary member of the Friends of the James Farm Board of Directors and has greatly assisted in the preparation of this history.[333]

Frank and Ann James moved to a farm near Fletcher, Oklahoma. Mrs. Samuel went to visit them but on her return trip home, she died February 10, 1911. She was buried in the family plot next to Jesse, Dr. Samuel and Little Archie. After her death, Frank James removed to the farm in Kearney, where he spent his final days. He died February 18, 1915 and his wife died at the age of 91 on July 6, 1944. He and his wife are buried in the Hill Park Cemetery, Independence, Missouri. Frank had his body cremated, preventing anyone from stealing it. He was always afraid that someone would attempt to steal Jesse's body.

332 Steele, *The Family History*, 58.
333 Steele, *The Family History*, 59.

The Ford brothers did not reign long after taking credit for killing Jesse James. According to Steele:

> *Charles Ford became distraught over the tremendous public ridicule he and his brother received over shooting the famous, unarmed outlaw Jesse James in the back of the head. Charles committed suicide on May 6, 1884, two years after their cowardly deed.*
>
> *Bob Ford, apparently with a good portion of reward money, journeyed to Creede, Colorado where he established a saloon and reveled in the notoriety he had earned as the man who killed Jesse James. A man named O'Kelley, apparently a fan of Jesse James, became inebriated and walked into Ford's saloon and shot and killed him on June 8, 1892. Buried in Colorado, Ford's body was exhumed a few years later by his family and returned to Missouri.*[334]

Bob Ford's sojourn into Colorado took him first to Las Vegas, New Mexico with Dick Liddil. After splitting with Liddil, he moved next, to Walsenburg, Colorado, where he opened a saloon. Ford then closed his Walsenburg saloon and went to Creede, where he set up another saloon. His first saloon burned down in Creede, so he replaced it with a tent, and he was planning to rebuild when he was shot and killed by Ed O'Kelley. O'Kelley then became the man who killed the man who killed Jesse James.

Both Ford brothers are buried in the Richmond Cemetery, Richmond, Missouri. Bloody Bill Anderson is also buried in Richmond, but in the Pioneer Cemetery.

And the legend of Jesse James continues.

---

334 Steele, *The Family History*, 101.

Part 4 Photo Section

*Monument at 1318 Lafayette Street, St. Joseph, Missouri
where the Jesse James house originally stood.*

Portrait of Jesse James painted by George Warfel. This painting was based picture that was taken shortly before Jesse James was killed. Jesse James House Museum, St. Joseph, Missouri, March 2006

Parlor of the Jesse James house. Bob Ford sat on a chair beside the organ when he killed Jesse James. Jesse James House Museum, St. Joseph, Missouri, March 2006.

Bullet hole in the wall of the Jesse James house. Souvenir hunters have gouged out that hole over the years in hopes of finding the bullet. The bullet did not leave the skull. Jesse James House Museum, St. Joseph, Missouri March 2006.

*Wall display on the life of Jesse James, Jesse James
House Museum, St. Joseph, Missouri March 2006.*

Jesse Woodson James and Zerelda Mimms James Gravesite,
Mt. Olivet Cemetery, Kearney, Missouri (2008).

Frank James at the farm in Kearney, Missouri, ca. 1911-1915

Part 5: Aftermath: Life in Adair

*The Levi Clay House, Adair, Iowa, Late 1880s/very early
1890s. Levi and Mary Clay are seated on the porch. The elderly gentleman is William Stillians, Mary Clay's father. Adelia
Viola Clay (my grandmother) is standing on the porch beside
him. Clyde Clay and Ida Clay are standing on the far side.*

Chapter 22: The Levi Clay Family, Adair, Iowa

After the dust finally settled, the town of Adair fell into a normal routine. Two disastrous fires in the late 1800s threatened the town more so than the James Gang had ever threatened it. The first fire occurred in 1884, while the second fire erupted ten years later. According to *The Adair News*:

> *The first fire was that of Friday night, April 18, 1884, which started in the Myers, Schnier & Co, clothing store. It spread rapidly to the Kelsey & Bodley hardware store, John Jackson Implement, store, William Ingraham restaurant, Charles Fisher saloon, R. S. Pinkerton livery stable, George Ish implement building and the E. Cate dry goods store. The residence of William Ingraham also was destroyed.*
>
> *The fire finally was checked by tearing the Henkle & Swart furniture store frame building.*
>
> *It was believed an arsonist started the fire. A number of citizens had passed the clothing store about 15 minutes before the fire started on their way home from a council and trustees meeting, and there was no sign of fire at that time. If it had not be raining at the time, the fire might have spread to additional business buildings.*[335]

The fire of 1884 was extinguished fairly quickly. But the fire of 1894 was much larger.

> *The really big fire which nearly destroyed the entire Adair business section started about midnight Monday, Aug. 6, 1894. As it was*

335 *The Adair News Special Edition*, Summer 1987.

only two brick business buildings were saved. Extreme drought had caused nearly all towns in the state to run short of water.

The fire started in an old building just south of the Smith and McKinney livery barn, and spread to the Thos. Flynn bakery and restaurant, Dr. Wishard drug store, C. H. Camper harness shop, E. Owen hardware store, Dan Hearn barber shop, Schwenneker & Bochart meat market, Raffensperger & Richardson paint shop, Mrs. Dodge's millinery store, Mrs. Valentine's millinery and dressmaking rooms, McManus & McEvoy general store and J. Myers & Co. clothing store.

Also destroyed were the J. D. Carroll restaurant, an unoccupied building east of it, Burger, Barnett & Morse barber shop, McClintock drug store, Scheeler meat market and ice house, Bank of Adair building, McClain & Thielen implement store, Porter & Son furniture store, Archer & Patten general store, W. H. Burr hardware store, E. G. Smith shoe shop, Post office building, the Reynolds House, as well as a number of residences and barns.

A number of burned-out business men hustled around and found temporary quarters in other buildings with other firms. Among them was the Burger, Burnett & Morse barber shop in The News Office.[336]

The first post office was established in Adair the spring of 1874, when John E. Moran was commissioned postmaster.[337] He held that position until October 21, 1881. His post office was located inside his store. After his resignation, Harvey Smith replaced him and was still in that position long after the 1894 fire.

The first school in Adair was located in the upper story of the drug store of D.W. Moss, and that was during the winter of 1873-74. According to the Adair County History:

The teacher, who held it for three months, was Mrs. H. P. Starr, who had about eighteen scholars. The next term was at the schoolhouse, that was built where it now stands, in the summer of 1875.

---

336 *The Adair News Special Edition*, Summer 1987.
337 *History of Adair and Guthrie Counties*, 1009

Mrs. Starr taught this school also, as she did the summer of 1876, the latter year of which she had sixty-six pupils enrolled. The next teachers were L. M. Hawes and his daughter, who have taught most of the time ever since up to the last term. The present corps of educators are Mr. Cowden and Miss Dolan. The first officer in this district was John Chestnut, Sr., director and treasurer.[338]

Levi Clay continued working for the railroad until 1876. He purchased a dray line from J. T. Ewing and operated that line for many years. By 1900, he became a blacksmith, and his shop is today the Adair Machine Shop. He was content to remain in Adair since life was good to him there, but not without a few unexpected experiences.

His first experience concerned his oldest child. When Adelia Viola Clay was approximately three years old (ca. 1872 or 1873), she was playing in a nearby field when she was bitten by a rattlesnake. Levi Clay was close by at the time, and was able to rescue her. The family then took her to the doctor, and she was fine. But she didn't play in weed-covered fields after that![339]

The second experience concerned the sudden death of Levi and Mary Clay's son, William Levi Woodward Clay. William was born in Adair, Iowa, May 29, 1884 and he died October 6, 1884. The cause of death is unknown, but there were so many infant deaths at that period of time. The Clays did experience the death of another child earlier prior to living in Adair. Their second child, Catherine Louisa Clay was born May 6, 1872 and she died April 4, 1874. She is buried at Bear Grove Tp., near North Branch, Iowa. William Levi Woodward Clay is buried with his parents in the Sunny Hill Cemetery.

The third experience was probably the most devastating and concerned Levi and Mary Clay's daughter-in-law Ethyl Crowell Clay.

Ethyl Crowell married Clyde Emanuel Clay (Levi and Mary's only surviving son) on December 25, 1906, and the young couple lived in Adair. They had two small children, Murray and Enolia. Ethyl died in a terrible fire August 22, 1911. The following is an account from *The Adair News:*

---

338 *History of Adair and Guthrie Counties,* 1009
339 Gordon Loren Inman, Personal Memories, 1953-1955.

Adair Lady's Awful Burns Prove Fatal

Mrs. Clyde Clay Victim of Terrible Accident Last Tuesday

Entire Body Badly Burned

Clothes Catch fire From Explosion of Gasoline Stove—Lived Fourteen Hours After the Accident Occurred

As the result of a gasoline explosion in the kitchen of her home Mrs. Clyde E. Clay sustained such severe burns that she died that evening at 10:45 o'clock. She was unconscious after 6:30 P.M. Her clothing was literally burned from her body, only the hands remaining in place. Her hands were so terribly burned that the finger nails dropped off when the physician attempted to dress the wounds. Most of her body from below the knees to her chin was charred and blistered in a frightful manner. Her face was not burned, and her hair only singed somewhat. At no time during the day did Mrs. Clay think she would die. About 6:30 she passed into an unconscious condition, from which she never awoke.

Cause Not Known

The cause of this accident, the most terrible that has ever occurred in Adair, is not definitely known. Mrs. Clay was working about a gasoline stove, evidently in the act of lighting it. Her little daughter was in the kitchen at the time and was slightly burned, but her mother succeeded in putting out the flames on the child's clothes. Mrs. Clay had some crabapples that she was preparing to can or preserve, but these had not been heated. It is evident that a small explosion of gasoline set her clothes afire, but how this should have happened cannot be ascertained. After putting forth her best efforts to extinguish the flames she ran into the front yard screaming. City Marshal Charles Ary happened to be working in the street a few feet away and Isaac Largent was passing through the alley in the rear and these two gentlemen quickly wrapped a quilt that was laying on the grass around the flaming figure. She was then carried into the house and a physician arrived in a few moments.

No Hope of Recovery

The extent and nature of her burns made it apparent at once that there was no chance for the unfortunate lady to live more than a few hours, during which she suffered untold agony. She was given every care that a physician and professional nurse could render. She suffered most immediately after the accident occurred. Later the pain was deadened by the use of drugs.

Mrs. Clay before her marriage was Miss Ethel B. Crowell. She was 22 years, 2 months and 2 days old. She was married to Mr. Clay December 25, 1906 and is the mother of two children, a son and a daughter.

Funeral services were held from the Methodist Episcopal church yesterday afternoon, conducted by the pastor, the Rev. Oscar F. Shaw. A more extended review of the left of the deceased will be published in The News next week.[340]

How ironic that an explosion would impact the lives of both the Clay and James families! The explosion impacting the Clay family was an accident, while the explosion impacting the James family was intentional with unintended consequences.

After his wife's death, Clyde Clay remained in Adair, Iowa where in 1915, he married his second wife, Myma R. Grim. Myma may have been a widow because she had a young child by the name of Lois J. Grim, born in 1906. Clyde and Ethyl's children were Walter Murray Clay (1908-1962) and Enolia Hazel Clay (b. 1910). From 1918 through 1920, the Clyde Clays lived in Ames, Story Co., Iowa, and in 1930, the family moved to Reno, Washoe, Nevada. Clyde then relocated to Los Angeles, California, where he became a fireman. His first wife, Ethyl, is buried in the Sunny Hill Cemetery in Adair, Iowa with the Clay family beside her sister-in-law Jennie (Mary Jane) Clay. Clyde died in Los Angeles, California on June 13, 1955.

Levi Clay and his family were members of the Methodist Church in Adair. His daughter, Adelia Viola, (my grandmother) moved to Marble Rock, Floyd Co., Iowa prior to her marriage to help one of her Clay cousins manage her household. The Floyd County Clays were Baptists, so Viola began attending the Baptist Church with them. It

340 Old Clipping from *The Adair News*, ca. August 22, 1911.

was there she met Loren Waiste Inman, with whom she had slept as an infant. Levi and Mary Clay and their infant daughter, lived on the upper floor of the Alonzo and Carrie Inman farmhouse in Floyd County, and the two families put the two babies together in the same crib. According to family papers, there was no further contact between the Clay and Inman families after the Levi Clay family left Marble Rock.

Adelia Viola Clay and Loren Waiste Inman were married in Marble Rock, Iowa April 4, 1893. And like Zerelda Cole James, she became a Baptist minister's wife. The Inmans had the following children:

Harold Clay Inman (b. Feb. 28, 1894, Marble Rock, Iowa; m. (1) Vera Rood, Nov. 14, 1922; (2) Frances Merle Bixby; d. March 2, 1958, Des Moines, Iowa:

Lelah Frances Inman, b. Feb. 17, 1932, Fort Des Moines, Iowa; m (1) Paul Bingham; (2) Ray Richards Sept. 10, 1955:

Judi Rae Richards (b. March 28, 1956)

Robert Dean Richards (b. Jan. 16, 1959)

Janet Lynn Richards (b. Nov. 6, 1960)

Joice Ellen Richards (b. June 30, 1965)

Carol Joyce Inman, b. Jan 15, 1934, Shellsburg, Iowa; m. Norman Gene Loll-- July 10, 1955. [No children]

Jack Loren Bixby Inman,(b. Aug. 13, 1935, Des Moines, Iowa; m. (1) Beverly Jean Caswell, Nov. 13, 1960; (2) Sandra Ball, Oct. 13, 1973:

Jeffrey Lee Inman (b. Oct. 1, 1961, Des Moines, Iowa)

Michael Loren Inman (b. May 7, 1963, Des Moines, Iowa)

Roxanne Inman (b. July 2, 1965, Des Moines, Iowa)

Shirley Ann Inman (b. July 8, 1937 (deceased); m. Donald Foreman April 26, 1957:

Dale Curtis Foreman (b. July 6, 1958, Des Moines, Iowa)

Gregory Scott Foreman (b. Dec. 31 1959),

Tammy Jo Foreman (b. Nov. 9, 1961, Des Moines, Iowa)

Martha Juanita Inman (b. Nov. 12, 1942, Des Moines, Iowa; m. Ralph E. Marasco, Sept. 7, 1964, Des Moines, Iowa:

Ralph Edward Marasco (b. Jan 6, 1966)

Melissa Jo Marasco (b. Sept. 14, 1967, Des Moines, Iowa)

Darren Joseph Marasco (b. Sept. 12, 1972, Long Beach, California)

Jennifer Lynn Marasco (b. Aug. 7, 1974, Des Moines, Iowa)

Arthur Kirk Inman,(b. April 9, 1944, Des Moines, Iowa)

Forrest Glenn Inman (b. Oct. 10, 1895, Marble Rock, Iowa; m. Mabel Ayers Templeton Jan. 15, 1901; d. Sept. 24, 1965, Kenmore, NY:

Charles Gordon Inman (b. 12 April 1929, Bronx, New York; m. Joan Elizabeth Counsell, Aug. 29, 1954, New Bedford, Massachusetts:

Elizabeth Anne Inman (b. July 29, 1956, Buffalo, NY)

Gretchen Christine Inman (b. July 5, 1958, Glens Falls, NY)

Jennifer Faith Inman (b. Nov. 13, 1963, Glens Falls, NY)

Lloyd Burr Inman (d. March 10, 1901, aged 19 mos.)

Lelah Inman (b. Jan 16, 1902, Coggon, Iowa; m. Arthur Eugene Peterson Dec. 24, 1936; d. 1982. (No children)

Gordon Loren Inman (b. June 11, 1908, Marble Rock, Iowa; m. Elva Gail Spence May 22, 1938, Marion, Iowa; d. May 7, 1974, Iowa City, Iowa:

Barbara Ann Inman (b. May 20, 1943, Cedar Rapids, Iowa; m. Howard Lee Beall April 25, 1964, Cedar Rapids, Iowa:

Brian Scott Beall (b. Aug. 6, 1968, Louisville, Kentucky; m. Mary LuAndra Gann March 9, 1991, Broomfield, CO). [LuAn's son, Brandon Dean Bueche was born during her first marriage to Brant Bueche January 6, 1983. Brandon's children: (1) by Joy Gionet—Trinity Rose Bueche, b. November 16, 2003, Lakewood, Colorado; (2) m. Jessica Rowe, Broomfield, Colorado—Brooke LuAndra Bueche, b. June 13, 2007, Louisville, Colorado, and Delaney Nicole Bueche, b. October 21, 2009. Lafayette, Colorado].

Deborah Lee Beall (b. Jan. 12, 1971, Cedar Rapids, Iowa; m. Dee Edward Wall, Jr., Aug. 22, 1992, Broomfield, CO)

Joshua Brian Wall (b. March 9, 1993, Denver, CO)

Jason Edward Wall (b. August 17, 1995, Denver, CO)

Amanda Nicole Wall (b. September 8, 1998, Denver, CO).

Beverly Jeanne Inman (b. June 17, 1944, Cedar Rapids, Iowa; d. August 25, 2007, Kalona, Washington, Iowa).[341]

Below is a summary of the Levi Clay family members and their activities:_____

341 Charles Gordon Inman, *Daniel Inman of Connecticut, Ontario, N.Y., and Sugar Grove, Ill. And His Descendants, ca. 1776-ca. 1976, with Ancestral Notes to the Early Seventeenth Century*, 1978,[with updated material for the Gordon Loren Inman family provided by Barbara Inman Beall.]

Adelia Viola (Viola)--removed to Floyd Co., Iowa, where she married Loren Waiste Inman and raised her family;

Catherine Louise—died at the age of 2 in 1874 and is buried near North Branch, Iowa;

Mary Jane (Jennie)--married Walter McCray/McRay June 30, 1901 and may have had one son (name unknown). They lived on a farm near Rockford, Floyd Co., Iowa, where they appear on the 1905 Census Record. Jennie's brother, Clyde Clay, was living with them at the time. This was the year before Clyde's marriage to Ethyl Crowell. They may have had one son. I have a photograph of the last time Levi Clay visited the McRays. Levi appears in the photo with Jennie, her husband, a boy and a dog. She died January 22, 1917 and is buried with the Clays in Sunny Hill Cemetery, Adair;

Frances Elizabeth Eldora (Elizabeth)—married Harry A. Robinson January 1, 1896 at Adair. They had one daughter named Elizabeth, who appears with them on the 1910 Des Moines, Polk Co., Iowa census. By 1915, they may have been living in Warren, Union Co., Iowa. Harry Robinson died by 1920. Elizabeth married David Ricker in May 1920 in Omaha, Nebraska. Elizabeth died in Boring, Clackamas, Oregon October 12, 1948.

Ida Artha Josephine (Ida)—married Newt Parkinson in Adair June 7, 1916. [No children]

Lydia Lowella Lorena (Lula)—married (1) John W. Baker December 25, 1901—John died in Oregon May 8, 1938; and (2) Mayberry Asby Splawn January 24, 1939. Berry Splawn was born May 26, 1880 in the Chickasaw Nation, Oklahoma Territory, and he died July 24, 1951 in Portland, Oregon. Berry Splawn's first wife was Nettie (surname unknown). His two children were by the first wife: Lillian Viola (b. 1903) and Edith L (b. 1906). Nettie died January 31, 1938. Lula died April 4, 1968, and is buried at Gresham, Oregon. It is interesting to note that Berry Splawn's family came from Ray and Daviess Counties, Missouri (part of Little Dixie). His father John William Splawn was born in 1853 in Nodaway, Missouri. Since the family originated in South Carolina,

I have an idea they supported the South during the Civil War. His father married Mary Cam Jaye in Denton, Texas in 1875, indicating that the Splawns left Missouri during the Civil War. Chances are Order No. 11 drove them from out of the state—an order that also impacted the James family.[342]

William Levi Woodward Clay—died as an infant.

Clyde Emanual—married (1) Ethyl Crowell in 1906, Adair, Iowa. The Clays had two children, Murray and Enolia; (2) Myma R. Grim in 1915. Clyde Clay eventually relocated to Los Angeles, CA, where he died June 13, 1955.

Agnes Suffiah Lucile Clay married Ray B. Wilkinson on March 11,1910. They lived for a while in Walnut, Polk Co., Iowa. By 1930, the Wilkinsons lived in Cottrell, Clackamas, Oregon. Ray Wilkinson died April 11, 1970 in Los Angeles, California. Lucille died March 26, 1976. The Wilkinsons had two sons: Dwight J. and Birchard C.

Ida Artha Josephine Clay is the only one who remained in Adair. Her husband, Newt Parkinson, took over Levi Clay's blacksmith shop and eventually turned it into a machine shop.

While visiting Adair in May 2002, I was given a sheet of paper about the old Adair Machine Shop. It is undated, but photographs that appear on the sheet are dated 1972 and 1996. A portion of that article follows:

Merle Moore of Adair has been in business in Adair at the Adair Machine Shop for 53 years. He started in the summer of 1944 and worked for Newt Parkinson, who owned the shop.

Merle purchased the shop from Mr. Parkinson October 11, 1954, along with Glenn Peterson. He learned the trade from Parkinson, who died Jan. 26, 1957. Merle bought out Glenn Peterson's interest in July, 1963. He has employed many different people through the years.

Merle's oldest son, Jim, began full-time at the Machine Shop after returning from the U.S. Air Force in November, 1971. His other

342 Yoakum-Jaye/Whitfield-Lancaster Family Trees, Ancestry.com, Provo Utah. Accessed June 23, 2010. Available: http://www.ancestry.com.

son, Mike, began full-time upon returning to Adair in June, 1984. The business was incorporated in January, 1986.[343]

Portions of the second page are missing, but enough information remains indicating that the shop underwent many changes from its days as a blacksmith shop to a modern machine shop. Because the machine shop is located at the end of the business district, it would have been built after the fire of 1894. Levi Clay went into business there as a blacksmith by 1900, although he appears to have continued his work as a drayman as well.

Levi Clay's wife, Mary Elizabeth Stillians Clay died September 11, 1915 in Adair, Iowa. Her death certificate indicates that she had a septic infection from her gall bladder, and palsy was listed as a contributory factor. Her occupation is listed as "wife of a drayman". She is listed as having been born in Pennsylvania and her parents (William Stillians and Catherine Lee) are listed as having been born in Virginia.[344]

Levi Clay lived for another two years. He died June 24, 1917 in Adair, Iowa. His death certificate indicates that he suffered from paralysis, so he may have been paralyzed by a stroke. His father's name is given as John Clay and his mother's name is given as Mary Hoy. His birthplace is listed as Akron, Ohio (spelled "Ackron"). The informant, whose name is listed as Viola Ingman (Viola Inman) did not know where the parents were born. He was 73 years, 6 months and 12 days old.[345]

The Clays are buried at Sunny Hill Cemetery with William Levi Woodrow Clay, Jennie Clay McCray, and Ethyl E. Clay. William Clay (1819-1894) and Elizabeth Fickles Clay (1824-1897) are buried not too far from Levi Clay and his family. William followed his brother to Adair and became a gardener there. William Stillians (1826-1907) and his granddaughter, Mary May Tift (1876-1893) are not too far from the William Clays. And in the newer section of the cemetery: Ida Clay Parkinson (1879-1957) and Newt Parkinson (1881-1957).

---

343 Adair Machine Shop, Source Unknown, Undated, 426-427
344 Mary Elizabeth Clay, State of Iowa Certificate of Death, County of Adair, City of Adair, September 11, 1915.
345 Levi Clay, State of Iowa Certificate of Death, County of Adair, City of Adair, June 24, 1917

***

As has already been noted, the Levi Clay family was the second family to move to Adair, and the first family to build a house there. That
house stood proudly on Cedar Street for many years, and for a long
time, the house was quite a mystery to me. I vainly hoped that the
original house was still standing, and I wanted to take a current picture of it. The Adair Historical Society sent me a picture of the house
that stands on the site today, but it didn't look anything at all like the
house in my old collection of pictures. And so for years, I ran around
that town, trying to match houses with the one in my old photographs.

Someone told us it was one of the houses across the street from the
Methodist Church. I took a series of pictures of that house before dis-
covering it looked nothing at all like the original Clay home. And I
was back at the drawing board again.

Next, there was a house on Cedar Street that somewhat resembled the
original Clay house. I took a series of pictures of that house and in the
long run, discovered that it wasn't a match either. Howard told me
that it was probably built in the 1920s or 1930s. I started my search
all over again.

I even compared my photo with the oldest house in Adair. In the 1980s,
the old section house was the local Jesse James Museum with a Rock
Island caboose sitting beside it. That house was built in 1868, but it
was the section house. The Clay house was built in 1873 or 1874 and
was a regular family home. Well, it was a try, I thought.

Finally, I stumbled upon four tiny snapshots in my grandmother's
photo collection and my question was answered.

In 1925, my grandmother, Adelia Viola Clay Inman, visited her old
hometown, and she took a series of pictures of the house. The first two
were labeled: "My Old Home." These pictures showed the old Levi
Clay house standing empty. The third one was labeled: "My Old Home
Being Torn Down." This picture showed the old Levi Clay house half
torn down. And the fourth one was ultimately labeled: "New Home
Where My Old Home Once Stood." And this photo showed a com-

pletely new house standing on the property (although that house has been greatly renovated over the years.)

"The original house was torn down!" I exclaimed. "The Historical Society was right! The house in the picture they sent me does stand on the old Levi Clay property!"

Laughing, I put the photos away. I would search no further. Then pausing a moment or two, I added: "Now, what am I going to do with all those extra pictures?"

Part 5 Photo Section

The Levi Clay House, Adair, Iowa, November 11, 1892. Mary Clay sent this photo to Adelia Viola Clay, who was living in Marble Rock by then. The young girls in the picture were leaving for school. Mary is standing on the upper deck. Levi is in the yard.

Levi Clay as a drayman. In 1876, Levi Clay bought a dray line and operated it for many years. This photo was probably taken late 1890s/early 1900s.

Adair Machine Shop, Adair, Iowa, May 2002. This building was originally the Levi Clay blacksmith shop, which he operated by 1900. His son-in-law, Newt Parkinson, took over the blacksmith shop and converted it into a modern machine shop.

*The Levi Clay family, ca. 1909 or 1910. Levi and Mary Clay
appear with four of their children: Clyde Clay and his wife
Ethyl Crowell appear with their small children: Murray and
Enolia; Lucille and Ida are in front; Adelia Viola Clay and my
father, Gordon Loren Inman are sitting beside Mary Clay.*

*Levi and Mary Clay Graves, Sunny Hill
Cemetery, Adair, Iowa, May 2002.*

Epilogue

Happy Face Tower, Adair, Iowa, May 2002.

Reflections, May 2002

Howard and I traveled to Adair, Iowa, where we spent a few days visiting the town some of my ancestors helped develop. We first went to Cedar Street, where I took pictures of the site of the Levi Clay house, and we toured the cemetery again. There I photographed all pertinent gravestones of family members. Since we were spending two days in the town, we also explored the Jesse James sites for the very first time. We went out to the location of the train wreck, took pictures of the monuments and tracks. We drove to Anita and Casey, where I obtained additional information and photographs. And then we asked about the location of the old Jesse James Museum and caboose that stood beside it. This was the house where the James Gang ate prior to robbing the train called "the oldest house in Adair."

In May 2002, the oldest house in Adair, built in 1868 as the section house, was still standing. The museum had closed. The caboose was gone. The windows were all boarded up with "No Trespassing" signs posted on the property. An elderly gentleman was cutting the grass when we pulled up across the street from it, so we decided to stop and talk with him.

"Is this the oldest house in Adair?" Howard asked him.

"Yes, it is," the man responded. "It's mine! I own it!"

"Where's the Jesse James Museum?"

"It's closed."

Howard paused for a moment, and then asked, "Well, what do you plan to do with it?"

The man began a long narrative. I don't know why the museum closed. I do remember visiting the museum in the 1980s, but at the time I was only beginning my interest in this project, so I only have vague memories of the experience. The essence of the man's narrative was that he was having a problem with the town of Adair over the disposition of the property.

"The Jesse James people down in Missouri called me and said they want it. They even offered to come up here and move the house back to the farm in Kearney. I was going to let them have the house, if they would move it," he told us.

But the town did not approve of that suggestion. And in the end, the man stated, "I'd sooner tear it down than let the town have its way."

I was able to take a photograph—perhaps the last photograph—of the oldest house in Adair. That was eight years ago, so unless they were able to work things out, I don't know whether the old house is still standing. My hunch is that it was probably disposed of and did not travel to Missouri.

***

In final analysis, what can be said about Levi Clay and Jesse James—two men with many similarities and vast differences?

Five years apart in age, they were both born into rural families with strong religious backgrounds. Levi Clay came from an Evangelical and Reformed background in the North. Jesse James was raised a Baptist in the South. Jesse James grew up in a household with slaves; Levi Clay did not. Both men lost their fathers at young ages. Levi Clay was six months old and Jesse James was two years old when their fathers died. Cholera appears to have claimed the lives of both men. Levi Clay's father was a farmer, and his father-in-law was a farmer and a minister. Jesse James' father was a farmer and a minister as well.

Both Levi Clay and Jesse James exhibited a certain amount of restlessness in their lives. Levi Clay moved to a number of locations in Illinois and Iowa before settling permanently in Adair, Iowa. Jesse

James appears to have been restless most of his life, settling down for short periods only to return to a life of crime. Concerning their fathers, Robert Sallee James has been described as a restless, driven man, who was full of passion. John Clay, father of Levi, has been called a worthy man who remained a lifelong Presbyterian. (He was probably Reformed Presbyterian since St. Peter's in Franklin Tp., Summit Co., Ohio was Reformed Presbyterian in the beginning.)

Both mothers were strong personalities who raised their children after their husbands' deaths. Mary Hoy Clay could not read or write while Zerelda Cole James was educated at a convent school. Mary Hoy Clay did not remarry, while Zerelda Cole James was married twice after the death of her first husband. Mary Hoy Clay appears to have been a gentle person who did not become easily agitated. Zerelda Cole James boldly and loudly expressed her opinions, and is reported to have had a temper.

Levi Clay and Jesse James both married cousins. Levi Clay married his first cousin once removed. Jesse James married his first cousin. Both men had children who died. Levi Clay's two-year-old daughter and infant son died, as did Jesse James' twin sons shortly after birth.

Regional violence impacted the lives of one of the men. Jesse James and his family members endured conflicts before, during and after the Civil War. Levi Clay did not live in a war-ravaged area. While members of his family may have fought in the war, his personal life was not torn apart by warfare.

Two men with similarities and yet with great differences—one who followed the straight and narrow, forgotten—the other who followed a life of crime, celebrated. And I began to wonder why.

Nestled along Highway 80 in Western Iowa, about an hour's drive west of Des Moines, the town of Adair, Iowa is advertised as the "Happiest Little Town in America." Its smiley face water tower is a favorite attraction. And there are people who visit the Jesse James site just for fun. Some of them lie down on the track as though tied to it. Some of them pose with the monuments displaying toy guns, with bandanas over their faces. Pictures of people doing this sometimes pop up on the internet. And Adair, Iowa does appear on a list of seven places to check out if you are ever in Iowa.[346] Those places include:

Grotto of the Redemption at West Bend

The American Gothic House at Eden

Buddy Holly Crash Site near Clear Lake

Canteen Lunch in the Alley at Ottumwa

The First Train Robbery in the West at Adair

Bank Robbed by Bonnie and Clyde in Stuart

Bank Robbed by John Dillinger in Mason City--

--in addition to the John Wayne birthplace in Winterset, The Bridges of Madison County, Bob Feller Museum in Van Meter and the house in Villisca, Iowa which was the site of the unsolved ax murders committed in 1912! That town is in the southwest portion of the state!

I was born and raised in Iowa and remember visiting the Grotto with my family while still a teenager. I also remember the Buddy Holly crash—and I knew about the Adair train robbery through my father's recollections. But I didn't know anything about the Stuart bank robbery by Bonnie and Clyde or the bank robbery in Mason City by John Dillinger. In addition to Adair's Jesse James Days celebration the third weekend every July, which includes a re-enactment of the train robbery, Mason City now holds a John Dillinger Days celebration called "Dillinger Meets Mason City" (including a robbery re-enactment), something they started doing in 2007.

What do we find so compelling about the dark side? Why do people like Jesse James capture and hold our attention long after they are gone? For that matter, why are some criminals celebrated while others are forgotten? The Reno Gang of Indiana committed the first train robbery, but we don't sing praises to them. There have been other outlaw

---

346 Stacy, in Neatorama Only, Travel & Places, Seven Places to Check out if you're ever in Iowa, March 26, 2008, Accessed September 17, 2010. Available online at http:// http://www.neatorama.com/2008/03/26/seven-places-to-check-out-if-youre-ever-in-iowa/.

gangs, but with the exception of a few, we don't remember who they were. And those we do remember, we don't attempt to attach ourselves to them and make them a part of us. So what is so special about Jesse James and why is he so appealing?

The answer lies in our celebration of the anti-hero and constant struggle we find within that person between good and evil. We like that tension because we find it in ourselves, and we connect with those who struggle with it. Jesse James was an anti-hero. He had a winning personality and the looks that helped him project his image. He also had a powerful newspaper man on his side, John Newman Edwards, who propelled Jesse's Robin Hood image in the press.

Jesse James came from a family of persuaders. His father was an evangelist, who could stir up the countryside. In the same manner and style, Jesse James stirred up the countryside in his own fashion. His mother was a passionate woman, who did not hold back her opinions from anyone. Jesse James had every bit of his mother's passion. His opinions were made clear with a gun. And he definitely had his mother's temper because it got the better of him from time to time. He was not a forgiving man and held a grudge. I think it is fair to say that he nursed his grudges.

On the other hand, he had a very devoted, caring side to him. He never rejected his family, although he did become angry with Frank on a few occasions. Though Frank was older and more subdued, Jesse was not one to sit still and ponder an issue. He wanted to plunge right in and take on the project immediately—something that led to his undoing. He was devoted to his wife and children. Some stories in St. Joseph describe a fun-loving Tom Howard cavorting about in the snow with neighborhood children.

Situations also enabled public opinion of the man. Civil War chaos in Missouri justified Jesse's guerilla activity. The inept Pinkerton bombing of the house in Kearney justified Jesse's continuation of his outlaw activities. People who were previously against him, were suddenly on his team. They could identify with the pain the Pinkertons had caused his family. The huge growth of the railroads and land grabbing behavior on part of the barons elevated the image of Jesse James. When you tie all of this together, you envision a nineteenth century Robin Hood righting the wrongs.

If the truth be known, Jesse James probably made a discovery. There were times when he tried to settle down and take up farming or ranching and put his past behind him, only to return to a life of crime again. I believe that he discovered he couldn't make an honest dollar fast enough. He wanted to go into ranching—but that took money—lots of money—something he didn't have and couldn't get unless he pulled another job. He was an impatient man who couldn't wait for something to happen. He had to make it happen—now!

I don't think he was a very good judge of character. That observation is apparent when considering the associations that he made. He first real hero in his life was Bloody Bill Anderson, the guerilla chief who showed no mercy. Bloody Bill was larger than life to him—a sharp contrast to the meek, quiet, gentle stepfather Jesse James was raised with. Bloody Bill was the first one to reach out and accept the angry, confused teenager and turn his anger into hate. And like Bloody Bill, Jesse James became a force to be reckoned with. However, the men who followed him were of varying degrees.

Most of the outlaws who rode with Jesse James in the beginning were guerilla fighters from the Civil War. They were seasoned fighters and were expert at getting what they wanted without getting caught or killed. Then they started disappearing and after the Northfield, Minnesota debacle, Jesse James was forced to start all over with a new breed of outlaw. This breed was quite "inferior" to the first. The men were younger and were not experienced on the battlefield. All they wanted was fame and a fast buck, so to speak. Some of them were so inept, they were killed or captured almost immediately. His acceptance of the Ford brothers proved fatal. In fact, his mother did not trust Bob Ford and warned him about it. But Jesse was not a good listener. Once he made up his mind, he was determined to follow through with it.

The James brothers had separate and distinct personalities, which was also true for Levi Clay. Astrological profiles show that Jesse James was a Virgo,[347] Frank James was a Capricorn,[348] and Levi Clay was a Sagittarian.[349] The Mystical Blaze website indicates people born under the signs of Virgo and Capricorn are compatible, which would explain one reason why the James brothers got along so well. On the other hand, Virgo and Sagittarius do not fare so well!

Virgo personalities are described as:

...a complex mix of intelligence, common sense, attention to detail, and commitment. This is a down-to-earth sign with a strong sense of responsibility, especially with regard to family and close friends. Although they are described as orderly and neat in most personality profiles, the modern day Virgo may not always stand out from the crowd in the neatness department. However, even if the Virgo's house or office is not always in perfect order, you can be sure that they still know where to instantly find whatever they need, despite it being hidden in a pile somewhere. The real stand-out feature of the Virgo personality is their commitment to excellence in everything they do. This is a person who once committed to a given task, will complete it to the very best of his ability. If something goes wrong, and the task is incomplete or not perfectly done, it will be on Virgo's mind for some time to come. Virgos can be quite critical of perceived flaws in others, but do not take kindly to criticism themselves. They are very aware of body and health, and will take a dim view of comments related to the physical, such as weight gain or acne, of which they are already painfully aware. If life becomes too complicated or their already fragile ego is damaged, Virgo may become depressed to the point of immobilization at home, but will probably still func-

347 Mystical Blaze, Personality Profile-Virgo, August 23-September 22. Accessed September 17, 2010. Available at http://www.mysticalblaze. com/AstrologyVirgo.htm

348 Mystical Blaze, Personality Profile-Capricorn, December 23-January 21, Accessed September 17, 2010. Available at http://www.mysticalblaze. com/AstrologyCapricorn.htm

349 Mystical Blaze, Personality Profile-Sagittarius, November 22-December 21, Accessed September 17, 2010. Available at http://www.mysticalblaze. com/AstrologySagittarius.htm

tion perfectly in the workplace. Virgo tends to be fairly careful with money and usually won't be caught without at least a small nest egg tucked away somewhere.[350]

The Mystical Blaze website also describes the Capricorn personality:

Capricorn on the outside is a cool, calm, reserved individual with powerful inner strength who possesses the innate ability to rise to the top through unflinching conviction and sheer perseverance. This is a rather stoic person who more than anything else enjoys power, respect, and authority, and who is willing to toe the line for as long as it takes to achieve his goals. Inwardly, however, Capricorn may not be the self-confident pillar of strength that he appears to be, and when his power or authority is compromised, he may make flawed decisions that could cause everything he has worked for to go down in flames in a spectacular way - think Richard Nixon or Mel Gibson. Even so, the Capricorn personality is one that is firmly grounded in reality and who will consistently be the voice of reason in a chaotic world. He understands why the rules are in place and conforms accordingly. Though he may seem unfriendly, arrogant, or without humor to outsiders, Capricorn is inwardly quite warm and sympathetic, often with a surprisingly quick wit. Capricorn's general outlook is fairly rigid, and once he forms a view of the world, he will often stubbornly hold on to that view despite compelling evidence to the contrary. He may also be subject to a degree of pessimism, often seeing the glass as half empty rather than half full. Socially, Capricorn is inhibited and uncomfortable in new situations, approaching others at first with caution and suspicion. As far as money is concerned, Capricorn approaches finances as he does everything else - with prudence, planning, and discipline. As such, there are not many Capricorns on the bottom of the barrel in society.[351]

Such comparisons facilitate an understanding as to why Jesse James (who was several years younger than Frank) became the leader of the

350 Mystical Blaze, Personality Profile-Virgo, August 23-September 22, http://www.mysticalblaze.com/AstrologyVirgo.htm
351 Mystical Blaze, Personality Profile-Capricorn, December 23-January 21, http://www.mysticalblaze.com/AstrologyCapricorn.htm

gang and also explain why Frank followed his younger brother, allowing him to lead, although Frank did step in on occasion and object to some of Jesse's ideas.

And even though there was only a one-time encounter between Jesse James and Levi Clay, it is important to note Levi Clay's personality profile as well. Levi Clay exhibited a great deal of restlessness when he was a young man in that he frequently moved from various towns between Illinois and Iowa before finally settling in Adair. He did not become really satisfied until after buying his own business and running it for many years. According to the Mystical Blaze website:

Sagittarius is the traveler of the zodiac and considers every day an opportunity for another adventure. This is a cheerful, spontaneous, and idealistic individual with an exceptional sense of humor. Though there is not a malicious bone in his body, Sagittarius often suffers from foot-in-mouth syndrome, giving honest assessments where a little tact might suit the situation better, then dancing merrily away with nary a thought as to how his comments have negatively affected others. Though not considered particularly deep by friends and acquaintances, Sagittarius does think deeply about the big picture, such as why he is here and where he is going, and can often see the end results with almost prophetic accuracy. As a lifelong seeker of knowledge, Sagittarius will likely be quite well-read in a variety of subjects, and will be equipped with a well-developed philosophy in which he maintains unshakable faith. Sagittarians retain almost a child-like quality throughout their lives, always remaining optimistic and never fully accepting the seriousness inherent in day-to-day living. Obviously, this degree of child-like naivety coupled with borderline reckless spontaneity can and does cause problems for some Sagittarius individuals, but if things don't turn out well, they will dust themselves off and cheerfully jump to their next adventure without any serious regrets[352].

While the nineteenth century press sang praises or condemnations of Jesse James, these tributes were carried over into the twentieth century

352 Mystical Blaze, Personality Profile-Sagittarius, November 22-December 21, http://www.mysticalblaze.com/AstrologySagittarius.htm

press and ultimately to Hollywood and to television. Over the years, a number of top grossing films portrayed the life and times of Jesse James. Jesse James is not just an American icon. His name is known world-wide!

One of the funniest of the Jesse James films was Bob Hope's 1959 spoof *Alias Jesse James*[353]. Although the film is inaccurate with the sole purpose of humor in mind, I laugh every time I watch that movie, and probably just as hard as I did the first time when I saw it. The IMDb website attests to a number of factual errors in the film, which lend more toward humor than toward anything else:

- *Factual errors: According to the date on Queasley's telegram, the film takes place in 1880. Yet Milford and Cora Lee sing a song mentioning Grant's Tomb, even though former President Ulysses S. Grant didn't die until 1885, and his tomb in New York City wasn't built until many years after that. Also, Milford sees a young boy playing the piano, who tells him his name is Harry Truman. Truman wasn't born until 1884.*

- *Factual errors: At the James' farm, Milford kills a Gila monster. The Gila monster is found only in the deserts of the American southwest and northwest Mexico. Jesse James's farm was in Missouri (in both the film and real life).*[354]

The film focuses on the experiences of a fumbling insurance salesman who sells Jesse James an insurance policy and then attempts to get it back! (I love the get-away in the wagon. That portion of the movie is hysterical!) In ways, the character Milford Farnsworth reminds me of the unfortunate John W. Witcher, the Pinkerton detective who thought he would capture the James boys singlehandedly and put an end to their operation! In *Alias Jesse James*, Milford Farnsworth took over the insurance company. In real life, John W. Witcher was killed!

Jesse James was a man who loved the limelight. Had he lived and not followed a life of crime, he probably would have made an excellent

353 Alias Jesse James, Director: Norman Z. MCLeod, Actors: Bob Hope, Rhonda Fleming, Wendell Corey. Release Date: 20 March 1959. Hope Enterprises.
354 Alias Jesse James (1959). IMDb Website. Accessed September 25, 2010. Available at http://www.imdb.com/title/tt0052545/

showman, or a preacher, or an actor. He would have commanded center stage in the civil world. Instead, he commanded it on a stage in his own theatre as an outlaw. And the public could not get enough of him. Reams of dime novels were snapped up by a thirsty public. Newspaper accounts, both positive and negative, filled the pages of the nation's presses. Headlines loudly proclaimed his activities. And he was the topic of many table discussions. Soon people began talking about personal encounters with the man, and that only fed the flames. People spoke of his generosity in helping poor widows pay off their mortgages. Whenever he stayed someone's home, he generously paid for the meal. People spoke of his politeness and courtesy. And because he was so widely proclaimed, people wanted to *be* Jesse James.

In 1995, the body of Jesse James was exhumed from the grave in Kearney, Missouri hopefully for one last and final time to settle the J. Frank Dalton claim from Texas that Dalton was the real Jesse James. DNA testing was to be performed not only on Jesse's body, but on the body of J. Frank Dalton as well. The body buried in Kearney carried a 99.7% proof that that it was indeed the body of Jesse James. There is no proof on the other side since the wrong body was exhumed in Texas.

***

September, 2010

Howard and I had just spent a weekend touring gold mines and ghost towns west of Boulder, Colorado. We circled through Central City in Gilpin County because I wanted to check out an old cemetery there. It was late afternoon when we arrived, and we discovered that the gates were locked and chained. The cemetery had to resort to that to keep vandals from destroying the tombstones.

Back inside the car, Howard said, "Hey! How would you like to visit a place where Jesse James stopped?"

My response went something like this, "Jesse James never stopped here!"

"Yes, he did! He stopped at Crook's Palace!"

This has to be some sort of joke, I thought as we pulled into the parking lot at Crook's Palace, which is located in the adjacent town of Black Hawk. Central City and Black Hawk run together, and Jesse James was never in Central City or Black Hawk!

Howard disappeared inside the building while I waited in the car.

"You're wasting your time!" I said.

Presently, he returned.

"Come on! You are about to see something great."

"What? They have his mummy in there?"

Stopping on the sidewalk, I took a picture of the sign noting the fact that this was the oldest saloon in Colorado having been founded in 1868. I wandered inside, wondering where the monument to Jesse James was located. I was greeted by a smiling bartender and some interested patrons, who were sitting at nearby tables.

"No, Jesse James didn't stop in this bar!" the bartender told me.

I looked at Howard as though to say, See? I told you so!

"But he drank at this bar!"

Say, what?

He introduced me to the long, old wooden bar in front of him.

"This bar came out of a saloon in St. Joseph. Jesse James used to drink at this bar!"

"They hauled it all the way out here from St. Joseph?"

"That's right."

I took a picture of the magnificent artifact to add to my collection. While Zee James told authorities that Jesse James never drank alcohol or used tobacco, he probably did those things when he was away from home. He became "one of the guys" when he was with them!

We left the bar and returned to the car. And as we drove away, I thought, "Everyone has a Jesse James Story—including Crook's Palace in Black Hawk, Colorado!!

Epilogue Photo Section

Downtown Adair, Iowa, May 2002

Another view of downtown Adair, Iowa, May 2002

Monument at the Jesse James Historical Site, Adair, Iowa, May 2002

Site of the Levi Clay House, Adair, Iowa, May 2002. The
Levi Clay house stood where the garage is now standing.

"New home where old home once stood." This photo was taken in 1925, shortly after the new house was built.

May 2002 version of the "new home." It has been re-modeled substantially over the years.

Bibliography

Letters, Manuscripts and Miscellaneous Documents

Adair, Iowa. Wikipedia.com. Accessed June 20, 2010 Available at http://www.wikipedia.com.

Adair Machine Shop, Source Unknown, Undated, 426-427.

Alias Jesse James, Director: Norman Z. McLeod, Actors: Bob Hope, Rhonda Fleming, Wendell Corey. Release Date: 20 March 1959. Hope Enterprises

Alias Jesse James (1959). IMDb Website. Accessed September 25, 2010. Available at http://www.imdb.com/title/tt0052545/

Annual Report, Chicago, Rock Island and Pacific Railroad Company, April 1, 1874. qtd. in Stiles, T. J. Jesse James: Last Rebel of the Civil War. [New York: Alfred A. Knopf, 2002] 234-235.

Application for Membership to the National Society of the Daughters of the American Revolution, Washington D.C., Betty Duvall Pollard, National Number 577008-A481 for Christian Clay (Klee), February, 1974.

The City of St. Joseph, Missouri Website, Accessed September 5, 2010. Available at http://www.ci.st-joseph.mo.us/history/history.cfm.

Clay, Mary Stillians, Inscription on back of photo, Summer 1873.

Clay, Mary Stillians. Letter (Addressee Unknown). Summer 1873.

Clay, Mathias Overview. McCabe Family Tree. Public Member Trees, Accessed June 15, 2010. Ancestry.com, Provo, Utah. Available at http://www.ancestry.com.

Col. Edward Dorsey, Owings Stone Family: A Genealogy of 20,000+ Ancestors and Relatives, Accessed July 27, 2010. Available at: http://whois.domaintools.com/owingsstone.com.

Cole, Richard, Jr. Last Will and Testament, Public Member Stories, Accessed August 5, 2010.

Ancestry.com, Provo, Utah. Available at http://www.ancestry.com.

The Dorsey Family, Descendants of Edward Darcy-Dorsey of Virginia and Maryland for five generations, Accessed July 27, 2010. Ancestry. com, Provo, Utah. Available at http://www.ancestry.com.

Fromm, An Mary Overview, Gibson Family Tree, Public Member Trees, Accessed June 15, 2010. Ancestry.com. Provo, Utah. http://www.ancestry.com.

Gaiser, Louise A. A Historical Sketch of Brown's Cemetery, January 2, 1963, Accessed September 17, 2010. USGenWeb Archives. Available at http://files.usgwarchives.org/mo/platte/cemeteries/brown.txt.

The Genealogy of Virginia Ann Snowberger Hagan, Ancestry.com, Provo. Utah. Accessed June 17, 2010. Available at http://www.ancestry.com.

Guthrie Co., Iowa Genealogical Page. Rootweb Website. Accessed September 17, 2010. Available at http://www.rootsweb.ancestry.com/~iaguthri/html/index.html.

Harris/Cannon Connections. Ancestry.com, Provo, Utah. Accessed June 15, 2010. Available at http://www.ancestry.com.

Hord, J. Mark, William "Bloody Bill "Anderson. The Southron Guerillas. April 22, 2008. Accessed April 23, 2009. Available at http://www.geocities.com/mosouthron/partisans/Anderson.html?200822.

Hurley, Joe. Joe's Route 6 Journal, Casey to Adair IA. Accessed September 17, 2010.

Available at http://www.route6walk.com/.

Inman, Charles Gordon, Notes on the Clay (Klee) Family, January 9, 1992.

Inman, Gordon Loren Inman, Personal Memories. 1953-1955.

J. Frank Dalton, Outlaws and Gunslingers Website. Accessed July 21, 2010. Available at http://www.theoutlaws.com/outlaws5c.htm.

James Kirkpatrick Records, Ancestry.com, Provo, Utah. Accessed June 14, 2010. Available at http://www.ancestry.com.

Jesse James. FrontierTimes.com Website. Accessed September 17. 2010. Available at http://www.frontiertimes.com/outlaws/jesse.htm.

Joyce, Clint and Cecil Houck. Brown Family History, Part 1, Roostweb Database Accessed June 30, 2010. Available at http://www.rootsweb. com.

Lee, Mary J., Oklahoma. Granddaughter of Garrett Lee. Letter ca. 1943.

Murphy Family Tree, Ancestry.com, Provo, Utah. Accessed June 12, 2010. Available at http://www.ancestry.com.

Mystical Blaze, Personality Profile—Capricorn, December 23-January 21. Accessed September 17, 2010. Available at http://www.mystical-blaze.com/AstrologyCapricorn.htm.

Mystical Blaze, Personality Profile—Sagittarius, November 23-December 1. Accessed September 17, 2010. Available at http://www.mysticalblaze.com/AstrologySagittarius.htm.

Mystical Blaze, Personality Profile-Virgo, August 23-September 22, Accessed September 17, 2010. Available at http://www.mysticalblaze.com/AstrologyVirgo.htm.

Oak Grove Cemetery, Morgantown, West Virginia, Record for William Lee (1803-1898). Find-a-Grave.com Website. Accessed September 1, 2010. Available at   http://www.findagrave.com.

The Official Site of Stuart, Iowa. Accessed September 17, 2010. Available at http://www.stuartia.com/old/ .

Pennington, William, Compiler. Roster of Quantrill's, Anderson's, Todd's Guerillas and other Missouri Jewels. 1998, Accessed July 28, 2010. Available at http://penningtons.tripod.com/roster.htm.

Platte County, Missouri Facts, Discussion Forum, and Encyclopedia Article, Wikipedia. Accessed July 19, 2010. Available at http://www.absoluteastronomy.com/topics/Platte_County%2c_Missouri.

Reno Gang—OutlawHistory.com Website. Accessed September 17, 2010. Available at http://www.outlawhistory.com.

Reno Gang. Wikipedia.com website. Accessed September 17, 2010. Available at http://en.wikipedia.org/wiki/Reno_Gang.

The Reno Gang's Reign of Terror, HistoryNet.com Website. Accessed September 17, 2010. Available at http://www.historynet.com/reno-gangs-reign-of-terror.htm.

Saunders, Frederic Z. "Edward Dorsey of Anne Arundel County, Maryland." Accessed July 20, 2010. Available at http://home.netcom.com/~fzsaund/dorsey.html.

Splawn, Lula, (Lydia Lowella Lorena Clay, daughter of Levi Clay. Unmailed letter found in her possessions, 1957.

Stacy, in Neatorama Only, Travel & Places, Seven Places to Check out if you're ever in Iowa, March 26, 2008, Accessed September 17, 2010. Available online at http:// http://www.neatorama.com/2008/03/26/seven-places-to-check-out-if-youre-ever-in-iowa/.

Stillians Family Bible, in the possession of Bruce Stillians, Villisca, Iowa

Stillians, William. OneWorld Tree, Ancestry. Com, Provo, Utah. Accessed June 18, 2010. Available at http://www.ancestry.com.

Summit County-Ohio History Central: A Product of the Ohio Historical Society. Accessed June 2, 2010. Available at http://www.ohiohistory-central.org/entry.php?rec=2016.

Welcome to Clay County, Missouri, An MoGenWeb Project Page, US GenWeb Project, Rootsweb Website. Accessed June 16, 2010. Available at http://www.rootsweb.com.

Wickham, Jane B., Genealogy Specialist, Tiffin-Seneca Public Library, Tiffin, Ohio, Letter dated March 19, 1993.

Wig, Clifford T., Stark County Chapter, OGS, Letter dated March 10, 1993.

"Wild Bill Thomason's Relationship to Anderson Boys and James Boys," Ancestry.com, Provo, Utah. Accessed July 25, 2010. Available at http://www.ancestry.com.

Wilson, Lois P. Jeremiah Klee Family Group Sheet, October 1, 1993.

Yoakum-Jaye/Whitfield-Lancaster Family Trees, Ancestry.com, Provo Utah. Accessed June 23, 2010. Available: http://www.ancestry.com.

You are There: The Capture of Jesse James. Director: Sidney Lumet. Release date: 8 February 1953. Narrator: Walter Cronkite: Cast: James Dean as Bob Ford; John Kerr as Jesse James. CBS Television Network. Information available at IMDb website, Accessed September 25, 2010. Available at: http://www.imdb.com/title/tt0751918/.

Newspaper Articles

Adair News, July 23, 1922. Reprinted Summer 1987 as The Adair News Special Edition.

Adair Lady's Awful Burns Prove Fatal. Old Clipping from *The Adair News,* ca. August 22, 1911.

Chinese Students on Train from Upper-Crust Families. (Taken from the Council *Bluffs Nonpareil* July 22, 1873) The *Adair News Special Edition, Summer 1987.*

Description Given of Five of the Train Robbers, (Taken from the *Council Bluffs Nonpareil* July 25, 1873), *The Adair News Special Edition, Summer 1987.*

Full Particular of the 1873 Train Robbery Near Adair, org. printed in the *Daily Iowa State Register,* Wednesday Morning, July 23, 1873. Reprinted in *The Adair News Special Edition,* Summer 1987.

Great Train Robbery Near Adair July 21, 1873, *The Adair News Special Edition, Summer 1987.*

The History of Adair and Guthrie Counties, 1884. Portions Reprinted in *The Adair News Special Edition,* Summer 1987.

The Iowa Robbers Identified as the Band who went through the Ste. Genevieve Bank and other Villainies. Orig. pub. In the *St. Louis Times,* 25 July 1873. Reprinted in *The Carthage Banner,* August 7, 1873.

Jesse James, *The Carthage Banner*, Carthage, MO, Thursday, April 6, 1882.

Pellett, Kent. First Train Robbery of the West, orig. published July 23, 1939, The Des Moines Register, Reprinted, Knights of Pythias, Anita, Iowa, 224-225.

Railroad Robbers Identified as Members of James Gang. Originally published in the *Council Bluffs Nonpareil*, July 29, 1873. Reprinted in *The Adair News Special Edition*, Summer 1987.

Rock Island Train Wrecked & Robbed Near Adair July 21, *Daily Iowa State Register*, Tuesday Morning, July 22, 1873, reprinted in *The Adair News Special Edition*, Summer 1987.

Train Robbing Started in Iowa by Jesse James in 1873, *The Cedar Rapids Gazette*, Section B, 1, August 18, 1963.

Original Files and Documents from State and National Archives

Clay, John Estate File, 1844, Court of Common Pleas, Summit Co., Courthouse, Summit Co., Ohio.

Clay, Levi Guardianship file, 1845, Court of Common Pleas, Summit Co., Courthouse, Summit Co, Ohio.

Clay, Levi Death Certificate, Department of Vital Records, Des Moines, Iowa.

Clay, Mary Death Certificate, Department of Vital Records, Des Moines, Iowa.

Clay, Mathias. Seneca County Ohio, Will Record, 1828-1849. Vol. I, p. 84-85. FHL Film 388,625.

Dorsey, Edward, Archives of Maryland 41:314.

Dorsey, Col Edward. Maryland Calendar of Wills: Volume 3.

Lee, Garrett Fitzgerald and Ann C. Bannister. Frederick County, Maryland Marriages 1777-1804, Records of the German Reformed Church, Filmed at the Maryland Historical Society, Baltimore, Maryland.

Stillings, John/John Lee Webster Deed, February 10, 1784, Washington Co., Courthouse, Washington Co., Pennsylvania.

Stillings, John Estate File, 1785-1786, Washington Co., Pennsylvania, Pennsylvania State Archives, Harrisburg, Pennsylvania. [Note: The courthouse file has been lost. The file is available on microfilm in Harrisburg. I obtained the copies from another researcher.]

Stillings, John Estate: Orphan's Court Records, Washington Co., Vol. 1. Washington Co., Courthouse, Washington, Pennsylvania.

Stillians, William Death Certificate, Department of Vital Records, Des Moines, Iowa.

Webster, John Lee File, Maryland State Archives, Annapolis, Maryland.

Published Sources

Armstrong Cemetery, Reed Tp., *Seneca County Ohio Cemetery Inscriptions*, Compiled by the Seneca County Genealogical Society, Seneca Chapter OGS.

Arrangement of Militia 1781-1782, Pennsylvania Archives 6th Series, V. 2, 25-26.

Bell, Raymond Martin, Compiler. *Lists of Inhabitants in Washington County, Pennsylvania 1800 or Before,* (Dated 1981).

Bliss, Sylvester. *Memoirs of William Miller, generally known as a lecturer on the prophecies, and the second coming of Christ.* (New York: AMS Press, 1971).

Brumbaugh, Gaius Marchas. *Maryland Records Vol. II*. (Baltimore: Genealogical Publishing, 1928).

Cholera Epidemics—Ohio History Central, A Product of the Ohio Historical Society. An Online Encyclopedia of Ohio History Central. Accessed June 5, 2010. Available at http://www.ohiohistorycentral. org/entry.php?rec=487.

Coldham. Peter Wilson. *More Emigrants in Bondage: 1614-1775.,* 186. [Baltimore: Genealogical Publishing Co., 2002] 217p.

Cox, Richard J. Maryland Runaway Convict Servants 1745-1780. National *Genealogical Society Quarterly*, Vol. 68, No. 2, June 1980, 105-215.

Crumrine, Boyd. *History of Washington County, Pennsylvania with Biographical Sketches of its Pioneers and Prominent Men.* (H. Everts & Co., 1882).

Dyer, Robert L. *Jesse James and the Civil War in Missouri* [Columbia: University of Missouri Press, 1994].

Funk, Arville L. *A Sketchbook of Indiana History.* Rochester, Indiana [Christian Book Press, 1969—revised 1983], 106.

Grill Cemetery Records, *Franklin Tp., Summit Co., Ohio, Vol. 2* (Summit Co., Chapter, OGS, 1980) 28-34.

Hasson, Hazel N., *The Early Mennonites of Joe Daviess County*, Mennonite Heritage, March 1977. Genealogy Trails: Jo Daviess Co., Genealogy & History. Accessed June 3, 2010. Available at http://genealogytrails.com/ill/jodaviess.

History of Adair and Guthrie Counties, Iowa, (Continental Publishing, 1884).

The History of Jo Daviess County, Illinois, H. J. Kett and Co., (Chicago, 1878).

Hodges, Margaret Roberts, Editor. An Alphabetical List of those who took the Oak of Fidelity and Support of the State of Maryland in Anne Arundel County, 1778. Genealogical Department, National Society, Daughters of the American Revolution, Annapolis, Maryland. FHL Film 0006302.

Howe, Henry. *History of Summit County: Historical Collections of Ohio, Vol. II.* (G. J. Krehbiel & Co., 1888).

Index of Passengers & Immigrants, Ireland from Belfast, 1789. Gale Group, Creator, Passenger and Immigration Lists: 1996-2000 Cumulation (Passenger and Immigration Lists Index Cumulated. Supplement. (Publisher: Gale—100 Edition).

Inman, Charles Gordon, *Daniel Inman of Connecticut, Ontario, N.Y., and Sugar Grove, Ill. And His Descendants, ca. 1776-ca. 1976, with Ancestral Notes to the Early Seventeenth Century,* 1978, [with updated material for the Gordon Loren Inman family]. 1978, Provo, Utah: Family Histories, 1978).

Kilburn, Lucian M., Editor. *History of Adair County, Iowa and its People,* 1915. Kinyon Digital Library, 2002. Accessed September 17, 2010. Available at http://www.kinyon.com/iowa/adair1915v1/contents.htm.

Love, Robertus. *The Rise and Fall of Jesse James.* [Lincoln: University of Nebraska Press, 1990].

Passengers and Immigration Lists, 1357.2, (1987 Index Supplement). (Publisher: Gale).

Pennsylvania Archives, Washington Co., Pennsylvania: Note regarding John Stillings Survey April 28, 1785. Found in an Index.

Portrait and Biographical Album of Jo Daviess County, Illinois. Chapman Bros., (Chicago, 1889).

Presbyterian Cemetery, *Tombstone Inscriptions, Mercer Co., Pennsylvania.* Micofilmed by the Pennsylvania Historical Society, Harrisburg, Pennsylvania. (Date Unknown).

Settle, William A., Jr. *Jesse James Was His Name.* [Lincoln: University of Nebraska Press, 1977].

Shaw, Don C., *A Genealogy and History of Some of the Descendants of Johan Nicholas Klee of Bern Township, Berks County, Pennsylvania,* (1968).

284 Barbara Inman Beall,Ph.D.

Sheller Cemetery Records, Loudon Tp., Seneca County, Ohio, compiled by the Seneca County Genealogical Society, OGS., Date Unknown.

Steele, Phillip W. *Jesse and Frank James: The Family History.* [Gretna: Pelican Publishing Co., 1997].

Stiles, T. J. *Jesse James: The Last Rebel of the Civil War.* [New York: Alfred A. Knopf, 2002]

Turner, George. *The Secrets of Jesse James* [Baxter Lane Co., Amarillo, TX, 1975]

Wright, C. Milton. *Our Harford Heritage: A History of Harford County, Maryland.* (French-Bray Printing Co., 1980).

Tax Lists and Census Records

Anderson, William C., 1840 Census, Randolph Co., Missouri, Ancestry. com, Provo, Utah. Accessed July 5, 2010. Available at http://www.ancestry.com.

Anderson, William C., 1840 Census, Liberty Tp., Marion Co., Missouri, Ancestry. com, Provo, Utah. Accessed July 5, 2010. Available at http://www.ancestry.com.

Anderson, William C., 1850 Census, Salt Springs, Randolph Co., Missouri, Ancestry.com, Provo, Utah, Accessed July 5, 2010. Available at http://www.ancestry.com.

Clay, Christian and Mathias. 1810 Census, Farmanagh Tp, Mifflin Co., Pennsylvania, Ancestry.com, Provo, Utah. Accessed June 4, 2010. Available at http://www.ancestry.com.

Clay, Mathias and John. 1820 Census, Nimishillen Tp., Stark Co., Ohio, Ancestry.com, Provo, Utah. Accessed June 4, 2010. Available at http://www.ancestry.com.

Clay, Mathias and John. 1830 Census, Nimishillen Tp., Stark Co., Ohio, Ancestry.com, Provo, Utah. Accessed June 4, 2010. Available at http://www.ancestry.com.

Clay, Mathias, Simon and David. 1840 Census, Loudon Tp., Seneca Co., Ohio, Copy obtained from Tiffin-Seneca Co., Public Library, March 19, 1993.

Clay, Simon and David. 1825 Tax Lists, Loudon Tp., Seneca Co., Ohio. Seneca Co., Ohio History, Records, Facts and Genealogy. My Ohio Genealogy Website. Accessed June 17, 2010. Available at http://www.myohiogenealogy.com/oh-county-seneca.html.

Clay, Simon. 1850 Census, Loudon Tp., Seneca Co., Ohio, Ancestry. com, Provo, Utah. Accessed June 24, 2010. Available at http://www.ancestry.com.

Clay, Simon. 1856 Iowa Census, Palermo, Grundy Co., Iowa, Ancestry. com, Provo, Utah, Accessed June 24, 2010. Available at http://www.ancestry.com.

Clay, Simon. 1860 Census, Felix, Grundy Co., Iowa, ancestry.com, Provo, Utah. Accessed June 24, 2010. Available at http://www.ancestry.com.

Dille, Caleb, David, Jr., David, Sr., Israel, and John. Washington Co., Pennsylvania Names on Petitions, 1776-1780 Raymond Martin Bell, Compiler, (Washington and Jefferson College, 1961).

Dille, Lewis, Israel, Isaac, Price and Ichabod. 1790 Census, Morris Tp., Washington Co., Heads of Families at the First Census Taken in the Year 1790. (Washington DC: Government Printing Office, 1908).

Lacock/Laycock, Elisha. 1850 Census, Amwell Tp., Washington Co., Pennsylvania, Ancestry.com, Provo, Utah, Accessed July 1, 2010. Available at http://www.ancestry.com.

Lee, David, 1850 Census, Amanda Tp., Allen Co., Ohio. Ancestry. com, Provo, Utah. Accessed July 8, 2010. Available at http://www.ancestry.com.

Lee, David, 1860 Census, Amanda Tp., Allen Co., Ohio. Ancestry. com, Provo, Utah. Accessed July 8, 2010. Available at http://www.ancestry.com.

Lee, David, 1870 Census, Amanda Tp., Allen Co., Ohio. Ancestry. com, Provo, Utah. Accessed July 8, 2010. Available at http://www. ancestry.com.

Lee, Garrett and Abraham. 1830 Census, East District, Monongalia Co., Virginia. Ancestry.com, Provo, Utah. Accessed July 3, 2010. Available at http://www.ancestry.com.

Lee, Garrett and William. 1800 Census, District 1, Montgomery Co., Maryland. Ancestry.com, Provo, Utah. Accessed July 3, 2010. Available at http://www.ancestry.com.

Lee, Garret F. 1850 Census, Clinton Tp., Wayne Co., Ohio. Ancestry. com, Provo, Utah. Accessed July 3, 2010. Available at http://www. ancestry.com.

Lee, Garret F. 1860 Census, Cass, Nebraska Territory. Ancestry.com, Provo, Utah. Accessed July 3, 2010. Available at http://www.ancestry. com.

Lee, Garret F. 1875 Census, Cottage Grove Tp., Allen Co., Kansas. Ancestry.com, Provo, Utah. Accessed July 3, 2010. Available at http:// www.ancestry.com.

Lee, Garret F. 1880 Census, Baker Tp., Linn Co., Missouri. Ancestry. com, Provo, Utah. Accessed July 3, 2010. Available at http://www. ancestry.com.

Lee, William. 1860 Census, Clarksburg, Harrison Co., West Virginia. Ancestry.com, Provo, Utah, Accessed July 3, 2010. Available at http:// www.ancestry.com.

Monroe, David M. 1850 Census, Hampshire Co., Virginia. Ancestry. com, Provo, Utah. Accessed August 8, 2010. Available at http://www. ancestry.com.

Monroe, David M. 1880 Census, Spring Creek District, Wirt Co., West Virginia.Ancestry.com, Provo, Utah. Accessed August 8, 2010. Available at http://www.ancestry.com.

Stealions, Joseph L. 1790 Census, Derry Tp., Alleghany Co., Pennsylvania. Heads of Families at the First Census Taken in the Year 1790. (Washington DC: Government Printing Office,   1908).

Stillen, William M. 1840 Census, Greene Tp., Greene Co., Pennsylvania. Microfilm No. M704, Reel 40, p. 351. National Archives Annex, 6th & Kipling, Denver, Colorado.

Stillens, William. 1840 Census, Canton Tp., Washington Co., Pennsylvania. Microfilm No. M704, Reel 44, p. 199. National Archives Annex, 6th & Kipling, Denver, Colorado.

Stillings, John. 1784 Tax Lists, Amwell Tp., Washington Co., Pennsylvania. Lists of Inhabitants in Washington County, Pennsylvania 1800 or Before with Maps of the Early Townships. Raymond Martin Bell, Compiler. (Washington and Jefferson College, 1961).

Stillings, Mary. 1850 Census, Amwell Tp., Washington Co., Pennsylvania, Ancestry.com, Provo, Utah. Accessed July 18, 2010. Available at   http://www.ancestry.com.

Stillians, Rachel. 1900 Census, Stuart, Adair, Iowa, Ancestry.com, Provo, Utah. Accessed July 18, 2010. Available at http://www.ancestry.com.

Stillians, Widow. 1800 Census, Hanover Tp., Washington Co., Pennsylvania. Lists of Inhabitants in Washington County, Pennsylvania 1800 or Before with Maps of the Early Townships. Raymond Martin Bell, Compiler. (Washington and Jefferson College, 1961).

Stillians, William. 1850 Census, Cumberland Tp., Greene County, Pennsylvania, Ancestry.com, Provo, Utah. Accessed July 18, 2010. Available at http://www.ancestry.com.

Stillians, William. 1860 Census, Woodbine, Jo Daviess County, Illinois, Ancestry.com, Provo, Utah. Accessed July 18, 2010. Available at http://www.ancestry.com.

Stillians, William. 1870 Census, Woodbine, Jo Daviess County, Illinois, Ancestry.com, Provo, Utah. Accessed July 18, 2010. Available at http://www.ancestry.com.

Stillians, William. 1880 Census, Bear Grove Tp., Guthrie Co., Iowa, Ancestry.com, Provo, Utah. Accessed July 18, 2010. Available at http://www.ancestry.com.

Stillians, William. 1900 Census, Lu Verne Tp., Kossuth Co., Iowa, Ancestry.com, Provo, Utah. Accessed July 18, 2010. Available at http://www.ancestry.com.

Stillions, William. 1820 Census, Hampshire Co., Virginia, Ancestry. com, Provo, Utah. Accessed July 18, 2010. Available at http://www. ancestry.com.

Stillions, William. 1825 Tax Records, Hampshire Co., Virginia. Wilmer L. Kerns. Historical Records of Old Frederick and Hampshire Counties, Virginia (Revised). Heritage Books,   Inc. May 1, 2009.

Tift, William. 1885 Census, Manning, Carroll Co., Iowa. Ancestry. com, Provo, Utah. Accessed July 18, 2010. Available at http://www. ancestry.com.

Webster, John Lee. 1776 Census, Spesutia, Lower Hundred, Harford Co., Maryland. Maryland Census 1772 to 1890, Accessed July 18, 2010. Available at Ancestry.com, http://www.ancestry.com.

Index

John Talbot 45
John T. Ford 214
John Thomas Samuel 114
John Vanada 35
John W. Baker 66, 243
John Webster 44, 45
John Wesley Ford 214
John W. Ford 214
John William Splawn 243
John William Stillians 42
John Wilson 46
John W. Lee 58
John W. Witcher 190, 208, 266
John Younger 187, 188, 189
Joice Ellen Richards 240
Jonathan Cropper 99
Jonathan Masser 45
Joseph Clay 28
Joseph Dilley, Sr 61
Josephine Francis James 221
Joseph Lee Heywood 200
Joseph O. Shelby 115
Joseph Robidoux 211
Joseph Stealions 49
Joshua Brian Wall 242
Joshua Dorsey 107
Joshua DORSEY's 111
Josiah Walton 206
Joy Gionet 242
J. S. Allen 199
J. Stone Land and Cattle Co 134
J. T. Lee 59
Judge James M. Sandusky 135
Judi Rae Richards 240
Julia Ann 153
Julia Ann Hair 34
Julia Bermer 20

K

Kansas City, Missouri 120
Kansas City Times 189
Kansas Jayhawkers 99

Karl Hoy 36
Kate Clarke 126
Kathcrine Organ 108
Katherina Grim 21
Kearney, Missouri 90, 267
Kelsey & Bodley hardware store 235
King Robert the Bruce 55
King William's School 108
Klee, 20
Know-Nothing Party 116
Knox Co., Tennessee 83

L

Lancaster, Pennsylvania 36
Larkin (or Lacon) Dorsey 107
Las Vegas, New Mexico 207, 223
Laura Reno 153
Lavenia Jane Howard 111
Lawrence Barr 222
Lawrence H. Barr 222
Lawrence, Kansas 125, 133
Leavenworth, Kansas 127
Lebanon, Pennsylvania 34
Lee's Summit 203
Lee's Summit, Missouri 98
Lee Webster 48
Lelah Frances Inman 240
Lelah Inman 241
LeSueur 38
Levi and Mary Clay 66, 240
Levi Clay 20, 31, 33, 37, 41, 59, 61, 65, 79, 80, 147, 150, 169, 237, 239,
    243, 245, 258, 259, 262, 265
Levi Clay house 257
Lew Nichols Carnival 203
Liberty, Missouri 135
Liberty Tp., Marion Co., Missouri 127
Liberty Tribune 95
Lisa Margaretha Staudt 21
Little Dixie 81, 93
Little Swatara 34
Lloyd Burr Inman 241
Lloyd Cole 101, 102

Reed Tp, Seneca Co., Ohio 29
Reno Gang 157, 158, 161
Reno, Washoe, Nevada 239
Reuben Gall 34
Reuben Samuel 127, 221
Reynolds House 236
Richard Cole Jr 101, 102
Richard Cole, Jr 99, 100
Richard Cole, Sr 97, 99
Richard James 89
Richmond Cemetery, Richmond, Missouri 223
Ringgold County, Iowa 175
Robert A. Ford 214
Robert and Elizabeth Woodson Poor 91
Robert Archie Parmer 134
Robert Dean Richards 240
Robert E. Lee 55
Robert Franklin James 123, 206
Robert Grant 150
Robert James 94, 95
Robert J. Kin 194
Robert Newton Ford 214
Robert Pleasants 45
Robert Poor 89, 91
Robert R. James 96
Robert Sallee James 89, 90, 91, 92, 94, 95, 102, 111, 113, 126, 259
Robert Thomason 103
Robt. Pleasants Jr 45
Rockford, Floyd Co., Iowa 243
Rockford, Illinois 20, 61
Rock Island Railroad 148, 150, 151, 162
Rohrbach, Birkenfeld, Oldenburg, Germany 21
Ronald Ross 221
Rowley Boyle 49
Roxanne Inman 240
R. S. Pinkerton livery stable 235
Ruth Gapen 51

S

Sallie Cole 99
Sally Yates 99
Salt Springs, Randolph Co., Missouri 127

T

Endnotes

Chapter 3

1 It should be noted that St. Peter's United Church of Christ, which is located at the edge of the Grill Cemetery in Franklin Tp., Summit Co., Ohio was formerly an Evangelical and Reformed Church and before that, it was a Reformed Presbyterian Church. No doubt, this is the church where the Clays worshipped in Summit Co.

It is also important to note that many of these Clay deaths occurred about the time when William Miller was preaching in Summit Co. I don't believe the Clays were swept up in the tides of "Millerism", but I believe they may have been curious about it. If they were fooled the first time, they certainly didn't go back a second time. In October 1844, John Clay had already died and members of the Christian Clay family were falling victim to cholera. And here's a point to ponder: if William Miller baptized some of his converts in streams and rivers polluted with cholera, he may have contributed to the epidemic!

Chapter 4

2 Yohogania: (1776-1786). "An Indian word [Youghiogheny] meaning stream flowing in an opposite direction" of which the name of the county is obviously a variant. (Robinson, Morgan P. Virginia Counties: Those Resulting from Virginia Legislation. Genealogical Publishing Co., July 1916 V. 9, Nos. 1, 2 & 3) 1992) p. 193.

Yohogania County only existed for ten years (1776-1786).

3 *Cecil was the third in the list of original townships of Washington County, and embraced in its territory the present township and all that portion of Allegheny County lying between Robinson Run and Chartiers Creek, and all the present township of Chartiers, as well as the northern portion of Mount Pleasant. The erection of Allegheny County in 1788 and the addition made to that county in 1789 reduced the territory of Cecil, which was further reduced to its present limits by the erection of Chartiers in March, 1790, and*

*of Mount Pleasant in 1808. The township is bounded on the west by Mount
Pleasant and Robinson; on the north and northeast by Allegheny County; on
the east by Peters and North Strabane townships; on the south by Chartiers
and Mount Pleasant townships. The only stream of any importance in the
township is Chartiers Creek, which marks its eastern boundary. (History of
Washington Co., Pennsylvania.)*

4 Concerning the identity of James Kirkpatrick, who paid a bond into the
John Stillings' Estate in 1785, Washington Co., Pennsylvania: according to
records from the Kirkpatrick family, available on Ancestry.com:

> *James Kirkpatrick was the son of Scotch-Irish immigrants. In 1776,
> he served in a company formed in Shippensburg to support troops
> fighting in the Battle of Long Island (incidentally one of the worst
> defeats the colonists suffered in the American Revolution. George
> Washington and his troops hadn't much experience yet.) For James,
> that must have been the end of the war, because in the fall of that
> year he moved to the Loyalhanna area of Westmoreland County.
> Either just before or just after the move, he married Mary Latimer/
> Larrimer. While they were living there, he served in two militia units
> formed to fight the Indians. In 1791, James and Mary were living
> on Cherry Creek, near Elderton (now Armstrong county). That was
> the site of the Indian attack that killed their baby son, John. Shortly
> thereafter, they moved to land between the present towns of Dayton
> and Barnards, still in Armstrong county. They built a new cabin,
> dug a well and planted an orchard on top of a hill overlooking
> Cowanshannock Creek and the rolling hills they farmed. Several
> other Presbyterian families settled nearby. One of the settlers was
> William Kirkpatrick, who was possibly James' brother.*

> *In 1804, James and William Kirkpatrick and some neighbors formed
> the Glade Run Presbyterian Church, which for some years met in
> William Marshall's barn.*

> *In 1807, the land James Kirkpatrick had been "squatting" on was
> sold for back taxes and he rode through the wilderness to Greensburg
> to bid on it. For $44, he bought over 847 acres in Armstrong and
> Indiana counties, including the tract he farmed. By 1821, James and
> Mary had four living sons. Another son, James, had fought in the
> War of 1812.*

> *In 1829, when James Kirkpatrick was more than 70 years old, he
> deeded 100 acres of his land to his son Moses and the balance to
> his son David in return for David's agreement to care of James and*

Mary in their old age. David and his wife, Elizabeth, lived on in the old home place.

James Kirkpatrick was born September 25, 1754, in Shippensburg, Cumberland Co., Pennsylvania to James Kirkpatrick (1728-1781) and he died April 22, 1839 in Wayne, Armstrong Co., Pennsylvania. (Armstrong Co. was originally part of Washington Co., Pennsylvania.) In 1774, he married Mary Margaret Larimer. They had a number of children and the names vary on the records. However, the common consensus follows:

James Kirkpatrick – d. 1876

Jane Kirkpatrick --1775 – 1835

David Kirkpatrick--1778 – 1845

John Kirkpatrick--1784 – 1800

Nancy Kirkpatrick--1784 – 1876

Sarah Kirkpatrick--1787 – 1876

John Kirkpatrick--1802 – 1876

Mary Kirkpatrick--1805 – 1876

Moses Kirkpatrick--1806 – 1876.

During the summer of 1993, while working on my doctorate in Indiana, Pennsylvania, Howard and I often went out for weekend jaunts. One of our favorite places to go was a town called Smicksburg. And during one of those jaunts, we took a detour through the town of Dayton, which is located in Armstrong Co. We stopped at the Glade Run Presbyterian Church Cemetery, on the Smicksburg Road. I took a picture of James Kirkpatrick's tombstone because I thought the inscription on it was quite unique, not knowing about his connection with my fourth great-grandfather. The man buried in the Glade Run Presbyterian Cemetery is same individual who paid a bond into John Stillings' estate. There were two James Kirkpatricks in Washington Co. at the time: James Kirkpatrick's father (who died in 1781) and James. That photo is included in the photo section at the end of Part 1. According to Kirkpatrick Family Records at Ancestry.com, the War of 1812 reference on the tombstone is in error. James Kirkpatrick's son fought in the War of 1812.

5 According to the History of Washington County, Pennsylvania:

Hanover is the extreme northwestern township of Washington County, having the county of Beaver and the State of West Virginia,

*respectively, for its northern and western boundaries. On the east
it is bounded by Robinson and Smith townships, and on the south
by Smith and Jefferson townships. The only streams of any size
or importance belonging to Hanover are Raccoon and Harman's
Creeks, which respectively mark parts of the eastern and southern
boundaries of the township, and King's Creek, which flows in the
southwesterly course across the northwestern corner of Hanover.*

6 Elisha Gibson Mitchell was a doctor, who practiced medicine in Beallsville,
Washington Co., Pennsylvania prior to the family's removal to Illinois.

7 Early Methodism before 1812, specifically 1784-1812, (exact source unknown since I made the notes for my own information. Early Methodists
generally fell into the following classifications:

1. Those who were Methodist in the East, especially Maryland, and
    moved West.

2. Those who had been Episcopalian and found it easy to switch.

3. Those with no religious affiliation, but were attracted to Methodism.

4. Those who were Methodists in Ireland and came to America.

Methodist Circuit riders generally moved after six months in one location.
(Source Unknown: Notes found scribbled in a notebook]

Chapter 5

8 The East District of Monongalia Co., West Virginia is an area in the
Northeast section of the county, bordering Pennsylvania and Maryland. I
found it on a locator map, and it is a political or voting district. Morgantown
is not in East District, and is southwest of the area. East District is primarily
rural.

9 A problem exists with the Garrett Lee family. Garrett married Ann C.
Bannister in 1790. Their oldest son was born in 1803. The next child was
born in 1821. Three possibilities exist: (1) Garrett and Ann may have waited
a long period of time between the birth of the first child and the second to
have any more children: (2) Garrett and Ann may have had a number of
additional children who did not survive; (3) Ann Bannister Lee may have

died and Garrett's second wife may have had the name of Ann. Garrett's later children are by the second wife. As yet, I have found no second marriage record for Garrett Lee.

10 A search of Monroe, Alexander, and Kidwell records shows that these three families intermarried on numerous occasions.

Chapter 8

11 In compiling the James family history, Steele notes, "A Tennessee James family indicates William was the son of John James and that William's brother, Thomas, founded the Tennessee James line." [Phillip W. Steele, Jesse and Frank James: The Family History, 23]

12 According to Steele, one of their children, Robert Newton Hite, who was a member of the James Gang. was killed by Robert Newton Ford in 1881. Ford killed Jesse James the following year. [Steele, The Family History, 32]

13 J. Frank Dalton, who claimed to be Jesse James, was once asked how he acquired the Woodson name. He said he didn't know.

Chapter 11

14 Steele notes: "Perry Samuel was the half-black son of one of Reuben Samuel's slaves. Some writers have indicated that John T. Samuel was his father. Since John T. was very young at the time, it is more reasonable to credit Reuben with being the boy's father.

Breinigsville, PA USA
15 December 2010
251480BV00001B/2/P